Paul Richardson is a former edit
Taste and *Wine* magazine, and a
For the last seven years he has w
Spanish cultural themes, includi
including *Harpers & Queen*, *Daily Telegraph*, *Independent* and *Condé Nast Traveller*. He is the author of *Not Part of the Package: A Year in Ibiza*, and *Our Lady of the Sewers and Other Adventures in Deep Spain*.

Londres
Junio 2007.

Also by Paul Richardson

Not Part of the Package: A Year in Ibiza

Our Lady of the Sewers and Other Adventures in Deep Spain

cornucopia

PAUL RICHARDSON

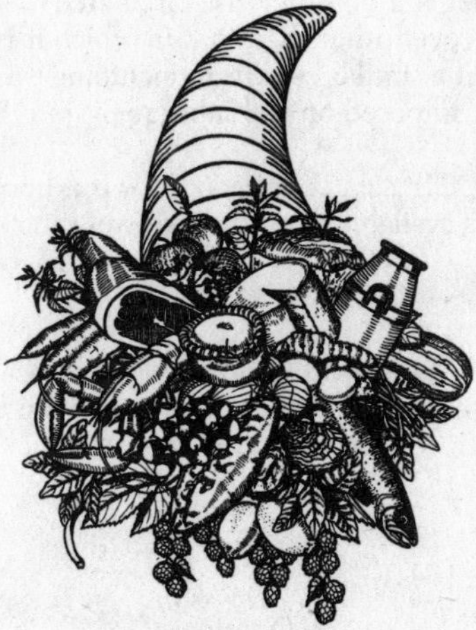

ABACUS

An *Abacus* Book

First published in Great Britain in 2000
by Little, Brown and Company

This edition published by Abacus in 2001

A CIP catalogue record for this book
is available from the British Library.

ISBN 0 349 11132 4

Typeset in Berling by M Rules
Printed and bound in Great Britain by
Clays Ltd, St Ives plc

Abacus
A Division of
Little, Brown and Company (UK)
Brettenham House
Lancaster Place
London WC2E 7EN

www.littlebrown.co.uk

acknowledgements

Some of my best friends are beautiful cooks. My thanks to Carol Griffiths, Marlena Spieler, Brenda Taylor and Colin Spencer for their inspiration. A book like this relies largely on inside information; thanks, then, to the multitude of friends and friends-of-friends willing to have their brains comprehensively picked. Several books inspired and guided me in my quest, notably Jane Grigson's *British Cookery*, Dorothy Hartley's *Food in England* and Henrietta Green's *Food Lovers' Guide to Britain*.

Much gratitude and love to Kate and Miles, Simon and Sarah, my mother and Rodger, and my father, for help and hospitality beyond expectation. Among those to whom I am indebted for bed and board, and in some cases subject matter, are: Adrian Arnold, Marcus Blee and Linda Felcey, Roger Clarke and Simon Su, Rachel Chisholm Batten, Simon Ann Dorin, Katy Emck, Susan Ferguson, Catherine Heard and Carla Pinto, Jason Lowe,

Thomas Mercer and Fi Searles, Emma Mahony and Adam Barker, Simon Prosser and Katie Owen, Sasha Schoenfeld and Lorençu Posa, Nick and Anne Stacey, Alex Willcock and Sophie Conran. Special thanks to Antonia and John Price for their unstinting generosity.

Thanks too to Richard Beswick, my editor, who gave me a mission I couldn't refuse, and to Julian Alexander, who provided the crucial logistical back-up.

To the cooks and farmers and fishermen of Spain, who taught me that good eating needn't be élitist, I say: ¡Gracias!

To the defenders of real food in Britain against the insidious forces of junk, I say: Fight the good fight!

contents

The Highlands
Glasgow and Edinburgh
Cumbria
Yorkshire
North West
North East Anglia
Wales
East Anglia
London
Kent
Sussex
Hampshire
Cornwall

1

normandy and sussex

an hors d'oeuvre

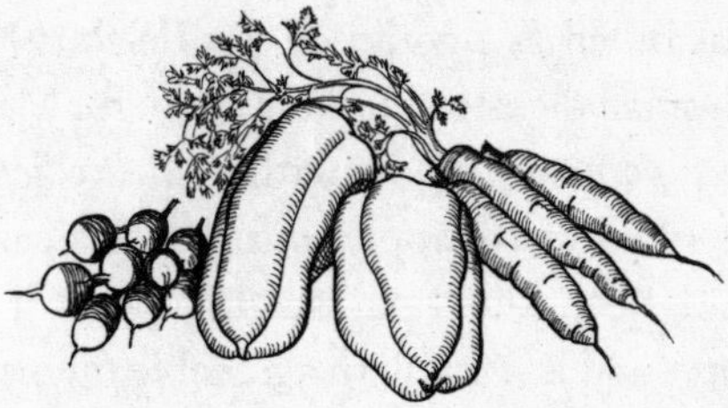

It was midday by the time the ferry pulled out of Dieppe harbour, and I was already feeling peckish again. I left the car in the hold, climbed up to the top deck and stood among the squalling seagulls, watching the old port become a pinkish smudge on the pale horizon. I took a big cold breath of sea air, gulping it down like the iced, acid Muscadet de Sèvres et Maine that I had been drinking rather too much of during my last few days in northern France.

The dinner last night was still fresh in my mind: a solitary, celebratory last supper at a small restaurant just off the Place Nationale, chosen practically at random from the hundred or so to be found in this seaside town of 36,000 inhabitants. Like many of the best meals, it had been memorable for the least spectacular of reasons. There was a white tablecloth, a crisp green salad, a basket of bread and a bossy mother hen of a patronne, clucking away among the busy evening tables. '*Vous voulez goûter la marmite dieppoise, c'est un plat typique*,' she said sternly, making my choice something of a fait accompli. The *marmite*, proudest boast of the local cuisine, is a rich mélange of monkfish, brill, sole, langoustine, scallops and potatoes, the sauce given an ivory smoothness by a generous splash of Normandy cream. I ate as much as I could of this delectable dish, taking care to leave a small digestive parking space for Madame's heavenly *tarte aux pommes*, made with delicate *feuilleté* pastry, superbly buttery, and with apples infused with calvados.

Dieppe had been the final staging post of my journey through Europe, and left me with agreeable memories of a culinary culture that, despite all the changes and chances of modern life, seemed still to be predicated on the relentless search for good quality. That morning, before boarding the ferry, I had given myself an overview of the gastronomic resources of Dieppe, which were only average by the standards of most small French towns: there was a lively weekly market, to which villagers brought their produce, and a series of trestle tables on the harbourside, run by Madame Jeanette Laine, where one could buy the morning's catch. Within a few steps of the harbour, I found a fine boulangerie selling the dense, tasty *pain de Dieppe*, a posh épicerie, a clutch of patisseries smelling irresistibly of fresh croissants golden and glistening with butter, and a famous cheese shop, Olivier's, where I enquired about a good Camembert au lait cru, to be given to an English friend I hadn't seen for years. Mademoiselle Olivier showed me several, removed them from their boxes and palpated them fearlessly.

For when did I want it, she asked? For two, three days' time? *Ah bon*, in that case, I should take this one, she said, and wrapped it up nicely and talked to me about the cheeses of this part of Normandy – Neufchatel and Sire de Créquy and Pont l'Évêque and Tomme d'Esgranges – so that I only just made the ferry before it pulled up the ramp and chugged away.

There had been few upsets in my progress through Europe – the occasional *magret de canard* a smidgeon overdone, the odd sauce oversalted or salad underdressed. Whatever I had heard about the sad decline of French cuisine, I found plenty of evidence to the contrary. Many was the time I had stopped by the roadside in some dust-blown provincial backwater to try the fifty-franc menu du jour, and been pleasantly surprised by a slice of homemade terrine or a plate of artichokes with vinaigrette, say, followed by a rabbit in mustard sauce or an *omelette aux fines herbes*, followed perhaps by a local goats' cheese or a homemade fruit tart, all plainly presented but with a smile.

I was now sailing into treacherous waters, however. Such good things might no longer be quite so easy to come by. I would have to keep my wits about me, my credit card and my Andrews Liver Salts closely to hand.

Travellers' tales had reached me of the horrors that might lie ahead. Dreadful, almost unbelievable tales of chocolate bars deep-fried in cheap fat and eaten with pommes frites, of artificially flavoured noodles in plastic pots to which hot water was added for immediate consumption on the move. In the last decade since I had lived in Britain, fast-food joints had sprung up like toadstools on a forest floor. Massive hypermarkets outside town centres had killed off many of the traditional grocers, and markets such as most other Europeans know them were a thing of the past. There were some towns, I had been told, in which there was neither a single proper patisserie, fishmonger nor charcuterie, nor were there restaurants offering anything other than Chinese, Indian, or other foods having their distant origin in Italian, American and Turkish traditions. Dozens of British towns and cities failed to boast a single really good restaurant.

What they had told me in Europe about the eating habits of the land that was my current destination sent my stomach into a nervous flutter. The British, it was said, regarded good food as a privilege, not a right. They had no living tradition of regional cookery, and to ask in local restaurants for *les specialités de la région* was to risk incredulity and ridicule. The concept of eating as a family was almost dead; most meals in the home were consumed in front of the television. The diets of many young people were almost entirely composed of snack foods, salty or sweet, and included no fruit or vegetables at all. Instant coffee, ready meals from supermarkets, microwave ovens for the heating-up of the same, breakfast cereals, spongy white presliced bread, devoid of taste or texture, biscuits, chocolate bars, and extruded starchy potato-based snacks were the mainstay of British eating. People's lives in the big cities were so hemmed in and twisted by the pressures of their work, I was told, that even those with money and an interest in good food often had neither time nor energy to shop and cook in the normal way.

When I told my French, Spanish and Italian friends that I intended to spend eighteen months researching British gastronomy, they tittered behind their hands and then commiserated with me. More than once I was made to listen to the hoary old joke about the English being the cooks in a dystopian Europe in which the Greeks are the organisers and the Swiss the lovers. '*La gastronomía británica, eso no existe,*' pronounced a Spaniard, whose year as a foreign-language student had left him full of affection for the British as a race but scarred by the memory of monotonous and shoddy cooking. '*Pour avoir réellement une gastronomie il faut aimer la cuisine, il faut l'adorer,*' said a Frenchman, apparently implying that our relationship with the food we ate was more or less a loveless marriage.

It seemed an awful panorama, yet I knew there was more to British eating than anyone who had not grown up here could possibly understand. The best British cooking, historically speaking, has been served not in restaurants but in family homes where dutiful mothers, not egotistical male chefs, took charge of the stove. As Jane Grigson puts it in one of her luminous books on our national food, 'our classical tradition has been domestic, with the domestic virtues of quiet enjoyment and generosity'. And it may be that I belong to the last generation of Britons to have proved this empirically.

I stared out to sea, losing myself in the flat horizon, and cast my mind back to the food I remembered from twenty-five years of life in the United Kingdom. It was true I'd been traumatised, as many of my compatriots must have been, by school meals and their malicious determination to remove all possible pleasure from the act of eating. The less said about the meanness, the sensual poverty of British institutional catering, the better. (In all its grim-faced pragmatism, that word 'catering' is to me one of the ugliest in the English language, and has no precise equivalent in any other, as far as I know.)

But there were good memories, too. What I remembered

best was the solid, savoury repertoire of English home cooking. Joints of roast meat, of course, with their various tracklements. Steak and kidney pudding and pie, two applications of the same ingredients producing dramatically different results. Faggots in gravy. Cottage pie. Ham with parsley sauce. Hot pot. Jugged hare. Sometimes we had pheasant, when someone ran one over in the road. Vegetables from the garden, boiled and gilded with a little butter and chopped fresh mint. Gooseberry fool, fruit pies, jam tarts, and the endless parade of sweet puddings: rice, bread and butter, queen of, summer . . .

There were almost no restaurants in those days, or at least, that was the way it seemed. Whenever there were restaurant scenes in TV sitcoms, they were always forbidding places where the waiters were haughtily French and you had to know the rules of the game – the correct and decorous way to taste wine, eat artichokes, and handle strange cutlery – else embarrassment would be the inevitable result. We were gastronomic innocents then, and the horizon of the exotic was not very far away. Spaghetti bolognaise, paella, coq au vin, chop suey, and the occasional anglicised curry sprinkled with raisins, desiccated coconut and chopped boiled egg: these were as far as our taste buds would go for the moment. But it wouldn't be long before we wanted more – much more.

I walked about on deck for a while, tasting the salty air, then went below to buy an English newspaper. It being a weekend, when perhaps people felt sufficiently liberated from the office to give vent to their culinary enthusiasms, there were pages and pages of cookery columns and restaurant reviews and features about particular ingredients – ginger or celeriac or seaweed – and what to do with them. A famous London chef who was once a footballer had just thrown a famous food critic, who happened to be accompanied by Joan Collins, out of his restaurant. Another film star, Kate Winslet, interviewed during an arduous session of filming on location in India, told how she and her boyfriend had lain in bed at night fantasising about bangers and mash washed down with pints of bitter.

Near the front of the paper, in the news section, was a short but intriguing story about Delia Smith, whose cookery books seem to have sold more copies than the Bible and undoubtedly exert a greater moral influence on contemporary Britain than the Good Book. She had been on TV the week before showing viewers how to make simple egg dishes: boiled, fried, scrambled. It was Delia's opinion that people in Britain had stopped picking up the basics of cookery from their mothers. Though they might be perfectly able to whip up a rustic Italian dinner party for six after poring all afternoon over *The River Café Cook Book*, what really mattered, she thought, was not the fancy frittata but the fresh, properly fried, free-range farmyard egg.

The day after the programme was shown, the newspaper reported, egg sales had risen spectacularly, soufflé-like, across the country.

It all added up to a picture of a nation whose relationship with food was far more complex, curious and passionate than I had perhaps allowed myself to realise. Gastronomy here was fashion, politics, gossip, glamour. But its dizzy, raging desire for the new, the trendy, the fanciful was tempered by a wistful hankering for the old plainness and familiarity – a kind of *nostalgie de la bouffe*. The excitement was tinged with insecurity. Reading that newspaper, I suddenly felt like the traveller who arrives in a familiar city whose streets seem as quiet as he has always known them, only to be told by the taxi driver that the place is actually in the grip of a revolution.

'We've just been on holiday, actually. We have a house in the Garonne, just outside Montauban. Lovely area. Do you know it? No, we go there every year for a few weeks, try and avoid the tourist crush, not always successfully I might add.'

The Phillipses were a Cornflake-packet family, Mum and Dad, a girl and a boy. He was an architect in Swindon, she worked part-time as a community nurse, and the kids went to local private schools.

'We love French food. Don't we, love? Well, it's a different world really, isn't it? Every year our neighbour, Madame Joly, we know her as, invites us over for lunch,' Mr Phillips went on. 'Simple, yet ambitious, if you know what I mean. Endless courses, so it's virtually impossible to pace yourself. This time we had a soup, made with some sort of herb she grew outside the kitchen door. What was that herb, love?'

'Sorrel,' said Sue shyly.

'Funny stuff, I thought. Rather bitter. Then there came some little rolls of meat, absolutely stuffed with garlic, and something like a quiche lorraine only with spinach, and a dish of carrots au gratin . . . Then a wonderful cheese she'd made herself with her own goats' milk.'

'There was a cake at the end,' piped up his daughter.

'Yes, she brought it out finally, just when we were thinking it was all over. Frankly it's all a bit much for me – I'll be quite happy to get back to some nice simple English food.'

'Cheese on toast! That's what you're getting tonight,' exclaimed the wife and mother, laughing as she slipped her arm around her husband's waist in a gesture that combined possessiveness, protectiveness and a gentle dig at his increased girth.

Down in the self-service restaurant, Brit Food was still looking more or less as I had been warned it might. Breakfast offered croissants in plastic bags and coffee in bizarre plastic beakers with lids and spouts for drinking from, like baby bottles. But it was nearly midday, and already a few homecoming Brits were tucking into mushroom stroganoff, chicken tikka, or jacket potato with tuna mayonnaise and sweetcorn. The indiscriminate use of tinned sweetcorn was a practice I fondly hoped would not have lasted into the twenty-first century, but this last dish showed that I was dreadfully wrong.

A young woman in a tailored grey jacket and glasses gently pushed away her half-finished potato and lit up a cigarette. Something about that gesture, which was accompanied by a frown of distaste that seemed to be directed mostly inwardly, told me that she was French. As it turned out, Marie was a boutique owner from Amiens, on the Somme, who was going on business to Brighton and found the ferry cheaper and easier than the Eurostar.

'British food . . .' she murmured when I told her my own business, and took a long meditative drag on her Marlboro Light.

'Okay, it has a reputation . . . not so good,' said Marie.

She was right, but it hadn't always been that way. For centuries, the reputation of British food was for a richness and variety at least equalling the cuisines of the Continent. A Venetian ambassador at the beginning of the sixteenth century described the English as 'great epicures and very avaricious by nature' who 'indulge in the most delicate fare'. Almost two centuries later the French traveller François Maximilien Misson wrote approvingly of the cookshops along the Thames in London, where good food could be had either to eat on the premises or to take away. These shops had been functioning at least since medieval times, as we know from a passage in William FitzStephen's *Descriptions of London*, written around 1183: 'There daily, according to the season, you may find viands, dishes roast, fried and boiled, fish great and small, the coarser flesh for the poor, the more delicate for the rich, such as venison, and birds both big and little . . . However great the infinitude of knights and foreigners that enter the city or are about to leave it, at whatever hour of the day or night . . . they turn aside thither, if it so please them, and refresh themselves each after his own manner. Those who desire to fare delicately, need not search to find sturgeon or Guinea-fowl or Ionian francolin, since all the dainties that are found there are set forth before their eyes.'

It seems likely that, historically speaking, British cooking has been admired for its sophistication a great deal longer than it has been disparaged for its mediocrity. I am always amazed by the brilliant complexity of the early 'receipts' that call for parsley, saffron, ginger, cinnamon, mace, cloves, sandalwood and cubebs to be pounded into a paste with chicken flesh and egg yolks, or for oysters to be parboiled in a mixture of almond milk, wine and fish broth spiked with onions, cloves, mace, sugar and powdered ginger. (My favourite medieval recipe, however, is very much simpler. It begins: 'Take a bear and seethe him.')

'*Bon, le niveau, c'est pas terrible. La cuisine, plutôt primitive.*

But you know something? It is not so bad as people say,' said Marie. 'I go back now to the UK very much, and the story is, things are, you say, looking up? The vitality, the variety, you know, is something new. Maybe it's because you don't have such a tradition, you have freedom, you know, freedom to experiment. In France, there is a lot of convention, ze young chefs, they feel the weight of that. Okay, I talk about London, and restaurants. How the ordinary people eat in the UK, at home, *ça peut être autre chose*, eh?' She raised her hand and cocked her head, in the uniquely French gesture of caution.

How the ordinary people eat in the UK, at home, was precisely one of the things I was most anxious to discover. For without that knowledge, as Marie seemed to be implying, my picture of the status quo would be radically skewed. 'A nation's gastronomical level should be examined by tasting both the products of the best private kitchens and restaurants and the dishes from the kitchens of the peasantry. Somewhere in between lies the true level of excellence,' wrote the great chef and gourmet Curnonsky in the preface to his 1959 masterpiece *Recettes des Provinces de France*. To have any real meaning as such, good food must be democratic, available to all income brackets and ages and parts of the country – not just to the metropolitan middle classes. The real greatness of all the world's great cuisines, surely, is that sophisticated French, Chinese, Italian, Indian and Japanese cooks are happy to acknowledge the debt they owe to the traditional food of those much further down the social scale.

The ferry docked at Newhaven on a sparkling autumn afternoon, and I found a room in a seafront B&B chosen at random from a row of net-curtained guest houses with names such as Dolphins, Dormez-Vous and Chatsworth. Mrs Lee fixed me up with a cup of tea – my first proper cup in months, orange-brown in colour and chewily tannic – and sat me down in the guest lounge, a front room whose decor, in common with that of millions of other front rooms across the country, would bring the staff of *Elle Decoration* out in a nasty rash.

'Come in on the ferry, did you?' she said. And we got to talking about the food she ate, and her children ate, and her guests ate, and what I would be doing on my trip to Britain. It wouldn't just be feasting in fancy restaurants, I told her. What I needed to know was what working people, children and the elderly wanted to eat in food-revolutionary Britain. What does Everyman find delicious? What does he dream of when hunger pangs take hold? Elizabeth David said our national delicacy is toast, and the landlady of the Sea Spray B&B appeared to agree with her.

'I like a nice bit of warm toast, oh yes. Hovis with the crusts off,' said Mrs Lee. 'Plenty of butter and strawberry jam.'

'Oi, Darren, what do you think's dee-licious? This man wants to know.'

Her youngest son, sprawled on the sofa, was making his way through a tube of Pringles.

'Bacon sarnies,' he said through a mouthful. 'Prawn cocktail crisps. Big Macs. Häagen-Dazs.'

'They do salads now, y'know, McDonald's,' said his sister, a teenage girl with a long swingy ponytail. Her tongue flicked delicately into the gooey morass of a Walnut Whip. The two of them had swung by the sweet shop on their way home from school.

'You're disgusting, you two,' said their mother, casting a conspiratorial grimace in my direction. 'They eat so much rubbish, it's not surprising they've got no appetite for dinner. I've tried to give them proper meals, you know, round the table, like in the old days. But they just go straight for the telly. As for Sara, it's a wonder she's still alive. Eats like a bird, she does, nothing but lettuce and chocolate, and not very much of either.'

Mrs Lee was a widow whose husband, a mechanic, had died five years earlier, pushing her into the hotel trade. Responsible, now, for the family's entire welfare, she seldom had time to cook properly unless you counted the guests' breakfasts of fried bacon, sausage, bread, egg, mushrooms and baked beans. Like over two-thirds of British homes – the highest proportion of any European country – Sea Spray possessed a microwave oven, and once or twice a day its cheery ping! announced the readiness of a cook-chill ready meal, bought in bulk from the Newhaven branch of Sainsbury's. On a given night there might be chicken korma, lasagne, mini turkey Kievs or fish fingers. As part of her weekly shop Mrs Lee also got in an industrial-sized sack of McCain Oven Chips – a pre-oiled frozen potato product whose ease of preparation is the only point in its favour – and by the end of the week the family had polished off the sack between them.

She regularly watched the cookery programmes on TV and had occasionally wondered about trying to recreate some of the dishes she saw being made before deciding it was more trouble than it was worth.

'I do like that Gary Rhodes, I think he's ever such a nice man. And I've got a lot of time for that Fern Britton, off *Ready Steady Cook*. I tell you who I don't like, and that's that Gordon

Ramsay. Effing and blinding. My husband would have had fifty fits.'

She sat forward on the sofa. 'Now, love, there's something I've been meaning to ask you. Will you be wanting the Full Monty in the morning, or will you be happy with the Continental?'

I walked off the Full Monty in the streets of Newhaven, looking for good things – a nice little pastry shop, perhaps, or a butcher selling homemade English pies, a weakness of mine. Perhaps it was unreasonable to expect great things. But in a harbour town one might have expected to find at least one fishmonger. There was none that I could find; neither was there a market, not so much as a single fruit stall, nor a proper delicatessen, nor a charcuterie nor a patisserie. The dining possibilities of the town were equally limited: there were several fish and chip shops, a curry house or three and a Greek restaurant by the name of Scoffers. There had once been an excellent simple fish restaurant, I was told, but it had gone out of business.

Such gastronomic paucity was puzzling, especially compared with the port town on the opposite side of the channel. On the other hand Newhaven was a smaller place with fewer pretensions. In the South of England, moreover, it is not to the towns and cities that you turn to look for good and interesting food, but to the bits of countryside wedged between them.

The pleasure of British food, I reminded myself, was never about lolling in a warm bath of perfection, but about unpredictability and risk, and finding delicious things in apparently unpromising surroundings. The thrill is not the choice, but the chase.

I climbed in the car and set off northwards, through a landscape of gentle hills, neat, fragrant and prosperous. It was harvest time, and combine harvesters rumbled in the fields, each surrounded by its retinue of greedy sea birds. Here and there, sitting smugly in their luxurious gardens, were farmworkers' cottages in Sussex flint and brick, once regarded as little more desirable as places to live than your average pigsty, now transformed into the hygienically rustic second homes of London millionaires. At the Ram in the village of Firle, the kind of country pub that looks like it ought to be patronised by harvesters in smocks supping pints of foaming scrumpy, the public bar was full of Glyndebourne-goers in their black-tie uniform, genteelly sipping on Sussex Chardonnay. Out in the car park, wickerwork hampers of operatic picnic food lay creaking gently in their Volvos.

A little further up the main road to Lewes, I made my first major gastro-discovery. All over England there are roadside stalls selling fruit and veg to passers-by – but Middle Farm was a farm shop with a difference. It sold what by any standards was an astonishing range of foods, all unpasteurised, unwaxed, unsprayed, un-genetically modified, un-everything. At Middle Farm I saw for myself what I had suspected for a while: that the wholesale industrialisation of food production in Britain has finally brought about a powerful backlash in the form of organic, natural foods, produced on a small scale with no artificial ingredients, if possible following traditional recipes. Here you could buy the whole lot in a single stop: organic fruit and vegetables from local farms; organic meats from rare breeds; dry-cured bacon and homemade sausages; bread from organic wind-milled English wheat and rye; free-range eggs laid by birds fed on biodynamic maize and barley; wonderful vegetables, organic of course, from the fields around the shop . . . All of it seeming to glow with a kind of self-righteous pride in its own impeccable pedigree.

Here at Middle Farm, I had my first revelatory taste of that thrilling phenomenon, the renaissance of British farmhouse cheese. For decades, while the French boasted of having a cheese for every day of the year, we were forced to content ourselves with a tiny range of dreary factory cheeses, made with pasteurised Friesian cows' milk on a massive scale and sold to us in sweaty plastic-wrapped blocks. The shock troops of the cheese revolution were men and women whose dedication went beyond the call of duty, expert *affineurs* such as Randolph Hodgson, Patrick Rance and Iain Mellis and stalwart producers such as Charles Martell, Ann Wigmore and Ruth Kirkham. The philosophy behind the movement combined innovation and daring with respect for the achievements of the past. Britain had once had a repertoire of glorious cheeses that creeping industrialisation, centralised food policies and public apathy had collectively put paid to. But Britain has some of the best pasture in the world, and therefore some of the richest milk. It would be possible, they reasoned, to make cheeses that were truly the equal of anything France or Italy could offer – but only by using unpasteurised milk, by working on an artisan scale, and by offering the cheeses for sale under the best possible conditions, not chilled to death and embalmed in plastic on some supermarket shelf.

The new generation of handmade on-farm cheeses have fought their way to life, and there are more of them than ever. In her invaluable *Real Cheese Companion*, Sarah Freeman gives the names and details of more than 130 of the new British farmhouse cheeses. A few have been made for centuries; others were invented last year. Some are made following indigenous British recipes, notably Cheddar; others take their cue from Dutch and French models, notably Gouda and Coulommiers. Among them are sheep's, goats', and cows' milk cheeses. For the first of my Great British gastronomical picnics, I sought out a selection of local examples, nibbling a morsel of each, marvelling at the fact that an all-Sussex cheeseboard was actually possible. Of the ones that have stayed in my memory, there was Flower Marie, a mould-ripened sheep's milk cheese that fully lived up to its exquisite name, with a voluptuous creaminess and a taste redolent of meadow grass and summer hedgerows. There was Old Plaw Hatch, produced on a biodynamic farm near East Grinstead where the cows are treated homoeopathically and fed on the farm's own hay, wheat and oats. It had a Cheddary fullness and tang, and a resonance on the palate that would be impossible to reproduce using pasteurised milk. And there was another astounding sheep's milk cheese called Lord of the Hundreds, nutty and almost caramelly sweet in taste. I bought a good chunk of each of the three, plus a loaf of bread and a pot of pickled walnuts, and sat in a cornfield to work my way through it all.

I spent most of that autumn in a country house under the first undulating chalky-flinty ridge of the South Downs, where I rented a flat in the attic. My landlady was a winningly robust, free-spirited and generous woman such as the English upper classes produce from time to time, who went barefoot around the house and spent half the year in Goa. Her food was as generous as her nature. It was English country cookery, our own comfortable and comforting national soul food. Roasts, stews, pies, vegetables, puddings, fruit, cheese. Life in her kitchen revolved around two pieces of furniture that had become institutions: a great black ancient smoking Aga, and a huge kitchen table strewn with the flotsam of family life – newspapers, ashtrays, butter dishes, candlesticks.

In a book Victoria had thoughtfully left by my bedside, I read up on old Sussex lore. There was once both a local dialect and a local character, I learned; the clichéd description of the Sussex countryman being that, obstinate and set in his ways, he 'wunt be druv'.

There is no genuine regional cooking in Britain, where our roots in the land are shallower than those of any other European people, and Sussex has nothing it can truly call its own. Or so I had always believed; but it was beginning, already, to seem that I was wrong. As I pored through piles of cookbooks in Lewes town library, I found tantalising hints of unexpected richness. Elizabeth David, who was born in a farmhouse just over the Downs from where I was staying, gives a recipe for Sussex Stewed Steak in her *Spices, Salt and Aromatics in the English Kitchen*, though I'm willing to bet there aren't many in the county who've ever tried it. It mustn't be forgotten, either, that Isabella Beeton's recipe for steak and kidney pudding, the first ever to appear in print, was given to her by a lady from Sussex, 'in which county the inhabitants are noted for their savoury puddings'. Of the old dishes, on the evidence of various pub menus in and around the city of Chichester, at least one has plenty of life left in it. That dish is Sussex Pond Pudding – a unique celebration of the fragrance of the lemon in the homespun guise of an English steamed pud.

Sussex Pond Pudding

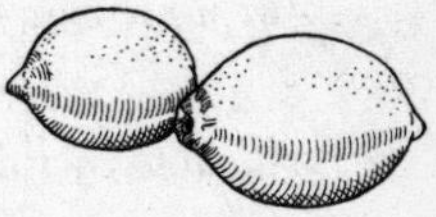

(serves 4–6)

Sift 225g of plain flour with 2 level teaspoons of baking powder and half a teaspoon of salt into a big bowl. Add 125g of shredded beef suet. Make a well in the centre of the mixture and mix in around 125ml of cold water with a knife to create a soft, smooth dough. Knead gently.

Roll out the pastry to a thickness of about 5mm. Grease an 850ml (1.5 pint) pudding basin, doing the top edge and rim as well as the inside. Cut out a quarter segment of the circle and use the remaining three quarters to line the basin. Dampen the edges and seal the joins. Into the basin put 75g of cold unsalted butter cut into flakes, followed by 75g of demerara sugar. Then add a fresh unwaxed lemon – avoid the old one that's been sitting sadly in your fruit bowl for months – pierced right through at various points with a skewer. Nestle the lemon nicely in the heap of butter and sugar, then cover it with a further 75g of butter flakes and 75g of sugar, until the basin is full.

Roll out the other quarter of dough to make a lid. Moisten the top edge of the pastry; place the lid on top. Pinch and seal the edges securely. Grease a square of tin foil and place it over the basin, making a 1cm pleat across the top to allow for the pudding to expand. Tie the foil down with a length of string under the rim. Steam for 3.5–4 hours, either in a two-tier steamer or in a saucepan half filled with boiling water (in either case the lid should fit tightly).

Allow to cool slightly, then remove the foil and turn out the pudding upside down on to a wide dish. When you cut into the pudding a 'pond' of lemon-scented liquid will form. Locate the lemon and cut into slices. Serve with egg custard, crème fraîche or Greek yogurt.

The days went on, and I settled back pleasantly into English life, remembering to eat lunch at one and dinner at eight, and discovering once more the national addiction to tea. In the mornings I shopped at Middle Farm, and at Infinity Foods in Brighton, a sort of New Age Fortnum & Mason, patchouli-scented and funky. The dark afternoons were spent combing the hedgerows for crab apples, blackberries and bullaces, and putting up jams and jellies and murky jars of sloe gin. And in the evenings I met up with old friends in disappointing restaurants that often seemed also to be over-priced – though a bad meal, as someone once said, is always expensive. Little by little the otherwise adorable city of Brighton revealed itself to me as a place where, sadly and mysteriously, it is difficult to find a first-class place to eat. As I padded the narrow lanes, vainly searching for a good, interesting, welcoming, affordable restaurant, I thought more than once of the great chef Antoine Carême, who came here to cook for the Prince Regent in 1816 and had harsh words to say about local culinary habits. 'Even the presiding deity of the Pavilion scarcely rose above the cowslips appreciation of a roast duck with its coarse and predominating accompaniment of sage and onion stuffing,' he wrote sniffily.

One evening I called up a couple of foodie friends from way back and went round to see them at their flat near the old West Pier. Mick and Jo grew up in an entirely new British gastronomic tradition, formed of a mish-mash, a sophisticated purée, of Thai, Italian and Provençal cuisines. They remain unamused by the notion of suet puddings.

'Eurgh! Yuk! I can't bear that sort of thing,' said Jo, pausing in her assembly of a particularly intricate salad of roasted peppers, shredded salt cod and garlic confit to assemble her features into a graphic expression of disgust.

'Stodge and slop,' said Mick dismissively, pulling open a bottle of Cloudy Bay Sauvignon Blanc he had managed to obtain at enormous cost from a New Zealand friend with contacts at the winery.

'I think most traditional English food's pretty revolting, if you want my opinion, which you probably don't,' said Jo.

'Yeah, though that may be just because you were presented with such a revolting version of it When We Were Very Young,' mused Mick, whose schooldays, like mine, were a Stygian procession of macaroni cheese, Spam fritters and tapioca.

'But then English cooking's always been inferior to French and Italian, hasn't it? It's just that we've always had a chip on our collective shoulder about it. Can you lay the table, Mick? Let's eat,' said Jo.

'Well now, of course that view reflects a common misconception,' said another friend of mine, a playwright and cook, when

I relayed to him the gist of the conversation. Just that morning he had been putting the finishing touches to a lecture he was due to give on the subject of English food and food history.

'Medieval cuisine in England, of course, one imagines to have consisted of bleeding hunks of meat, bread, and a large amount of beer. In fact it was a quite marvellously sophisticated and varied cuisine, whose influences came largely from Persia and very little from France. The love of fruit with meat, the use of ginger, cubebs, and all that tremendous repertoire of spices. As a nation, I believe, we really have such a rich heritage in cooking, but it became submerged in the sixteenth and seventeenth centuries by a feeling of inferiority to the French. In medieval times, you know, the French called the English "men of Cockaigne", Cockaigne being the mythical land of food, a byword for plenty, where the rivers ran with wine and honey – there's a Breughel painting of it, all these porkers running about with knives strapped to their sides so that you could slice off a bit.'

I sat in the walled garden of Chris's old house while he busied himself inside, and fell into a mild state of trance at the beauty of this quiet cottage garden in its full autumnal splendour. The best English gardeners have always allowed a certain amount of chaos to temper their natural liking for order and control. Chris switched on the fountain under the pergola and it leaped into life, adding to the Mediterranean note already provided by a fig tree climbing the wall behind me, scenting the air with its sweet waxy reek.

'We've been wondering about moving to Brighton,' he announced from inside as I turned my face towards the sunlight. 'I know Brighton from way back, as you know. The trouble is our quality of life would absolutely plummet, since we'd have no access to our supply of absolutely fabulous fresh vegetables.'

He brought out a plate with some sea salt in a little pot and a big clanking jug of iced tea and I munched rudely through an entire plate of stumpy little carrots, long strong radishes, pale green and juicy peppers, and miniature tomatoes called Sweet One Hundreds that had the best flavour I had ever encountered in a British tomato. These crudités were but a prelude to a lunch for which Chris apologised, perhaps a touch disingenuously because he knew as well as I did that there is nothing in the world more delicious than home-grown vegetables untimely ripped from the garden, good bread and butter and cheese. He brought out a bowl of beans, French and baby broad, steamed and tossed in sesame oil, and a salad of various leaves, not all of which I could identify, with Parmesan shaved into it. Already on the table was the pièce de résistance – an unpasteurised local butter from Fraysland Farm, an irregular squarish pat wrapped in paper, that tasted of meadows and hayricks and the aroma of fresh milk in cool dairies. After the ton of yellow spread we have all eaten in our lives, this was like eating butter for the very first time. Chris pushed the pat to the end of the table – 'I mustn't, you know; it gives me terrible health problems' – but not before he had smeared a good knifeful on his brown bread and raised his eyes to heaven.

Chris's kitchen garden was even more beautiful than his flower garden. Everything was planted out in a series of raised beds. 'Easier on the back,' said Chris.

Artichokes, asparagus, two or three types of chard, red cabbages, red Brussels sprouts, red basil (red vegetables were fashionable that year), beans of four kinds, including yellow ones especially for drying, peas, potatoes, courgettes, onions, elephant garlic: these are some of the things I remember from the bright tableaux formed by the neat rectangular beds. The salad section rustled and creaked with lettuces and herbs and edible flowers. It was hard to find my way among it all until Chris pointed out various of the leaves that had played starring roles in the salad at lunch.

'This one – now what do you think it is?' he enquired, holding up a stalk of something.

'That's purslane.'

'And this?'

'Could it be some kind of mustard?' I hazarded. It had a deep green lobe-shaped leaf; I chewed on the sweet-hot crunchy stalk.

'Yes, but what kind exactly? I'll give you a clue. Think of the Far East.'

'Chinese.'

'Japanese.'

He chuckled at my near miss. 'What about this, then?'

'God knows. It's weird, isn't it?'

The leaf was purple and slightly crinkly and had a bizarre and completely unpindownable flavour, with overtones of elderflower, vanilla and the bittersweet skin of a barely ripe apple.

'Now this is something I've just got hold of. It's the extraordinary shiso or perilla or beefsteak plant. It is supposed to combine the flavours of oregano, mint and basil, though I can't quite see that myself. A bit of a novelty, from Japan – where of course all the best novelties come from. It's very nice in salads, and gives a wonderful zizz to certain soups. I also plan to use it in pickles,' said Chris excitedly, nibbling away. 'Oh, the possibilities are endless. Shall we move on?'

2

kent

hops, salads and an encounter with knobby russet

Along the sides of the roads in the South-East of England the countryside spills out its wares in roadside stalls, farm shops and Pick Your Owns. In an hour or so, as I whizzed along a B road from Sussex into Kent, I could have bought honey, fresh herbs, goats' cheese, bread, duck eggs, pheasants, rabbits, endless roots and salads and a whole summer pudding's worth of strawberries, loganberries, currants and cassis. There were nuts, apples, cream and farmhouse cider. My mind bubbled and squeaked with plans for all this produce: the pheasant could be roasted with cider; the goats' cheese chopped into a heap of bittersweet herbs and sprinkled with chopped toasted cobnuts or drizzled with local honey.

As if drizzled with honey by a hungry God, the landscape

around me seemed to take on the autumnal richness, the luscious curvaceousness of an English Tuscany. I drove across the border and lost myself in the deep countryside around Lamberhurst, the surprising shapes of oast houses rising up from time to time within it, their white 'cowls' like sails in a sea of woodland, cornfields, vineyards and orchards. The county seemed to be empty. Perhaps its inhabitants were all in Tuscany.

'Welcome to Kent: Garden of England', said a roadsign, predictably enough. In the gaps between the motorways and railways and the cute little Kentish towns this is still the most prodigiously fertile agricultural land in Britain, but the crops it supports are not what they used to be. The county's economic mainstay was once its luscious cherries, its apples and pears, its cobnuts and pungent hops, hung on their towering poles. At Sissinghurst Castle during the 1960s, when Harold and Vita were still hard at work on their great garden, the estate was largely taken up with hops, fruit and dairy farming. When I visited it had long been given over to wheat, barley, oilseed rape and pasture for sheep. Most of the cherry trees in Kent have been grubbed up or abandoned to their fate. Cobnut or filbert plantations – 'filbert' being the anglicised form of *noix de Philibert*, St Philibert having been a seventh-century Abbot of Jumièges in Normandy – used to cover 7,000 acres of prime Kentish countryside and now occupy just 250 acres. 'I've given up on cobnuts,' said a lady farmer I met in a pub in Plaxtol. 'It's a waste of time. For all the profit you make on the damn things, you might as well throw them away. Though I do know where you can get hold of a ten-pound box of cobnuts, if you're desperate.'

Was there ever a Kentish cuisine? There surely was, though as Jane Grigson pointed out, why Normandy should have developed a coherent culinary style and stuck to it and Kent should not, when the two regions share many of the same ingredients, is a very good question.

Within the memory of the middle-aged, there are at least a few Kentish delicacies. Huffkins, a kind of small flat pale oval-shaped teacake, were once baked all over the county. I found them in a bakery in Ashford. And in spring, when the hops were bright green and tender, there were hop shoots. 'They are boiled in broth and eaten like asparagus with butter toast,' says Dorothy Hartley in *Food in England*, using the present tense when the past would now be more appropriate, since you don't see many bubbling pots of hop shoots on English stoves these days.

In a village outside Tunbridge Wells I found the hop farm that once supplied the hops for Whitbread beers. It was now a Hop Farm Country Park, with a gift shop, an interactive museum and rural rides. The few remaining acres of hops were now farmed privately and had nothing to do with the Hop Farm itself, which was now entirely devoted to leisure.

'It is a little sad, I suppose. But they do say that hops can be grown an awful lot more cheaply in China,' said the cheerful lady at the cash till. 'Would you like to take one of our leaflets?'

I walked for a while among the hop fields – a cool earth-bound Sargasso Sea of cascading greenery. I pulled a fistful of the tight, aromatic little bundles, crushed them in my hand and buried my nose in them. They were astonishingly beery, very like the smell of the head on a pint of good bitter. I put a few in my pocket and they stuck there for days, falling out occasionally when I groped for coins in car parks.

It was a struggle to imagine, in the silence of these green canyons, the extent to which hop-farming dominated the social life and economy of Kent. Come September, gangs of pickers would arrive in charabancs from the East End of London. For some of them hop-picking was a holiday; for others it was a lifeline. Either way it was tough work. Hops must be harvested as quickly as possible, while the flower still has plenty of colour and aroma. Until 1968, when the first machines came in, it was all done by hand, the cutting of the bines with a long hop-hook and the plucking of the hop flowers and the loading of the 'pockets', the long hop sacks. (Hop-picking had its own pungent vocabulary.)

George Orwell picked hops in the autumn of 1931. I love his fine description of the working day with its nice detail of the hop-pickers' menu: 'At about quarter past six in the morning we crawled out of straw, put on our coats and boots (we slept in everything else) and went out to get a fire going – rather a job this September, when it rained all the time. By half past six we had made tea and fried some bread for breakfast, and then we started off for work, with bacon sandwiches and a drum of cold tea for our dinner. If it didn't rain we were working pretty steadily till about one, and then we would start a fire between the vines, heat up our tea and knock off for half an hour. After that we were at it again till half past five, and by the time we had got home, cleaned the hop-juice off our hands and had tea, it was already dark and we were dropping with sleep.'*

On the way into Faversham, as I drove through the well-upholstered Kentish villages, they were already making bonfires with

* *Collected Essays, Journalism and Letters of George Orwell*, Vol. I, Secker and Warburg, 1968.

the leaves and stems of the hop bines. The skeletal structure of the wires and poles looked stark and sad against the greying sky.

But as one crop peters out, another kicks in. Over at Brogdale they were bringing in the apples in plastic fruit boxes, each meticulously labelled with the variety. This is important at Brogdale, because with more than 2,300 different varieties grown on the estate there is plenty of room for confusion. In the little shop where you gathered for the guided tour the apples spilled out of sacks and baskets, a Baroque still-life of colour, shape, surface shine and bloom and pittedness that would certainly surprise anyone who thought that apples were just apples. You were encouraged to buy a selection of varieties and I did so, making my choice as much on the basis of nomenclature – there were apples in the shop that proudly announced themselves as Pig's Nose Pippin, Poor Man's Profit, Scotch Dumpling and Winter Banana – as on gastronomic criteria alone.

There is nothing quite like Brogdale Horticultural Trust anywhere else in Britain, and for all I know in all the world. The Trust is responsible for the care of one of Britain's great treasures, the National Fruit Collections, a living museum of fruit trees covering sixty acres of prime Kentish farmland. Since they were set up in 1800 the Collections have had a chequered history that nearly came to an inglorious end in 1991, when the Ministry of Agriculture decided they were an irrelevance and should no longer be supported by the State. The Trust was set up in part with funds provided by the Duchy of Cornwall – a generous act, except that if the Duchy wanted its money back, Brogdale would have to sell an awful lot of apples.

On a cold September morning it seemed at first an unpromising sort of place. The shop and café, housed in a dreary piece of post-war functionalist building, were harshly decorated and had a charity shop feel about them.

What Brogdale lacks in resources, however, it more than makes up for in enthusiasm. The Collections can only be seen as part of a guided tour. Perhaps the people in charge feel that so much fruit, ripe for the picking, might be a temptation difficult to resist for the unsupervised visitor. But the guides are rare varieties in themselves. Mr Harmsworth sensibly arrived in a zip-up anorak, his notes encased in a plastic file.

'Well, you seem to be the only one today. Are you ready to look at some fruit?' he said briskly. Then he swivelled on his heel and marched me off through the incipient rain and the steamy labyrinth of trees.

Mr H. was born in Sittingbourne, in the heart of the fruit-growing country of east Kent, and spent his childhood Saturdays working as a farmhand on an old mixed farm. In those days the corn was still cut, stooked and stacked into ricks and the apple trees were picked by means of long ladders.

'That was before these new dwarfing rootstocks came in – see, how you can practically pick the whole tree standing on the ground?' he said, reaching me down an example of an Asian pear, a soft golden orb quite different from the rock-hard lump of green wood that is the British supermarket shopper's usual experience of the pear. It had a mild, sweet, delicate taste, with exotic overtones of cucumber and roses.

'We might as well start with the pears. Now, all pears these days are grafted on to quinces – they're the same genus, you see. Here at Brogdale we grow roughly five hundred different varieties. Now, of those five hundred, how many do you think are grown commercially worldwide on any kind of scale?'

I knew it wouldn't be very many, but I didn't expect his answer. 'Somewhere in the region of six.'

'Some of the five hundred that you won't see are Clapp's Favourite, Swan's Egg and Bishop's Thumb. Here's one of the few that you will. It's a cross between Doyenne du Comice and Concord, bred in the 1970s, and one of the up-and-coming pears on the UK market.' It had a bright, almost fizzy, user-friendly sort of sweetness. 'And here's one that's hardly grown at all these days. It's a Russian pear; from the Crimea, I believe.' This was a lovely 'weeping' tree, its graceful boughs just now so weighed down with fruit it seemed not so much lachrymose as stricken with terminal Weltschmerz.

'On your left are the medlars,' Mr H. went on in his clipped yet amiable fashion. 'Again, not much used these days, although I do hear Tiptree make 5,000 jars of medlar jelly every year, so there must be some demand. Before refrigeration, of course, they were a very useful fruit, since they ripen in late November, when there's nothing else about.'

Brogdale is a lesson in history as well as horticultural reality. Before technology allowed us to bring in foreign fruits and the price of our own crops dropped through the floor, British farms produced a far wider variety and quantity of fruit than is imaginable today. It seems to me that our native fruit is tragically undervalued. The medlar, eaten 'bletted', which is a euphemism for 'rotten', I could live without. But not the English plum, the cherry, the quince, the strawberry, and certainly not the finest-flavoured, most nourishing and most inexhaustibly varied fruit of all, probably the first cultivated fruit in history: the apple.

Understanding the development of the genus *Malus* from

the wild crab apple into the mainstay crop of today requires a very particular expertise. All I would have time for today was to scratch the surface, to nibble through the skin, so to speak, and briefly taste the rich flesh beneath. Mr H. took me on a whirlwind orchard tour of the prize items in this priceless gene bank. Decio, brought over to Britain by the Romans; the splendidly named Green Custard, which the Elizabethans first spelt Costard; and Hunthouse, a Yorkshire apple whose historical significance is greater than its culinary value: it was taken by Captain Cook on his voyages to ward off scurvy, and is as mouth-crinklingly bitter as to be almost inedible.

Then came the curiosities: the Dutch Lemoen, with its clear-as-daylight lemon tang, and the Scottish Bloody Ploughman – oh, those names! – with its ribbed scarlet skin and its seeping redness underneath. Brogdale visitors are always delighted to see the ugliest apple in the orchard, the Knobby Russet, which has a skin so pitted, wrinkled and scrofulous it looks diseased. One should never judge an apple by its skin, however, and the Knobby Russet had a dry and fragrant aroma and delicious hard crunch, with a final whiff of aniseed at the back of the mouth.

'Here, now, is one of my favourite eaters. Appropriately enough, it's called the Kent. Now in my view it's quite superb. But the thing is the supermarkets won't take it. Because it won't all grow the same size, and it has a tendency to roughen on the skin. Which is no good, because of course the supermarkets want a shiny apple,' said Mr H. as he strained his arms through the dripping foliage of another heavy-laden tree.

Slicing off chunks of cool fresh apple with a little knife he carried especially for the purpose, he gave me a piece of Kent and we munched together in silence. It was quite an experience, that apple: crisp yet yielding under the teeth, richly aromatic, holding sweetness and acidity and depth of flavour in perfect balance. I took another bite, and another look at this fine old tree whose fruit had been judged so inadmissibly irregular. And I inwardly cursed the supermarkets and their arrogant disdain for something that, by virtue of being a decent, unmanipulated piece of good food, falls foul of their preposterous rules.

There were apples at the Harvest Festival in the village church, though they looked to me more like Golden Delicious than anything I'd seen that morning. They sat in boxes on the floor beside the pews, alongside sacks of potatoes, boxes of eggs and the inevitable stash of vegetable marrows. Around the altar, however, was the site of the real traditional British Harvest Festival as I remembered it; the altar area was the site for the proud display of Heinz Baked Beans, Ambrosia Creamed Rice, John West Pink Salmon, Cassoulet Traditionnel de Toulouse and other products of the good earth for which we should all give our humble and hearty thanks.

It can't have been as grim as the McHarvest Festival, which I'd read about with amazement in the *Telegraph* that morning. A priest in the West Midlands was planning to hold her harvest celebration in the local branch of McDonald's, and would be asking her parishioners to bring fast-food items – packets of crisps, tinned curry, Pot Noodles, boil-in-the-bag rice – to adorn the 'church'. It made more sense, she said, for the McHarvest Festival to reflect the real urban culture of the parish and not some mocked-up idyll of nineteenth-century country life. And of course she had a point: if what you eat is Pot Noodles, then Pot Noodles, not farmhouse cheeses and free-range eggs, are what you have to be thankful for. But the bare fact of such dietary impoverishment, not to mention the Reverend's untroubled admission of the status quo, weighed upon my heart.

It will always be a problem for food writers to come to terms with the central place that McDonald's occupies in many British lives. Despite acres of bad publicity, jokes about the McJob and widespread loathing by the middle classes, Britain is still a hungry market for the McDonald's hamburger. Many mothers keep it in reserve as the ultimate weapon in the charm offensive they permanently wage with their kids – something special that will shut them up once and for all. Many kids, thereby encouraged to see the McDonald's hamburger as something utterly delicious, never make the leap from the instant gratification of fast food to the incomparably deeper pleasure of real food. In return for their loyalty Ronald McDonald treats them rather well. For all their shortcomings, McDonald's restaurants are a good deal more child-friendly than the average real food emporium.

In order to test out my theories, I dropped in to the Canterbury branch in St George's Street. A gaggle of kids had dropped in after school, all pencil cases and attitude. I canvassed their thoughts on this, the country's single most popular dish.

'Yeah, it tastes sort of meaty.'

'I like the special sauce, and that green thing.'

'Gherkin, dick'ead.'

'Yeah, and them McNuggets things, normally I'll have a Big Mac but if I don't have a Big Mac I'll have a McNuggets – wiv curry sauce.'

'It's just really nice.'

By the window sat a group of older female customers, merrily gobbling. One of them wore a pale-blue shirt and a dark-blue sensible skirt. They looked like they might be shop assistants or till girls in a supermarket.

How many times did they dine at McDonald's in any given week?

'Ask 'er, she's in here all the time!' said one of them, poking her friend on the shoulder.

'No, I might come in two or three times a week. Usually I'll have the Big Mac and a small fries and a small Coke. My little brother, though, he's the worst. He can't live without McDonald's. I reckon he's on ten or twelve Big Macs a week. He'd have breakfast, lunch and dinner in here if he could.'

'Sometimes I'll just come in for a coffee and a chat with some friends. I don't really go for the burgers much, anyway I'm lucky, my mum cooks at home,' said a pretty Asian girl, the quietest of the group.

'Yeah, well I love 'em. And they're cheap,' retorted the loyal customer.

'I mean, where else can you get a meal for two quid?'

A few years ago McDonald's launched a series of advertisements that showed people in all sorts of situations suddenly being compelled to go in search of the nearest branch of the Golden Arches. Those ads had it uncannily right: the need for a Big Mac is a feeling that goes way beyond simple hunger or even greed, and in a way has more in common with the dizzying power of lust. The success of the product lies in a calculated combination of almost every edible texture and flavour that human beings have been found to enjoy, from savoury to sweet via piquantly vinegary and bracingly salty, from chewily meaty to gooily unctuous via warm and pappy and cool and crunchy. The first bite of a Big Mac sets up an explosion of flavour and sensation akin to whacking the tastebuds with a large mallet.

A popular urban myth claims that fast-food chains employ psychologists to create an ambience so cunningly, indefinably unpleasant that the average human being can only endure it for an average of six minutes and thirty-eight seconds, in order to ensure that patrons flow efficiently through the system. Failing to reach this average, I returned to my car and spent half an hour brushing the crumbs off the seats, neatly piling up the road maps and the guides to Good Pubs and Good Food Shops and Ever So Charming Places to Stay.

I had been on the road for a week, and already the car was beginning to take on the subtle aroma of a municipal skip. Taking stock, under the driver's seat I relocated a mini-truckle of Cecilia cheese from Nepicar Farm near Sevenoaks that I had bought in a cheese shop in Chichester because I'd heard it was matured by being buried for two weeks in a barrel of hops. Under the passenger seat were more ageing goodies: a paper bagful of plums, a packet of hot-smoked salmon from the Dungeness smokery and a dusty, furry apple, plus a half-empty bottle of mineral water and a dried-up heel of Tesco ciabatta. In the boot, finally, a leg of frozen Gloucester Old Spot Pork had broken loose from its moorings and had spent the day careering left and right with every bend in the winding Kentish lanes, colliding noisily – though with less of a crack! and more of a whack! as it gradually defrosted – with the bottle of Chapel Hill English red wine with which I had been planning to accompany it.

I was too tired to drive back to Sussex tonight, and the thought of another fried-bread B&B made me nauseous. So I got on the mobile to a couple of old friends who had moved from Clapham to a village outside Tonbridge when London property prices went insane, and begged them for dinner and bed.

Quentin and Tamsin were gastronomes belonging to the brave new world of balsamic vinegar, arugula and sun-dried tomatoes. On the night I called they had just got back from a friend's house in Umbria laden with gastro-souvenirs. Their parents' generation might have brought back ashtrays, terracotta flowerpots and lace handkerchiefs. When I arrived, at dusk on Friday, they were still unpacking the olives, the slabs of lardo, the hard chunks of coppa and tins of rustling amaretti, and scurrying around the kitchen reciting recipes from Marcella Hazan. But I brought in a bagful of swag from the car and we arranged the Cecilia next to the Taleggio, the brine-cured Winchelsea ham next to the sliced coppa on a board, and drank a bottle of Gospel Green méthode champenoise cider – the Veuve Clicquot of apple drinks – to celebrate their homecoming, and for a brief while we basked in the pleasurable illusion that in terms of food and drink South-East England had little reason to envy Umbria.

By the back door was a pile of trugs – that inevitable adjunct of any fashionable garden de nos jours. I took one from the pile, stumbled out of the house into the cool dewy night and groped my way round the back to the vegetable patch. From beyond the stream, beside the cricket pitch, came the muted throb of dance music. The cricket club was holding its annual rave.

Tamsin and Quentin lived in a small brick house in a clearing in a wood that had once been the apple orchard for a nearby country estate; their house had been the apple store. I picked a big bag of spinach, lollo rosso and fresh herbs from among the green riot that had grown up unmolested over the last fortnight and stood for a while to watch the moon, which was just emerging from the tops of the trees like a great Orange Pippin, bringing up the pinks and yellows of the giant hollyhocks that stood guard on the fringes of the woodland.

We built an impromptu salad out of that bag of prodigal, dew-washed greenery. Since we were in trainspotting foodie mode, I pulled out my notebook to locate a wonderful quotation from John Evelyn, the seventeenth-century writer on horticulture whose influence on our own attitudes to veg has been incalculable, and read it aloud while Tamsin dressed the dish with Umbrian olive oil, Kentish cider vinegar, a little mustard and a clove of crushed garlic. 'In the composure of a Sallet, every Plant should come in to bear its part, without being overpower'd by some Herb of a stronger Taste . . . like the Notes in Music, in which there should be nothing harsh or grating . . . Reconcile all Dissonancies, and melt them into an agreeable Composition.'

'Mmm, that's nice. But I've got an even better one,' said Quentin, who had taken down from the bookshelf an anthology of writings about food. 'This is Pietro Aretino in 1537, apparently thanking his friend Girolamo Sarra for sending him some salad. I see it as one of those ready-mixed bags of leaves, you know, like in Marks and Spencer. Here we go: "I gape open-mouthed at the way you compensate for the sharpness of one herb with the sweetness of another. It takes no small skill to match the pungency and the bite of one leaf with the savour, neither pungent nor biting, of a different one until the whole is a mixture so tasty that it would satisfy satiety itself."'

We ate the salad, and Tamsin had knocked up a concoction of roasted vegetables and feta cheese, and as a lazy coda to the feast we polished off a half-bottle of Vin Santo with its duty-free polystyrene vest still on it, passing round a tub of Häagen-Dazs Macadamia Nut Brittle Ice Cream that Quentin had managed to dredge up from the bottom of the freezer, and felt that we had eaten well.

My hosts were tired after their journey, and wanted to vegetate in front of some inane TV. Flipping through the television guide, I noticed that on the afternoon of the previous day there had been three cookery programmes in succession. In the evening on the other channel there had been a travel programme with a feature on Thai markets, then a documentary on the booming London restaurant scene, which according to the dubious blurb was turning London into the food capital of the world. There was at least one food-related programme on every channel every day. In one single week I counted fourteen cookery programmes of all possible types, from the down-home daytime housewife type (spinach roulade, gazpacho, cider punch) to the studio beat-the-clock frenetic-activity type and the fly-in-the-soup behind-the-scenes portrait-of-a-loutish-genius-chef type.

Tonight there was something about rustic Italian food.

'Flick it over to four, would you, darling?' called Tamsin across the room. 'You might just recognise a few things here.'

We were halfway through a programme presented by two elegant though casually unkempt rich women in a minimalist kitchen, calmly cooking their way through some simple pasta.

Pappardelle with lemon juice, olive oil and Parmesan, a dish that would have fought hard to be more ravishingly plain. 'Now this will take you, I sh'd think, no more than about quarter of an hour to prepare, if that,' one of the women was saying as she poured the gorgeous-looking green-gold sauce on to the thick flat ribbons of steaming pasta.

Then it was the end of part one, and the commercials barged in with their jangle of messages. The first was for a kind of cook-chill pasta, sold on the speed with which it could be taken out of its cardboard sleeve and be heated up and ready in minutes. 'I'm not one of those people who actually enjoys waiting for things. Tagliatelle with ham and mushrooms – and without all those pots and pans', said a chirpy female voice. It made us laugh, the ridiculousness of the suggestion and the odd juxtaposition of ways with pasta, one so full of care and good taste and the other so mean, so impatient, so shallow.

Next day was a Saturday, and the village of Bedlington was holding its annual Grand Harvest Fête and Show.

'We've got to go. I promised Mrs Willis I'd take along some of my Sri Lankan pumpkin pickle for her stall, and the poor old thing's been banging on about it for weeks,' said Tamsin as we sat drinking coffee in the pale sunshine.

The Fête and Show was the major event of the year in the little Kent village, and it had galvanised the community into a state of tremulous excitement. The tea tent and the exhibition marquee had gone up on Friday afternoon, each kitted out with mushroom-shaped heaters in the expectation of a freeze. The tea-urn and the candy-floss machine had been booked for weeks, and the ladies of Bedlington had been up late last night buttering and slicing, buttering and slicing, while their neighbours baked cakes for the cake stall and their husbands guzzled pints of bitter down at the Railway Arms.

The Fête and Show was a few steps away from the old apple house, on a diminutive village green next to the cricket pitch. Late on Saturday morning we sauntered over. There was a coconut shy and a guess-the-weight-of-the-cake and a couple of bric-à-brac stalls manned by grannies charging pre-war prices for post-war junk. ('The pair of cocktail glasses? A shilling, dear.') Somewhere in the background a brass band chuntered its way through what the programme described as 'musical interludes'. This was a vision of England at its most innocent, gentle and appealing.

Inside the produce tent the winning items were laid out on trestle tables, inviting inspection. Everything was in scrupulous order and scrubbed to within an inch of its life. Potatoes chosen to show off their shocking pinkness and/or the eyeless smoothness of their skin, which had apparently been moisturised by Clinique. Shallots, tops neatly cut and tied with green cotton, deposited in shy groups in plates of sand. Onions with slices removed from their sides so that the judges could peer inside at their perfect internal structure. Runner beans of precisely matching lengths, ramrod straight and lined up on trays in military fashion. The usual impressive parade of vegetable marrows, so grotesquely distended they would surely be inedible.

It crossed my mind, faced with such a visual cornucopia, that one of the reasons for England's historical poor showing in the culinary arts might have been our national decision to invest more of our energy in gardening than in gastronomy.

The vegetable marrow, that triumph of horticultural values over culinary ones, represents some kind of proof. I had seen rank upon rank of them on roadside stalls in Kent and Sussex, offering themselves with a kind of desperation, like overweight overblown whores, to anyone who'd have them. Though what you would do with one of these creatures once you got her home is another question. You can boil a marrow and steam a marrow and stuff it and pickle it and make a jam of it and fritters of its flowers and Dorothy Hartley even suggests making a cold salad of it with baby carrots, peas and cress and mayonnaise. 'It makes a pleasant light lunch,' she says. She is right: it is probably the vegetable marrow's finest hour.

Dorothy Hartley's Marrow Salad

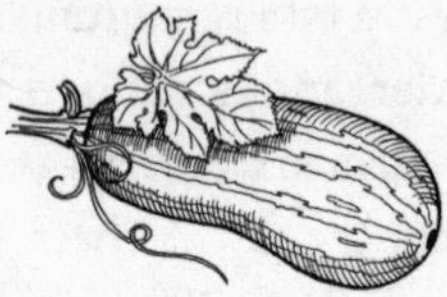

Take a small, fat marrow – the old, long ones can be stringy and flavourless. Hollow it out and flatten the base by cutting off a thin slice. Loosely stuff the marrow with fresh mint and steam it upright until cooked through. Allow to cool. Remove the top of the marrow to create a 'lid'.

The salad consists of cooked fresh peas, baby carrots, radishes and cress. Make a mayonnaise, combine the salad vegetables with it and fill the marrow with the mixture. Decorate the top of the 'bowl' with sprigs of watercress. Serve with brown bread and butter.

To drink with this dish, Mrs Hartley suggests 'hot coffee'. I should prefer a cool white wine.

First Prize in the Marrow Class was won by Mr Freeman, of Station Cottages. First Prize for A Group of Potatoes (Baking), I saw, also went to Mr Freeman, as did the First Prizes for Shallots, Runner Beans and An Arrangement of Vegetables on a Tray.

'You should see him when there's only a few weeks to go before the Show – the tension, it's terrible!' smiled a dumpy lady in a flowery skirt who stood at his side, his wife. 'He won't let me go near his vegetables. I tend to stay out of the way, really.'

We were standing by her husband's Savoy, a magnificent jade-green orb hooded with crinkly outer leaves of a deeper, darker racing green. 'Lovely, isn't it,' she said with a quiet pride.

'And what would you do with a cabbage like that?' I asked her.

'Oh, I might make a stuffing, you know, with mince meat and onion, and then tie it up and put it in the oven all together. Or I might just boil it up, not too long or it loses all the colour, and then a few bobs of butter on top, and a little bit of pepper.'

'Mmmm, delicious!' exclaimed Mr Freeman, overhearing his wife's plans for his esteemed creation.

Tamsin, Quentin and I wandered round the rest of the tent, giggling with delight at the size of the produce and the smallness of everything else, the way people laugh at a child's earnest innocent gestures. There were categories in the show that I remembered from my own childhood, when we were co-opted every year by our mother to submit hastily assembled Lentil

Collages and Flower Arrangements in a Piece of Kitchenware (Under 16s).

In the last quarter of a century the land of my fathers has changed almost beyond recognition; but there are some things that never change. Here they were still: An Edible Necklace; An Individual Pizza; A Favourite Sandwich (Named). The winner in the latter category was an eight-year-old boy who had cut his tuna salad sandwich into a fish shape and surrounded it with a necklace of greenstuff. Interestingly, all of the sandwiches entered used pre-sliced Hovis-type brown bread, except for one poor child whose mother had provided him with two slices of white Mother's Pride and a slice of Kraft cheese that curled greasily beyond the crust.

By the time we left for the Railway Arms the Favourite Sandwiches had been lying all day on their paper plates. Since they had been wrapped in clingfilm, they were beginning to sweat gently and odorously in the gaseous blast of the mushroom heater.

'Well, I don't know about you,' said Tamsin behind her hand, 'but if tuna salad on Hovis is what kids in Britain dream of, then I'd say we've got rather a long way to go. By the way, I gave Mrs Willis the pumpkin pickle. She actually bought a pot herself.'

'And what did she say?'

'Well, she unscrewed the lid and took a sniff and it nearly blew her head off, poor thing. She said it was possibly, no offence, but perhaps just a little bit too spicy for, you know, the village.'

'And what did you say?'

'I said I knew what she meant.'

3

into the west

real meat and wild mushrooms

I grew up in Hampshire, but my knowledge of Hampshire food is still regrettably scant.

I suppose there must be Hampshire dishes, just as there is a Hampshire dialect. (Two old women in our village spoke it. They were known as This and That. They, and it, were completely unintelligible to outsiders.) The phrase 'Hampshire hogs', which I remember hearing as a child, suggests it was a bacon-and-sausage county, like neighbouring Wiltshire. William Cobbett in *Cottage Economy*, a bedside book I love for its forthright and, as it now seems, prophetic view of the relationship between food and well-being, describes the Hampshire equivalent of the *matanza* of Southern Europe, in which the hairs were burned off the skin of the freshly killed pig rather than being scalded off with boiling water. 'The taste of the meat is very different from that of a scalded hog,' he contends, 'and to this chiefly it was that Hampshire bacon owed its reputation for excellence.'

Peer a little more closely into local lore, and a few small items of Hants gastronomy begin to emerge. Jerusalem artichokes ('Jerusalem' being a half-heard intimation of '*girasole*', the Italian word for the sunflower to which it's related). They were a favourite in our family, but I had no idea until recently that they were first grown in England at Buriton, near Petersfield, Hampshire, where the botanist John Goodyer had his trial garden. 'I stocked Hampshire,' he said proudly in 1617, having doled out the knobbly grey root to everyone he met.

Buriton Artichoke Soup

Thoroughly clean and peel half a kilo of Jerusalem artichokes. Cut the artichokes in thin slices into a bowl of water acidulated with a good splash of vinegar or the juice of a lemon.

Cook a chopped onion in 4 tablespoons of melted butter until translucent. Add the artichoke slices, a chopped leek and a chopped carrot. Cook the vegetables for a few minutes in the butter over a low heat, stirring. Then pour in a litre of good chicken stock. Season with salt, pepper and a little freshly grated nutmeg. Simmer, stirring occasionally, until the vegetables are soft.

Reduce the contents of the pan to a purée with a hand-held blender or Magimix. Finally stir in 3 tablespoons of double cream. Serve with hot toasted brown bread.

I roamed the county from east to west, racking my brains all the while for fascinating local foodstuffs. As I swung around the Winchester bypass I remembered I was not far from Alresford, where I was once taken to see the watercress beds lying in their thick rectangular masses, the cress so green it was almost blue, stretching away over the quiet watery flats like a Southern English equivalent of paddy fields. There is no more evocatively British salad vegetable than watercress, though its refreshing piquant bite has been eclipsed in modern minds by the all-conquering arugula (aka rocket), and there is no more authentic treatment of it than the watercress sandwich made with brown bread, plenty of good fresh butter and sea salt, with the optional addition of a few peeled shrimps.

At Robinson's, the butcher's in Stockbridge, where most of the denizens of the well-heeled villages hereabouts come for their meat, I had another food flashback. It was here that my friend Colin Sanderson had once ordered a huge slab of Scotch sirloin. Roasted with Yorkshire pudding and washed down with two bottles of Colin's excellent Château Beychevelle 1970, this had stayed in my memory as a Sunday lunch to conjure with.

I parked in the High Street and took a little tour round the premises, letting Mr Robinson point out the various activities of the traditional British butcher. In a yard out back a boy was skinning a fallow deer, while another was hanging up a row of fat Christmas geese – for the upper-class market, which increasingly shuns the tasteless chalky meat that turkey has become. A whole side of Aberdeen Angus, deep and marbled red, was tagged with a label 'For Collection, Mr Sanderson' and a London phone number.

At the back of the shop a second Mr Robinson was stuffing sausages, while a third brushed salt off a thick slab of bacon. Since the shop had given up on wet-cured bought-in bacon and began dry-curing their own, said the butcher, bacon sales had trebled.

'Why, then, aren't there more butchers like you?' I had to ask.

Mr Robinson scratched his head under his white butcher's hat. 'Hmm. I suppose we've sort of gone on doing what we always did, and other people sort of stopped,' he said.

In the oak woods around Michelmersh, I sat down on a heap of leaves to eat a ham sandwich and swig on a bottle of apple juice from Leckford Farm, just up the road. The woods were russet and dusty brown and rustled mysteriously with each gust of the autumn breeze. Under an oak leaf, as I rummaged idly among the forest bric-à-brac, I saw a small mushroom. A small orange-yellow fungus beside a rotten bough, peeping up from among the peaty, blackish-brown soil; I would have sworn it was a chanterelle. I found another, and another and another. They had the sweetish, faintly nauseating smell of over-ripe peaches.

For a long time, British tolerance of fungi extended to just two varieties: the omnipresent 'button mushroom', of which 30,000 tons a year are sold in the UK alone – mild morsels of squeaky white flesh with only the vaguest semblance of mushroom flavour – and the big field mushroom, so good sautéed in a little butter or stuffed with a mixture of parsley, breadcrumbs and finely chopped bacon. While in France more than thirty species of edible wild mushroom are commonly found in markets, on this side of the Channel they were almost all beyond the pale in polite society.

In the old days, when the subject of wild mushrooms came up in conversation, the words at the back of everybody's mind were those that described the medical consequences of consuming the death cap: 'nausea, stomach cramps, convulsions and death'. As for those individuals who habitually collected and consumed the things, they were thought at best daringly unconventional, at worst reckless, eccentric and anti-social. In pre-foodie days, fear of fungi was a touchstone of British attitudes to eating. Wild mushrooms, with their curious and disturbing names – trompette de mort, slippery jack, the deceiver – were something Continentals did. We would stick to what we knew and liked, the reassuring button and the nice big honest-looking field mushroom, thank you very much.

Why such attitudes prevailed may be a matter for the anthropologists to explain. Robert Graves suggested that fungi fear could be traced back to the ancient taboo on the hallucinogenic fly agaric mushroom, whose consumption was reserved for the priestly class and their shamanic rituals and prohibited for the rest of the population.

In point of fact, if you look into the history of our human relationship with the fungus kingdom, you find that the old English attitude of timorous circumspection was at least partly shared by some of the greatest gastronomical cultures of all time. Until the fifteenth century there were no reliable guidelines for mushroom collection and consumption, which obviously made it an activity fraught with risk. 'Only the boletus, among fungi, ought to be touched,' declared Galen. Even this could be toxic, thought Pliny the Elder, especially if it grew close to rusty iron, rotten rags, or snakes. 'For by horrible and almost daily examples, these fungi can be charged with killing households and whole banquets of people.'

In spite of the danger they presented, or perhaps because of it, the ancient world still considered wild fungi a tremendous delicacy. In his fourth-century *Art of Cookery* Apicius gives no less than fifteen recipes for mushrooms. Some of them might be worth a try even today. How about 'ash tree fungi boiled in water, served with salt, oil, wine and chopped coriander', or this very Roman-sounding treatment for ceps: 'Chop the stalks, place in a shallow pan, having added pepper, lovage, a little honey. Blend with *liquamen*' – the famous fermented fish sauce; Thai *nam pla* might be the best modern substitute – 'add a little oil, and cook'?

Interest in the gourmet properties of fungi died down until the Renaissance in Italy and France, but then it exploded again. Pope Clement VII was passionate about spinuli, prunuli and cardeoli, and consumed vast quantities of each. Jean Baptiste Buyerin's *De re cibaria* of 1560 remarked: 'Everyone agrees that truffles were treated with singular esteem at the meals of great men in Rome, and they have firmly kept their position today in the great Roman and French houses . . . (but) certain people judge fresh boleti that they cook over coals, with butter and a little mound of salt thrown in, the highest delicacies.'

By the late eighteenth century the French and Italians were committed connoisseurs of all edible fungi, and the large number of fatal accidents caused by the non-edible ones didn't seem to put them off. When in 1754 a man died after eating wild mushrooms in the Bois de Boulogne, Parisian police tried to place a ban on fungi-gathering – without a shred of success. Jean-Jacques Paulet, whose *Traité des Champignons* of 1793 was history's first truly reliable mushroom field guide, described the fungi cultists who knew all the horror stories – the deaths of the Emperor Claudius, poisoned by a dish of mushrooms, and of the Emperor Charles II, and nearer their own time, of the Princesse de Conti at Fontainebleau in 1751, not to mention 'those that one observes daily in the areas around Paris, Rome, Naples, etc., and nevertheless they have not yet lost the taste. While one is speaking to them of these accidents, they regret not being in the Béarn in order to make use of oranges, rougillons, coquemalles, poules, savatelles, etc; in Guyenne, to gather cèpes; in Provence, to find the pinède, the baligoule; in the Piemont, to eat the truffe-à-l'ail; in Burgundy, to collect the mousseron; in the Bourbonnais, to find coches; at Fontainebleau, to eat barbes-de-chèvre; in Italy, to water the stone that produces fungi – all dishes that they call, with the Roman emperor, the food of the gods.'

Down among the dense oak woods of the New Forest in Hampshire, there have always been a few stalwart mushroom hunters. For years they had the place to themselves. But then I suppose people grew used to eating porcini in Italian restaurants and shiitake in Japanese ones, and mycological maestros such as Roger Phillips and Stefan Buczacki published guidebooks for prospective mushroom gatherers, and foreign chefs appeared on TV expressing their puzzlement at our lack of interest in the riches to be found on our own front lawns, and little by little the whole subject of wild mushrooms became rather fashionable, and increasing numbers of the British began to eat them with almost as much relish as those daring Continentals have traditionally done.

On a cold October night I had dinner at Le Poussin, a small restaurant in the town of Brockenhurst, at the edge of that patch of suburban wilderness known as the New Forest. On the menu were boudin blanc with wild mushrooms, fillet of brill with wild mushrooms, breast of guinea fowl with wild mushrooms . . . In the visitors' book by the front door, I spied a list of people who had come down from London to take part in something called a 'mushroom foray' a few days earlier. It seemed I had accidentally stumbled on the secret headquarters of a fungiphile ring.

'I've just been out to my favourite chanterelle patch today. I'm not going to tell you where it is, no. Roughly behind the big hotel there, pretty much in mid-forest,' said Alex Aitken, chef, while I rounded off the mushroom feast with a delicious slice of caramelised apple tart. He had in his hand a big white plate with a few of the items he had found today on his furtive early morning forage, and he held it out for my examination. A waft of something pungent, earthy, redolent of fallen leaves and laundry baskets, arrived at my nostrils from the plate.

It was a beautiful sight, the various shapes of the mushrooms and the curious colour combinations of grey, brown, orange and purple against the background of cool white china. There were saffron-yellow chanterelles and three big *Boletus edulis* – I call it the picture-book mushroom, with its thick bulbous pale stem and tight brown cap. That was as much as I recognised. It was left to my host to point out the blewit, with its deep purple colour and fruity aroma, the brown chanterelle, the slippery jack and the poetically named amethyst deceiver.

Much of the pleasure of wild mushrooms, as of fine British food in general, lies in the search and the encounter.

The following morning was chilly, dark and dew-drenched. I had come to the forest alone. Mushrooming is a solitary activity, and most serious hunters regard the group excursion or foray en masse with horror. I had come armed with the mushroom gatherer's typical equipment of basket and knife – the knife for cutting off fungi at the roots, and the basket so that, once cut, they remain open to the air (a plastic bag would make them sweat and rot) and can still cast their spores to the wind. I'd also brought a field guide that purported to show, by means of fastidious descriptions and lurid photographs, which were the edible fungi and which the ones that if eaten would bring on the nausea, stomach cramps, convulsions, et cetera.

Dawn was dappling the fallen leaves with orange light. Somewhere in the depth of the forest the mushrooms were calling – but would I be able to understand their language?

I sat on a tree stump and flicked through the field guide, feeling that I had perhaps bitten off, so to speak, more than I could digest. The variety was bewildering, and the number of species I was familiar with distressingly small. There were hundreds I had never even heard of, a parade of exotic beauties whose names were as strange as their shapes and surface textures. There were the characters: the miller, the charcoal burner, the weeping widow and the old man of the woods. There were the sinisterly precise taxonomies: the moss pixy cap, the foxy orange web cap, the yellow cowpat toadstool and the two-toned wood tuft. Even the names of the inedible fungi – the sickener, the stinking parasol, the weeping fairy cake, the yellow stainer – had a certain toxic, Baudelairean beauty.

Like someone entering a minefield, I ventured gingerly across the expanse of grass that lay before the entrance to the wood. A man out walking his dog crossed in front of me, muttered something, then seemed to see my basket and vanish at speed into the depths of the forest.

For a while I wandered about on the fringes, finding nothing but a collection of slimy little toadstools and one small geriatric puffball with scaly green skin. Then, as I was kicking through the fallen leaves underneath the first row of oak trees, something caught my eye: a purplish-brown mushroom with white patches where something had nibbled away at the surface of the cap. I knelt down on the damp grass and consulted the guide. What it said about the charcoal burner – the purplish cap, the white flesh, and the fact that you rarely find a perfect specimen because mice and rats find it irresistible – gave me the thrilling sense of being on the verge of my first real fungi find. And I got out my knife, cut off the mushroom just below the soil level, as is correct foraging practice, and placed it proudly in my picker's basket.

Mushroom hunting requires a certain degree of concentration and a particular mental attitude, somewhere between razor-sharp observation and nonchalant detachment. The novice is so desperate to search out his quarry that he dashes from tree to tree and sees nothing, while all around him the old hands are calmly and quietly filling their baskets. Reminding myself of this, I closed my eyes for a minute and tried to visualise a large, tasty mushroom, then, holding the vision in my mind, I plunged once more into the fray.

And suddenly I saw it. Up ahead, some five or six yards before my eyes, looming out of the dense backdrop of orange and brown, was the white shape of a mushroom. It was such an unmistakable sight, with its tall slender stem and its overarching cap, that it seemed to be sending out a signal.

Even at a distance I could tell it wasn't one of the highly prized culinary aristocrats, the ceps or morels, but something plainer and more common. Close up, it had a wholesome look to it, with none of the slimy patches and peculiar colours that often characterise the unwholesome types.

'Quite common in wood margins, grassy clearings, roadsides. One of the best of our edible fungi, and can be seen from afar,' said the book, going on to point out that the parasol mushroom should not be confused with its cousin, the *shaggy* parasol. The shaggy had a more unkempt-looking cap than that of the normal parasol, and a stem that was completely smooth, whereas the non-shaggy had a ring of flesh about halfway up to which the parasol was once attached before it opened out and formed its current graceful shape.

Into the basket it went, and before long I spied another parasol, and another, and a whole family of them clustered together in the patch of grass under an oak tree, where they caught my eye when the mid-morning sun through the branches picked out the contrast of white and green. Before eleven o'clock I had a basket full of booty. I was still looking out for chanterelles, hankering after the sight of what someone once compared to a torn golden shawl thrown down among the leaves and sticks, the egg-yolk yellow of the mushroom and the gills on its underside like the fan-vaulting of a Gothic cathedral.

It began to seem unlikely, however, that I would find any this time. A kilo or two of parasols would have to do for now. So I took my swag back to the restaurant, where chef was just making up a batch of muscat sauce for a dish of guinea fowl and wild mushrooms.

'Now then, let's have a look here,' he said genially, picking over the contents of my basket. 'These are parasols, no problem there. This one, though, hmmm . . . I thought it might be a shaggy, but it's actually a shaggy ink cap. You want to eat that pretty soon, they sort of liquefy, become a bit disgusting.'

'What about this one, then? I thought it might be a charcoal burner,' I asked.

'Could be, could be . . . but it ain't,' said Mr A. 'Dunno what it is, but I don't like the look of it. These are all inedible. This one's quite good – it's a fairy ring champignon, so called for obvious reasons – usually you find more than one. But *this* thing . . .' His voice took on a mild excitement as he fished it out, a yellow comb of fungus I'd found on an old fallen bough and prised it off as a curiosity.

'Chicken of the woods. Lovely texture, really does have a bite a little bit like chicken. You haven't done too badly, all in all.'

I felt an absurd little flush of pride.

Alex said sure, I could cook up my parasols for breakfast. So I cut them into strips, rolled them in egg and breadcrumbs, salt and black pepper, and fried them up in butter in a big restaurant-kitchen frying pan. They were savoury and nourishing, with a meaty texture and cream-coloured flesh that reminded me of veal cutlets alla milanese. I nibbled on my parasol fritters and drank a cup of milky coffee while Alex expounded his food philosophy, which turned out to be just the sort of ideology you'd expect from a man who loves to hunt for wild things and cook them.

Le Poussin was a provincial restaurant, and the glory of a good provincial restaurant in France or Britain, as opposed to an urban one that can draw from the whole country, is its connection with the intimate environment around it. Brockenhurst is on the fringes of the New Forest, and from the New Forest comes game: wild venison, rabbit, pigeon, and squirrels. It seems odd that so few people have thought of eating squirrel, since it is hardly an endangered species and they often look rather temptingly plump around the hind quarters. Mr A. serves them up in the restaurant – only the saddle and legs are worth bothering with, he says – describing them on the menu as 'Tree Rabbit'. At Rhinefield the local farmers let their pigs out into the forest to graze on acorns – see, I *knew* Hampshire was a repressed pork county – and he likes to get hold of that pork whenever he can, because the acorn diet gives an extra dimension of richness to the meat.

His ingredients are local, and so are his clients: the provincial bourgeoisie of coastal Hampshire, owners of yachts, bigwigs in the businesses of Portsmouth and Southampton. He would love to attract a wider social mix, get more ordinary people in, more real locals like the old guy from the New Forest who brings in bits of game from time to time. 'This guy's a born and bred Forester, you know. This is probably the last sort of place he'd think of coming, but he brings in his family every now and then. I can't tell you how delighted I am to see him in here. In France or somewhere, the locals will always save up for a big splurge in the best restaurant in town; it's only here it seems odd.'

In a B&B just off the M27, with my stomach still reeling from the onslaught of that last large and excellent meal, I dreamed dyspeptic dreams of the West Country, where I was now heading. They were food nightmares, laced with horror and repulsion. Vast vats of clotted cream, bubbling in a quivering thick-skinned mass with the colour and texture of school custard. Dorset Blue Vinny, stinking of old boots, whose dark blue veins turned into the varicose veins on the legs of a dead tramp. Cornish pasties bulging and then bursting, like something from a splatter movie. Grannies gorging like lager louts on cream teas, the genteel clink-clink of their tea cups gradually turning into a maddening industrial clatter that woke me up in a raging thirst.

Needing a restorative swim before the big push westwards, I turned off the A35 at West Bay and hurled myself into a greasy grey sea, ploughing frenetically up and down for a few minutes while a group of tea-swigging grannies in heavy winter coats looked at me as though I was completely mad.

Then, feeling virtuous and peckish, I repaired to the Riverside Restaurant to eat a nourishing meal of local air-dried ham, scallops on a bed of cous-cous with a copious sloosh of pesto sauce, and a baked cod steak scented with rosemary and scattered with a very large handful of extremely pungent and vinegary capers. It was heavy-handed cooking, and expensive in the context of this Hi-de-Hi holiday town. Still, to find an airy light-filled restaurant with quick, pleasant service, a proper wine list and fresh locally sourced raw materials in a seaside town in the South of England was something akin to finding a sun-dried tomato in a haystack.

So I sat at the only table for one, by a window overlooking the river, next to a frumpy posh couple who stared at me as I tucked into my food and made me wonder idly why there was no equivalent in English of the French expression '*Bon appétit*', except for the inadmissible American 'Enjoy your meal'.

Once again I was eating alone; once again struggling to fend off the feeling that people around me were wondering what this person was doing on his own on a Saturday lunchtime, when the rest of the restaurant was full up with chattering tables of two, four and six.

Existential angst in brasseries is an occupational hazard for the lone diner. In order to combat it, you need to have your ego armour firmly in place. Self-confidence is the key. The following tips are the fruit of my own experience: (1) If anyone glances at you, it will only be through mild curiosity. This is natural. Bear in mind that you will not occupy their attention for more than a minute at most. (2) Without conversation it is easy to gobble your food. Take it slowly. Put down your knife and fork from time to time, and pause. Look around the room. Eavesdrop on other people's conversations. Have a good laugh. These are the perks of the table for one. Enjoy them. (3) If you decide to read a book at your table, try to ensure that you read a number of paragraphs in succession, not just the same one over and over. (4) Never be tempted to think that anyone else in the restaurant thinks that because you are eating alone you must be a sad loser. In emergencies, try repeating the following mantra: 'I AM NOT A SAD LOSER. ALONE DOES NOT MEAN LONELY. I HAVE MANY FRIENDS.'

If the restaurant has a window and a view, of course, it is always a good idea for the lone diner to sit beside it. In the huts along the waterfront, overweight families were immersed in their weekend routines. The garden nearest the restaurant was a perfect square of grass edged with borders heaving with phlox and nicotiana, showing a mastery of colour and form that seemed natural and inborn. A wobbly girl on platformed trainers was currently jiggling out of the hut with two enormous bags, practically sacks, of Cheesy Wotsits. Ripping open one of them and hurling the other towards her sister, she sank her hand deep inside the bag and collapsed giggling into a white plastic garden chair. I watched in fascination as her father caught a large wriggling fish, despatched and gutted it in front of the shrieking girls, and shoved it on the gas-fired barbecue, naked and unadorned, to be mercilessly flame-grilled until it resembled a piece of fossilised tree trunk.

On the way back west I saw a sign to Denhay Farm, makers of the sweet chewy air-dried ham I had eaten at lunch. The land round here was almost suffocatingly verdant, thick grass pasture bisected by wide hedges hiding tiny lanes that switchbacked among the modest hills. This was what Thomas Hardy knew as the 'vale of small dairies' since, until the invention of the Milk Marketing Board, it was known as a cheese-making region par excellence. I was met at the farm shop by a no-nonsense Dorset lady who was, today, a little brisk and business-like, being about to set off on her weekly midnight drive to London with a van full of cheddar cheese, dry-cured bacon and sausages, not to mention the ineffable Denhay air-dried ham.

'We call it "English prosciutto",' said Mrs Streatfeild as she pottered around noting down orders. Which is in fact a fair description of the product, especially as part of the inspiration for it came from a trip Mrs S. took to Parma when it was decided to 'add value' to the pigs they had always kept without ever really thinking of them as money-spinners.

'The hams all come from our own pigs, and those pigs are fed on the whey from the cheese-making, which is of course perfectly sound farming practice. The meat is matured on the bone and cured in a mixture of Dorset apple juice and honey, salt, and various herbs. Then it's smoked, just lightly, and hung up to dry. See?' She picked up half a ham from the chill cabinet and waved it about in front of me, and I could see that this particular bit of meat had plenty of what butchers call Intra-Muscular Marbling.

'Must be the way you feed them . . . *Whey* you feed them?' I ventured, eliciting a thin smile from the redoubtable Mrs S.

Outside in the valley it had started to drizzle, marking the final end of one of the meanest summers in living memory. I looked around the farm, peering in at some of the six hundred sows Denhay keep in three different palatial residences. They got up from their straw divans and set up a general irritated snuffling when they saw me. I felt a little like an intruder in a luxurious harem.

Hungry again, I ripped open a packet of ham as I walked back to the car, wolfing down half-a-dozen thin slices. It tasted even more succulent and sweet than it had in the restaurant – perhaps the open air and the background aromas of wet green grass had something to do with it. As a whole ham, freshly sliced according to need and hunger pangs, the taste would surely take on yet another dimension of bright and zingy saltiness. Either way, if Dorset can come up with a product as good as this, Parma and Jabugo and Westphalia had better watch their step.

The flesh of animals has always been close to the hearts of the British. For centuries it appeared to foreign visitors that we ate almost nothing else. 'I always heard that they were great flesh eaters, and I found it true,' wrote the French traveller François Maximilien Misson in his *Mémoires et Observations faites par un voyageur en Angleterre* (1698). 'I have known people in England that never eat any bread, and universally they eat very little; they nibble a few crumbs, while they chew meat by whole mouthfuls.'

When you read accounts of the kind of diet enjoyed by wealthier citizens in the seventeenth and eighteenth centuries, you begin to understand that, in the consciousness of the age, meat was almost the same thing as food. If you ate vegetables and fruit, it would only be because you were too poor to afford meat. Fruit, indeed, was thought to produce fever. 'In the afternoon had notice that my Lord Hinchingbroke is fallen ill, which I fear is with the fruit that I did give them on Saturday last at my house: so in the evening I went thither, and in great fear of the small-pox,' wrote Samuel Pepys in 1661.

Two years later, on 4 April 1663, Pepys records in his diary a celebration dinner: 'We had a fricasse of rabbits, and chickens, a leg of mutton boiled, three carps in a dish, a great dish of a side of lamb, a dish of roasted pigeons, a dish of four lobsters, three tarts, a lamprey pie, a most rare pie, a dish of anchovies, good wine of several sorts, and all things mighty noble, and to my great content.'

At the dawn of the twenty-first century, the relationship between the British and their meat is under fire as never before. The old intimacy and trust has gone, to be replaced by the deepest suspicion. There can be no more loyalty to something that, whatever its status as a national symbol, has made some of us terribly ill.

Meat now falls into one of two categories. Old Meat, which

still takes up the lion's share of the market, is an industrial product like any other, produced in accordance with the industrial criteria of efficiency and economy. The best that can be said of the results is that they are cheap. New Meat, on the other hand, has other priorities: welfare, health and taste. It is made, for example, from animals that have not been fed on hormones, growth promoters, excrement or proteins derived from other animals. The beasts are humanely treated in life, and slaughtered with the avoidance of undue distress.

All this inevitably means that the finished product is not cheap; but that does not seem to have stemmed the huge demand for it. Now it may be that only the wealthy are buying this stuff, which would be a shame. What I'd prefer to believe is this: belatedly, consumers are waking up to the fact that, if you eat less meat and supplement your diet with other forms of protein (the pulses, for example, a food source which British cooking inexplicably underrates), you might be able to pay the premium on a really good joint of organic lamb or beef from time to time.

In Devon alone there were at least half a dozen suppliers of New Meat, from the Pure Meat Company in Moretonhampstead and Village Farm and Deer Force 10 in Holme, to Pipers Farm in Cullompton and the queen of the green-meat scene, Anne Petch at Heal Farm in Kings Nympton. It was towards Pipers Farm that I now turned, taking a long route through countryside that seemed to have become even more swollen and languorous after the October rains. There was such a rich, golden look to this landscape that I felt that if you could gather up a patch of it and squeeze it in your fist some kind of thick, sweet and highly nutritious liquid would drip through your fingers. Meandering hedges developed casually into triangles of lush deciduous woodland. Hayricks stood like ziggurats in freshly harvested cornfields. Of the candidates for southern Britain's rural centre of gravity, few places have a more convincing claim than Devon.

I first heard about Pipers Farm from a London friend who had ordered a slab of sirloin from them one Easter, as a perverse reaction to the BSE scare, and said it was unlike any beef she had ever tasted before. And now I was standing on a hillside outside the hamlet of Clyst Hydon, gasping a little from the uphill tramp through the shining, waving upland grass, and the animals I saw before me were the Red Devon cattle whose forebears had produced that remarkable lordly beef.

'They're called Ruby Reds, and they're the typical North Devon breed. South of the A30 you get the South Devon breed, which are larger and coppery-coloured,' explained their owner, a tall, lean, voluble, intelligent man wearing the kind of green-and-brown check Viyella shirt now worn only by country people and the elderly.

The A30 roared beneath us in the valley bottom. But beyond the road were hills and dales chequered yellow with wheat stubble and green with pasture. It was Mark Twain who said the English countryside was so beautiful it ought not to be left outside.

Since the Greigs arrived from a hill farm in Wensleydale in search of good land, an old-fashioned family-based society and a tradition of what Peter Greig called 'low-input, high-welfare' farming, they had built up a business that cleverly harnessed the resources of these hills and dales by co-opting neighbouring farms to rear their livestock for them.

'You see, something like twenty-four family farms contribute to this enterprise in their various ways,' said Mr Greig, opening his arms wide in an expansive gesture that took in the whole valley below him.

Peter Greig's conversion to the real food gospel came while he was standing in his father's farm watching broiler chickens being 'processed' for a supermarket. It came to him in a flash: if that supermarket's clientele could see what was going on in that factory farm, they would never eat a chicken again. 'We had two young sons; we knew we could produce wholesome food that we'd be happy to feed our children. So we started doing things our way, and ten years on we're a going concern.' He taught himself the art of butchery, taking lamb and beef carcasses apart muscle by muscle and throwing the bits in the pan to see how they contract in the cooking.

His two sheepdogs, Fly and Tessa, lay panting on the grass at our feet, and the group of Ruby Reds set up a gentle lowing. Their backs were curiously flat, like velvet-covered dining tables.

We wandered along the hedgerow along the brow of the hill. The farmer picked a sprig of wild honeysuckle and sniffed it, closing his eyes in a brief olfactory ecstasy before tossing it back into the hedge.

We strode back down to the office and he plied me with samples, unloading a bagful of rock-like frozen lumps that he talked me through one by one. There was a substantial-looking, dark-hued chicken breast; and a Ruby Red steak; and a boneless leg of lamb from a Suffolk/North of England cross that had been hung for two and a half weeks with the hole left by removing the bone stuffed with a thin tube of apricot and crushed hazelnuts; and a ham hock that I decided then and there I would use for a soup of dried green peas; and a boned loin of six-year-old Swaledale mutton, immaculately tied into a perfect roll, a thing of butcherly beauty; and a gorgeous rose-pink joint of gammon, which I cooked a few nights later. Simmered in a court-bouillon, cut into thick, juicy slices and slathered in parsley sauce, that piece of gammon was beyond all doubt the best I've ever eaten in my life.

Twice-Cooked Gammon with Parsley Sauce

(serves 6–8)

Place a 2kg gammon joint (organically produced if possible) in a large casserole. Pour over it a 75cl bottle of English dry cider, adding a large chopped onion, 8 cloves, 8 juniper berries (lightly crushed), 4 bay leaves, a teaspoonful of peppercorns and 2 tablespoons honey. Top up with water until the joint is covered. Bring the casserole gently to the boil and simmer for 45 minutes with the lid on.

Remove the meat into a roasting pan. Add 2 or 3 cupfuls of the boiling liquid to the pan. Make a mixture of 4 tablespoons of thin honey and 2 tablespoons of grain mustard. Coat the surface of the joint with this mixture and roast in a medium-hot oven for another 45 minutes. Baste occasionally with the pan juices.

Allow the gammon to stand for ten minutes before carving into thick slices.

For the sauce: *Remove the onions and spices from the boiling liquid and reduce until a nice strong stock is obtained. Make a roux with butter and flour and gradually add the stock, stirring all the time. When sauce has thickened, throw in 3 handfuls of finely chopped parsley (the fresher the better, and the more the stronger), allow to cook for a minute or two, then finally add a generous dash of double cream.*

Pipers Farm may be the utopian future of meat farming, but the present looked a good deal grottier. The following day was Tuesday – livestock market day in Hatherleigh, north Devon, and a perfect opportunity to take the temperature of a rural English society that mostly has its being thanks to the trade in meat and milk.

It was a fair jaunt from the creamy pastures of south Devon to the much more rugged and lesser-known lands of the north, where men are men and kaffir lime leaves, mojama and chipotle chillies are hard to find.

Pushing dazedly through the excited market crowds down Hatherleigh High Street towards the market ground, I felt I was sleepwalking into an older, scruffier, slower-paced England than the one I'd seen hitherto. Even the physiognomies, long noses and thin taut faces, seemed to come from an older genetic seam, and the fashion editors of London-based glossy magazines would find it shocking that people in Britain should live in such ignorance of even the most basic principles of style. Big-buttocked farmers' wives with long swinging dirty blonde hair wore stretchy leggings and wide-striped rugby shirts. There were acres of jumble-sale nylon, hectares of stonewashed denim, and probably several hundredweight of cheap Korean trainers.

I wandered around the pre-sale exhibition of items laid out for the weekly auction, deciding I had never seen a stranger, poorer selection outside the more prosperous countries of the Third World: there were balls of twine, music centres, coffee mugs, old saws, various unidentifiable bits of rusty metal and bundles of old sackcloth tied up with orange string. There was a nice old hazelwood walking stick that I coveted myself until I saw that an elderly couple (he in his Market Best of clean blue farm trousers held up with braces and a brown tweed jacket with plastic patched elbows) had their eye on it. It was a good strong one, fat as a man's wrist at the top, but light and comfortable to hold. 'That'll be good for you, when you go up to the dogs,' said the wife to her husband in a Devonian burr as thick as clotted cream.

There were wooden sledgehammers, and a chainsaw, and milk churns, and ugly country furniture. Further on, in the small livestock section, big white geese squatted quietly in their cages. A yellow-haired country boy with brown hands reached down and pulled up a clutch of brown birds.

'Two-ducks-and-a-drake-hundred-and-fifty-pence, two-ducks-and-a-drake,' intoned the auctioneer.

In a wooden shed fixed up for the purpose, farmers could pop in for their monthly haircut at preferential rates. Next door they could stock up on feeds and medicines, taking note of the latest chemical products, each with their particular claims to make a silk purse out of a sow's ear. Like LiquiThrive, a feed supplement for sheep that claimed to bestow the multiple blessing of 'Tighter Lambing, Less Barren Ewes, More Lambs, Less Lamb Losses, Heavier Weaning Weights, and Increased Sale Value'.

If anyone felt hungry after their exertions in the auction room, a canteen at the back provided sandwiches and fry-ups and mugs of tea in a fug of steam and grease. Elsewhere there was a tiny kiosk given over to cheese, in which plastic-wrapped triangles of industrial French Brie and block Cheddar dominated the display, while a Dorset Blue Vinny ('a special treat') sat, sweaty and unloved and getting bluer by the day, in a corner of the cabinet. There were makeshift veg shops and a Transit van spilling over with cabbages, and several produce stalls with only the most canonical and tedious of English preserves: pickled onions, pickled eggs, lemon curd, runner bean and green tomato chutneys . . . It was all very cheap – but then it would have to be, because these market-goers in their dowdy hand-me-downs had precious little change from the weekly shop to spend on luxuries.

There was in the air at Hatherleigh Market a held-in let's-make-the-best-of-it feeling, behind which lurked the double-headed phantom of financial insecurity and political frustration. The top prices offered for animals at auction – ninety-six pence a kilo for lamb, sixty-two pence for heifer and eighty-five pence for steer – seemed shockingly low even to one who knows nothing of the trade. All around the market walls handwritten notices advertised clever scams for easy money. 'Pigeons? Rabbits? Farmers: Turn Your Problems Into Cash'. The estate agent's window was full of farms for sale. People were selling up and getting out, and if their farmhouses were 'suitable for holiday letting' they might get a few thousand more for the property. 'All goats offered for sale must be accompanied by a Goat Movement Form,' read one of the dozens of notices pasted up on the walls of the auction room.

Compassed about with laws that they lose money by obeying, chastened by supermarket economics that only allow them ever tighter profit margins, reaping the whirlwind of intensive farming practices that have damaged first the environment and then their own livelihoods – how will it all end for British farmers as a society? As it is, they are marginalised, morose, increasingly mired in something very close to poverty, and if we are not careful they will soon become a dispossessed and angry class of people. The inner cities as a social threat may have had their day. The danger now comes from the outer provinces.

4

cornwall

life beyond the pasty

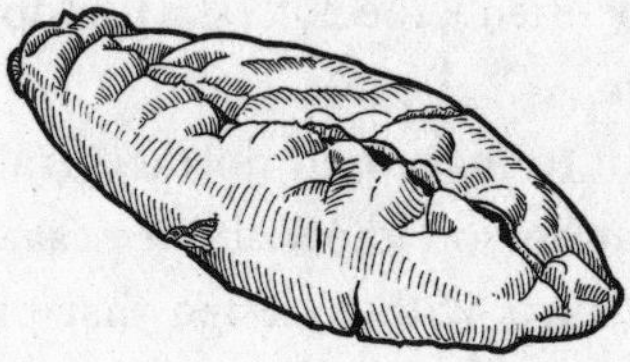

It was only a matter of crossing the Tamar, the river marking the boundary between what are ostensibly merely counties, before I caught a discernible flavour of something very like foreignness.

My first stop in Cornwall was the sensible town of Liskeard, where next to the fish stall was a branch of the *Kowethas an Yeth Kernewek* or Cornish Language Fellowship. The Fellowship was staffed by three people with that bad combination – time on their hands and an axe to grind.

If I had wanted to know that *Pandr'a vynn'ta dhe eva?* means *What do you want to drink?* in Cornish and that *Koffi/korev/gwin mar pleg* means *Coffee/beer/wine please*, I could have spent many a happy hour at the Fellowship. But I was more interested in what these people knew about the pasty, cornerstone and symbol of Cornish culture the world over. It being a slow day for prospective students of the Cornish language, they had plenty of time to tell me.

Here was a plastic recipe card written out in Cornish in Led Zeppelin album-cover script.

'So that's the ingredients, right?' I guessed them from the first few lines. 'What are the basic elements: beef, potato, swede . . .?'

'Yes, but we never say swede, always "yellow turnip",' said a woman in an Indonesian tablecloth skirt, adopting a slap-on-the wrist reproving air.

'I see. I'll try not to make that mistake again.'

'Hey, Pete, what do you know about paaaasties?' she called, across a rail of T-shirts with a design that probably said, 'My friend went to Cornwall and all they got me was this lousy T-shirt' in Cornish. I fancied she dragged out the multiple *aaaahhhh*, as in 'heart', as if to emphasise the fact that most visitors from the other side of the Tamar commonly mispronounce the word pa-sty, with a short a as in 'hat'.

'What does the gen'leman need to know? The paaasty, why, it goes back centuries, it's one of the world's great dishes,' said Pete, coming out from behind the counter and his beard, perhaps scenting the distant possibility of a sale.

Well now, I wouldn't go so far as to put pasty up there with bollito misto, paella and boeuf en daube, but I do think, at its best, it must be rated one of Britain's great fast foods. It is such a familiar sight in Cornwall, the lunchtime pasty-muncher filling his or her face from a paper bag, that I doubt whether McDonald's, Wimpy and Spud-U-Like can make much of a profit in the region.

'There's a tremendous mythology about pasty-making, of course,' continued Pete, warming to his theme. 'The other week there was a story in the papers about a man who was up in court for attacking his wife with a broom handle because his pasty wasn't up to scratch. That gives you some idea of how seriously we think of our national dish down here.'

A notorious test of a good pasty used to be that they could fall down a mineshaft and remain intact. All myths have their roots in homespun practical wisdom, of course, and this one clearly referred to the importance of making sure there was a solid enough crust on the thing that the juices didn't leak out.

The Cornish relationship with the pasty seems quaintly intimate and oddly passionate.

I remember being impressed by two things about Cornwall as a child: one was that people called each other 'my lover', and the other was that pasties contained a savoury section and a sweet section, providing an entire meal in a handy edible box. To a child's mind this was a wonderfully appealing concept, so it was disappointing to discover from Hettie Merrick's *Pasty Book* that the beef-in-one-end, jam-in-the-other pasty is now firmly discredited by pasty experts. Mrs Merrick, who was born and bred in Cornwall and ran a pasty place in Porthleven for years and whose daughter Ann now runs the famous Pasty Shop in the Lizard and presumably therefore knows what she's talking about, points to a possible confusion with the Bedfordshire clanger, which is a suet roll with meat and vegetables at one end and jam at the other. (The clanger, incidentally, according to an old book on English farmhouse cookery, 'is supposed to have been invented by resourceful lady hat-makers of Luton as a complete meal to be left on the hob for their husbands, while they themselves were at work'.)

'There's several fascinating things going on in paaaasties nowadays,' Pete was saying. 'You know the beef crisis, it really has had an effect on cuisine in Cornwall. Before, you would just ask for a pound or two of skirt or chuck, and if they thought you were local you might get the offcuts of very much better meat. Now, of course, there's been an explosion of all these alternative recipes, like pork and yellow turnip—'

'That's "swede" in English, right?'

'Right. I've seen lamb and mint, cheese and pickle, egg and sausage, you name it.'

'What about the commercial brands? What do you make of them?'

'You know what, it's a funny thing, but I've never seen a Ginsters van delivering in Cornwall. Cornish people don't much like 'em.'

The lady in the tablecloth skirt lumbered over to our side of the shop to announce her lifelong and profound hatred of Ginsters pasties, whose natural habitats are petrol-station chill cabinets and inner-city late night stores.

'I wouldn't touch a Ginsters with a ten-foot bargepole,' she fumed. 'In fact I think they should be banned, for giving paaaasties a bad name.'

'It's a fact that outsiders can't make proper paaaasties,' said Pete. 'There's a famous restaurant in Padstow and the man there makes something that he describes as one.' I guessed he meant the Seafood Restaurant and its proprietor/chef Rick Stein, whose rapidly growing gastronomic empire now includes a delicatessen. 'Well, I tried it and it wasn't very good. It was just too meaty, and there was too much pepper in there. To me, he's just trying to be clever.'

'Well, what did you expect?' said the lady contemptuously, fanning her face with a plasticated Cornish recipe card. 'I mean, who does he think he is, trampling all over our culture like that and doing very nicely, thank you, from the benefits? It's imperialism, isn't it? Nothing less than culinary imperialism.'

I flicked through the rest of the recipe cards: apart from pasty, there was stargazy pie, saffron cake and heavva cake, and fudge. Add to that hog's pudding, groats pudding, a few good local cheeses, Cornish splits and fairings, ice cream and, it goes without saying, clotted cream, and you have more or less the full range of Cornish culinary achievement. Hardly a vastly impressive repertoire by Southern European standards of regional cuisine, but by British standards the county is rather rich in local dishes and admirably jealous of its culinary patrimony.

At the delicatessen in Market Street I sampled my way through the best of Cornwall's fine foods, some of which were finer than others. The most famous brand of a kind of wide ginger biscuit called Cornish fairings, packaged in a red box with blue naval trimmings, bore a list of ingredients that should inspire shame in every red-blooded Cornishman or -woman, including as it did annatto, curcumin, E160b, E100, E475, E500, E450a and E503, and studiously avoiding all mention of ginger.

A white wine from Bodmin Moor was, in the words of the *Monty Python* sketch, a wine for laying down and avoiding. If you read the small print on the packet of Duchy Originals, which are some of the best cheese biscuits I have ever come across, you will see that they're actually made not in the Duchy of Cornwall but in Scotland.

On the other hand, I would be happy to recommend Callestick Farm ice cream, especially when drizzled with Mr Bunney's excellent honey, and a clutch of decent Cornish cheeses: firm-textured and tangy raw-milk Menallack, and a nice fake goats' milk feta from the village of Gweek, which enables it to be known, with a felicitousness that almost makes you suspect they chose the cheese and the village to fit the pun rather than the other way round, as Gweek feta. I bought a slab of Yarg, too, to keep in the car. This Caerphilly-style cheese, with its peculiar grey-green coat of nettle leaves, both looks and sounds as if it must have been made from Cornish milk by Cornishmen for the last five hundred years and was probably taken down the mines along with the homemade pasty. The truth is somewhat different: Yarg was first made around fifteen years ago, one of the first of the new farm cheeses in the county, and christened as such because its makers' surname was Gray (try spelling it backwards). I tried a little – it had a dry, pleasant crumbliness and a faint taste-memory of sweetness that might just have been a hangover from Mr Bunney's honey.

What should be the next stop, then, in my grand tour of *la cuisine cornouaillaise*?

'Well,' said the man behind the deli counter, 'you could do worse than go for a paaaasty from that bakery just across the street.'

So I stood in the lunchtime queue at Barnecutt's and bought one for a few pence less than a pound and munched half of it from its paper bag as I walked back to the car park, feeling the mild glow of smugness foreigners experience when they manage to do something that chimes in with local practice.

The man at the deli had told me the best saffron cake in Cornwall came from a small village ten miles from Liskeard. In ten minutes I was there, outside a neat Victorian house with bright green windowframes where the Pearce family have been bakers for the village of Kelly Bray since 1865.

If I hadn't been sure I had come to the right place, my doubts would have been dispelled by the small delivery van that stood by the door, which said on the side in unmistakable black letters 'Pearce's Noted Saffron Cakes', and bore a painted naif picture of a bright yellow cake speckled black with currants, the crumbs gently eroding on to a plain white plate.

'We make, oh, I should think about seventy or eighty saffron cakes a day, and 1,500 or so of these little buns a week. I counted it once,' said Mrs Pearce as she pulled apart the stuck-together square of saffron buns, arranging them in an old-fashioned glass-fronted cupboard at the side of the shop.

From the bakery behind her came a thick fug of heat and bread smells, in the midst of which I detected an aroma unusual in British kitchens: the pungent, piercing, almost antiseptic reek of saffron.

'Come through to the bakery, dear,' said Mrs P., beckoning me back. I followed her into the floury sauna where her husband, a tall, rangy, grey-haired, gloomy-countenanced man, was following his usual routine.

'Another batch ready?' said Mrs P. to Mr P., and he, nodding, flicked open the oven and a delicious hot stink of saffron came out.

'On its way,' he grunted.

The ovens were once coal-fired and the 'peel' he was using now for taking out the bread – a long pole made of some handsome hardwood, lightly toasted by the heat, with a polished-up metal paddle at one end – once reached twice its current length to the far end of the cavernous oven. The buns on the tray were so yellow it was hard to believe the Pearces didn't use turmeric or tartrazine rather than large quantities of finest Spanish saffron. To prove the point, Mrs P. scuttled into a storeroom and came back with a highly decorated tin that she hugged in her arms like the precious thing it was. The stamens of *Crocus sativus* are, literally, worth their weight in gold.

'That's finest Valencia. We paid two hundred pounds for this tin. We *have* paid up to a thousand – if there's a poor harvest. How long does it last? A few weeks.'

She put her hand in and teased out a few threads from the dark reddish-orange mass and examined them idly in the palm of her hand, seeming to remember something of the heart-breakingly time-consuming process by which these threads are removed from the heart of the crocus flower. 'Of course the pickers are paid an absolute pittance . . .' she murmured, pursing her lips.

On the window ledge stood a white jug with streaks of deep orange sticky down its sides – the saffron steeping in water overnight for tomorrow's bake. I put my nose in the jug and caught another blast of that smell, so nearly medicinal it doesn't seem surprising that the Cornish once regarded saffron as a cure for coughs and bronchitis.

Apart from the saffron, Pearce's cake uses Canadian bread flour, eggs, fats and an enormous quantity of currants so that the finished product is quite crammed with them, the golden yellow dough thickly speckled with black just like the picture on the side of the van outside. Some of the raisiny sweetness of the fruit must seep out, too, because the cake is rather squidgy and sticky though still crumbly, with a rich highly aromatic flavour from the saffron. It is one of the classic cakes of Britain.

Saffron Cake

Steep a packet of saffron in a cup of water overnight. Rub 200g of lard and 175g of unsalted butter, cut into small cold pieces, into a kilo of good strong white flour. Add 275g of sugar, 100g of sultanas, 25g of mixed peel and 325g of currants and mix. Then add 40g of yeast, the saffron and its water, a beaten egg and a little milk if more liquid is necessary. Knead well. Leave the dough to rise in a warm place, covered with a clean cloth, until it has doubled in size. Knead again and place in a greased bread tin, leaving again in a warm place until the dough has filled the tin. Bake at 170 °C, Gas Mark 3 for an hour. Turn out the saffron cake on to a wire tray.

Outside Kelly Bray was a long-abandoned tin mine, a mysterious place set amid woods and meadows, towers and walls overgrown with ivy, elder, briars. Too many of Cornwall's mines have been over-restored, tamely kitted out for the tourist trade, complete with clotted cream tea rooms and Virtual Tin-Mining Experiences. The ruined mines that remain are powerfully romantic experiences in themselves, Cornwall's industrial cathedrals, as highly charged with *genius loci* as any ruined religious building. I sneaked between two walls – gaping arches above me ready to crumble – and found myself in a deep dark Celtic wood. Then I sat outside in the sun on an old slagheap and snaffled the rest of my paaaasty, wondering if there was anything at all in common between what I was eating now and what the mineworkers might have eaten a few yards and a hundred years from where I sat.

Down by the stream at Rilla Mill I saw a notice, posted by the makers of Yarg cheese, recruiting nettle-pickers for that distinctive grey-green coating. 'Due to recent good weather nettles have been growing well and need to be picked before the frost.' The dairy would pay six pounds a kilo. I ate some saffron cake and Yarg – the two went well together, the rich fruity sweetness of the cake offsetting the salty crumble of the cheese – and lay down in the grass beside the stream, daydreaming of life as a part-time nettle-picker. Would protective clothing, gloves and antihistamine cream be provided? Was six pounds a generous wage, or were nettles like saffron, and a kilo would take an age to pick? How much would a plastic supermarket bag of nettles weigh, if you packed them in tight, pushing down with your gloves making sure the tips didn't sting your wrists?

I fell asleep for an hour or two in the thin sunlight, then drove the few miles towards the coast and found a room at the top of the steep-sided gorge of West Looe, right above the harbour. I sat on my window-seat until the sun set, staring down at the jostling crowds and the kids shrieking at crabs and the piles of nets and the tarry old fish trawlers coming in at East Looe quay and the old sea-dogs apparently provided by Central Casting, so perfect were their grizzled beards and oil-stained blue dungarees, who stepped off the boats and side-stepped the tourists with their white plastic boxes . . . The fish market at Looe is still functioning, though nobody knows for how much longer, as the British fleet goes into apparently terminal decline and Penzance and Newlyn take the lion's share of whatever fish is left swimming off the Cornish coasts. Most of the harbourside business nowadays seemed to consist of charter fishing trips, at night for the Hemingway types, in search of mackerel, shark or conger eel.

My Looe landlady was married to a fisherman. She was a pretty blonde girl in her mid-thirties, too busy to cook very much and far too squeamish to mess around boning and filleting, another example of that quite unfathomable and peculiarly British characteristic, not recognising a good thing when you see a polystyrene box of it, still quiveringly fresh, every morning of your life.

'I know, I know. I should cook it more than I do,' she said smilingly as she fried up my bread next morning. 'I just find it such a pain in the bum to fillet and all that. Though it *is* nice when he brings back the odd lobster, the odd crab. But lemon sole, that's what he mostly brings back . . . Well, I'm sorry, but I can live without it.'

I ran through the oral questionnaire that I usually put to Bed and Breakfast landladies in an attempt to discover whether there is any proper traditional regional food any more in Britain or whether it has all gone to that great cook-chill cabinet in the sky. But Liz was a modern Cornishwoman, to whom stargazy pie (so-called because the fish-heads poke out of the pastry) and heavva cake meant a lot less than ciabatta and quattro formaggi. 'That starry-gazy pie – one of the fishermen's wives made one up a few weeks ago. You're supposed to make it with pilchards, aren't you? She did it with mackerel. As for paaaasties, I think they're 'orrible. They're the most disgusting thing in the world. I won't touch 'em.'

It was possible that her profound dislike of the national dish had its roots in her previous occupation. By coincidence, it turned out that, before she got into Bed and Breakfast, Liz had been a food analyst for a well-known cook-chill company.

We exchanged knowing glances as she laid my Full English on the table in front of me.

'Actually their micro-analysis wasn't bad, I seem to remember,' she said mildly. 'There aren't too many bacteria in their products. I shouldn't really be telling you that, now should I?'

My most memorable meals in Cornwall have, on the whole, not been in restaurants. They have been on clifftops.

When a picnic on a clifftop is really good, it can be unforgettable. There was one I'll remember for ever, a decade ago on a warm day in March when the sky was as blue as lapis lazuli and the gorse flowers lit up the hedgerows with yellow flame, above the still beautiful harbour village of Port Isaac. Like all good picnics, this one was a miraculous conjunction of place and time and food and drink: I bought a dressed crab from a stall in the harbour, some soft white splits – the Cornish bap, made with a milky dough – a jar of mayonnaise and a bottle of fabulous, fat, buttery Meursault from the minuscule selection in the town grocers.

Why was it so good? Impossible to say. Whatever magical qualities that meal possessed, it would be a mistake to try and recreate them. Which is just what I tried to do this time, nevertheless, on the clifftop at Pendrannack on the Lizard peninsula, when the sky and the colours of the landscape had been chilled and darkened by the autumn afternoon. On the winding path to the sea, for the first time in twenty years I saw a slow-worm – a legless lizard on the Lizard – looking like a thin stream of melted bronze. It felt like a sign, a natural 'This Way Please'.

At Pendrannack, I spent the afternoon gazing at the untarnished beauty of the green jutting arm of cliff across the wild bay, and the streams clattering down through the bilberry bushes into the sea, and ate my way through a banquet of crab-meat stuffed into little brown Cornish buns, a 'heavva' cake that really lived up to its name – a flat dense cake made with lard, milk, sultanas, currants and fruit peel, bought from Eddy's, the baker in Newlyn – and most of a pot of clotted cream I had bought that morning, realising that I could put off my encounter with this pivotal West Country product no longer.

The cream was made at Pengoon Farm, where the Easts were some of the last people in Cornwall still making clotted cream the old way, in small batches on top of the stove without recourse to oven-baking, steaming, microwaving, artificial yellowing or any of the techniques employed by certain modern-day industrial creameries who only have themselves to blame for the inferiority of their products. Mrs East suffered from arthritis and preferred to stay indoors these days, but her husband came to meet me in the yard – another smelly farmyard strewn with rusted machinery and plastic fertiliser bags. Pengoon had seventeen Jersey cows. Clotted connoisseurs believe only Jersey or Guernsey will do, because of the higher fat content of the milk. Because fat is of the essence here. The minimum legal butterfat content of clotted cream is 55 per cent. There is also butter oil, which is what gives a good cream its gorgeous deep yellow crust.

The milk is heated and cooled, then separated and clotted in Pyrex bowls set in gently simmering water on the top of the Rayburn. Bubbles come to the top, making a surface of tiny golden craters. In a glass-fronted fridge in the corner of the tiny farm shop, there were the bowls of clotted cream from yesterday's session at the Rayburn, and I asked Mr East for a nice big scoop from one of them.

'How do you eat it?' I wondered aloud, meaning how did the Easts eat it at home, if indeed they could bear to touch the stuff any more.

'On the end of your finger, if you like,' said Mr E. He said it again, for emphasis. 'On the end of your finger, if you like.'

Now, on the clifftop, I ripped off the lid of the pot he had given me and ate the cream in just the manner he had recommended. It was a beautiful pale yellow-gold cowslip colour, speckled with bits of darker yellow crust. It had a vibrant, fresh flavour redolent of lush grass, and an unctuous cool creaminess that inevitably meant the first fingerful was followed by another and another, and that I ended up breaking off bits of heavva cake and loading them with cream before conveying them to my mouth, feeling my arteries clotting by the minute.

The Lizard was a shabby little seaside town with single-storey houses painted shabby colours, the grey of overcooked meat and the off-white of melted Wall's ice cream. Ann Muller's Lizard Pasty Shop was a little hut in a side street painted a bright buttercup yellow not unlike the surface of a good fresh farmhouse clotted cream. When I arrived there in the early evening Ann was just closing up after a long day, but she kindly found time to make me a cup of tea and tell me something of pasty lore, of which she knows, by the way, probably more than any woman alive.

If Ann is the Pasty Queen of Cornwall, then logically her mother Hettie Merrick, who wrote the book about Cornish cuisine, must be the Pasty Queen Mother. It was Hettie who kicked off the family's business interest in the dish at an agricultural fair in Brittany at which she set up a pasty stall only to see demand dramatically outstrip supply. Her daughter Ann was drafted in to help on the stall and, by the end of the day, as she explained to me, 'I could crimp as fast as Mother.' Crimping, of course, being the arcane Cornish art of sealing the pasty, about which battles have been fought and controversy still regularly rages.

She stood by the stove in her floury apron, a tall handsome woman with long grey-blonde hair and muscular arms both acquired and maintained by pulling at the oars on rowing boats. As a spokeswoman for the pasty and Cornish food in general, Ann was so voluble, enthusiastic and good-natured that she ought to have been receiving a salary from the Cornish tourist board. Her blue-grey eyes shone with joie de vivre.

'Okay, the thing is, I make several hundred of these things every day, so it won't be any trouble to make one more. That way you'll really understand the process,' she said, tying her hair back with a rubber band.

In a few minutes I saw before me a circle of dough made with Dove's Farm strong flour, lard and margarine, kneaded a little to make it slightly stretchy.

'The constitution of the dough is crucial, because if it's too flaky or fragile you'll have filling leaking all over the place, and the whole point about the pasty is it's got to be properly sealed. Okay, now the filling.'

It was a circular pile of flakes of potato, yellow turnip aka swede, and a few small pieces of meat. It was a plain, not to say drab sort of mixture, and hardly seemed likely to yield up anything even half as intensely savoury as the Italian calzone or the Spanish empanadilla, which are the pasty's nearest foreign relatives. But there are hidden complexities of flavour in the pasty, and subtle technical twists. Because of the way the ingredients are layered and generously seasoned with black pepper in between, when the pasty is cooked the sweetness of the swede alternates with hot blasts of pepperiness.

'The beef's chuck, virtually fat-free, and no gristle,' said Ann. 'As far as filling goes this is just the simplest. I also make a "herby" pasty, which is traditional too, with spinach and parsley. You can actually put anything in and call it a pasty. There's also my Lizard breakfast pasty, and it's very popular. Baked beans, sausage and egg. Pasties were something that all the women in my mother's Cornish family did,' she said as she used those rowers' wrists to grind one last scattering of pepper before taking up the edges of the pastry and beginning to seal them together with a series of quick little twisting movements of finger and thumb. 'But my mother, and I think her mother, used to crimp from right to left, and I crimp from left to right. And that's one of the great differences between us.'

In a minute or two the pasty was finished, and Ann lifted it on to a tray and pushed it into the big oven at the back of the shop. The oven must be really hot, she explained, so that the temperature inside the pasty rises quickly, effectively pressure-cooking the filling while not overcooking its pastry container.

Now she could pour us both another cuppa and take the

weight off her feet, and let her mind roam over a lifetime of Cornish eating.

She had a fund of stories. As a child growing up in the village of Gunwalloe, between Mullion and Porthleven on the western edge of the Lizard peninsula, she remembered 'Chapel teas' with buttered splits and jam, and saffron buns, and slab (fruit cake). The greatest childhood treat of all was Thunder and Lightning, a slice of fresh bread spread with treacle or golden syrup and smothered with clotted cream. 'We used to walk up to Tregiddell Farm, where Mrs Curtis made the most fantastic cream. She made it on the top of her Aga, and we'd collect it in our little cans. Sometimes we ate it on top of junket. I used to like it sprinkled with a little nutmeg. At the farm, maybe it's just my rose-coloured specs, but there always seemed to be caraway buns and fruit cake on the table, too.'

Cornish people enjoy their own cooking, which is plainly the reason they've managed to keep hold of some of it, while the rest of the country has sold its soul to pizza and pasta. There was the time when Ann's son Fergus had a car accident and ended up in hospital, and when she visited him there she would pop down to the canteen to get them both something to eat. Usually the menu featured Under-Roast Potatoes, a classic Cornish dish whose name has nothing to do with undercooking but refers to the fact that liquid is added to the potatoes halfway through the roasting so that they braise underneath and brown on top. 'I love Under-Roast, but there never seemed to be any left, whatever time I got there. The Cornish people working in the hospital had got there first and eaten the lot, you see.'

Of pasty lore, of course, Ann knew all there was to know. She told me that it was still bad luck to take a pasty on board ship;

that Cornish children still learn the playground ditty that starts off, 'Matthew, Mark, Luke and John /Ate a pasty five foot long'; and that if a pasty is too lightly seasoned (hardly a problem with Ann's own pasties) the local word for it is 'fresh'. She might well have gone on all night, expatiating on the pacifying virtues of saffron ('it's the high concentration of riboflavin, or something') if her cook's body-clock hadn't told her my special pasty was done to a turn. She leaped up and pulled the oven door open, and an aroma wafted towards me that had something of the all-enfolding warmth of newly baked bread but overlaid with a delicious savoury richness, like a steak and kidney pie that has just arrived, steaming hot, on the table at Sunday lunch.

Ann Muller's pasty was a triumph: the pastry golden and crispy on the outside, meltingly tender on the inside where the juices of meat and vegetable had been drawn by a process of osmosis. Deep within the core of the pasty, I saw that the chunks of beef had cooked so thoroughly that they almost fell apart in the mouth, and that together with the potato and swede they had actually created a little thick gravy, clinging to the interstices between individual pieces. I bit off a crisp corner and worked my way towards the thick middle of the pasty, where the pastry bulged humidly underneath and seemed like it might burst with the weight of filling. And the black pepper caught the back of my throat and warmed me as I gulped greedily.

Ann smiled at me wearily as she set about closing up for the night, her face wearing the quietly indulgent look of someone who is used to pleasing people with her work. 'Nice, eh?' she said, untying her apron.

The Classic Pasty

Rub in 125g lard with 500g of white flour and a pinch of salt. Put 125g of margarine in the freezer for ten minutes, then grate into the bowl. Add 200ml of cold water and mix with a knife. Knead lightly, gather the dough into a ball and refrigerate for an hour.

To make the filling for one pasty, slice 50g of swede (oops, 'yellow turnip'), 25g of onion, and 175g of old potatoes. Trim 100g of skirt of beef and cut into small pieces.

From the made pastry cut off 100g for each pasty and roll it out into a circle the size of a dinner plate.

Lay out the chopped onion along the middle, then the turnip. Season with salt and plenty of black pepper.

Then lay the meat along the top. Season again. Finally add the potato to the pile.

Moisten the far edge of the circle, fold over the dough and gather the two edges together. 'Crimp' along the seam to seal the pasty, folding the edge repeatedly in a rope pattern. Brush the pasty with milk or egg-and-water.

Transfer it on to a greased and floured baking tray and bake in a hot oven (220 °C, Gas Mark 7) for 20 minutes. When the pasty has browned, turn the oven down to 180 °C, Gas Mark 4 and cook for a further 20 minutes. Finally turn the oven off completely and leave for another 15 minutes. Remove and leave to cool a little before eating.

From the sweet southern coast I made my way overland towards the rougher craggy moorland of the north, along the sunken Cornish lanes whose sides are so high that tourists crane their necks in frustration to see the changing scenery. The hedges were studded with clumps of purple heather, foxgloves and white convolvulus, and sometimes the lanes dipped through deep wooded gulleys, dark and lush. But beyond those high hedges the hillsides were treeless and stony. The Cornish landscape is a microcosm of the wider British countryside, offering you generosity and barrenness almost at a single glance.

In terms of food there is a similar disparity going on, an emulsion sauce compounded of the atrocious and the exquisite, which is a truth equally applicable to Cornwall in particular and Britain in general. The exquisiteness tends to be concentrated (to continue the mayonnaise metaphor) in individual drops or globules which, if the sauce is to become consistently smooth and rich, one can only hope will eventually become blended into the whole.

One such droplet of excellence is the harbour town of Padstow, headquarters of the genial Rick Stein, who, as everyone in Britain who is slightly interested in food and also possesses a TV knows, is chef-patron of the Seafood Restaurant and star of the fish cookery series *Taste of the Sea*. Not everyone in Padstow thinks the world of Stein, but few would be foolish enough to deny that the culinary impact he has had on this town has been dramatic. In point of fact, it seems to me that there is nowhere like it as a place to eat anywhere else in the South-West.

The signs of Steinery are everywhere in Padstow. Not only in the scale of his mini-empire, which at the moment of writing included a bistro, a delicatessen, a cafe and twenty-seven rooms for rent at various premises in the town, in addition to the original upmarket restaurant. Not only in the half-dozen good restaurants that have sprung up as a reaction, and/or under the influence of, his own. The tiny but excellent Bistro Margot Thomas, with a mere eight tables, is a stalwart of local gastronomes. Brock's, a recent arrival, is more new-fangled and classier, an airy, beamed upper room, all yellow walls and seagrass floors, where the menu is clearly pitched at the Seafood market though considerably cheaper, with a chef whose CV reads like a primer of London restaurant chic: Chez Nico, Soho House, The Square . . . And then there is No. 6 Cafe and Rooms, next to the deli in Middle Street, which has nothing to do with Stein but a fish logo not unlike that of his own bistro and a menu of trendy stuff like deep-fried squid with salsa fresca and seared scallops with black pudding and potato cake that has Rickery written all over it.

Even at modest places there has been a hike in quality whose origins are not hard to trace. The Waterfront, with pub dining-room chairs and fanned pink serviettes, looks like it should be serving chicken in a basket but actually does seared monkfish with Thai fragrant rice and roast cod with onion, garlic and bayleaf. And Granny's Pasty Shop across the way, which might once have restricted itself to the usual fillings of meat and turnips, cheese and onion and pork and apple has branched out daringly, post-Rick, into such mad sophistications as bacon, leek and cheese, Indian chickpea and chocolate and banana.

Even on a gruesome late autumn day, with the wind flapping the masts in the harbour and the yachties rolling up their Authentic Cornish Fishermen's Sweaters around their necks against the wind, it was tough finding a parking place in Padstow. As a pretty little Cornish fishing port of the sort that makes a jolly day out, it never had a problem attracting visitors, but the coverage given to the town by Stein's TV shows had given it another massive boost. When the BBC replayed the Padstow episode of *Taste of the Sea* the local tourist information centre was swamped with enquiries. 'It was wonderful weather for that one, and it did look absolutely gorgeous,' said the girl at Stein's Delicatessen. 'You can understand why people want to come here. But a lot of it's got to do with Rick, as well. People like his enthusiasm, his ordinary-guy sort of appeal. And if that's what you need to get people in the kitchen, so be it.'

Like a lot of good delis in England Stein's had the feel of a space a little bit too small for the sheer amount of stuff crammed into it. For a while I simply rootled contentedly, like a boar let loose in some bit of woodland full of succulent nuts and berries.

'There are things here you won't find for hundreds of miles around. Like this black pepper,' said the manageress, pulling a small cloth bag almost at random from the groaning shelves beside her. 'It comes from a remote valley in Kerala where you can still see tigers and elephants, and the only fertiliser they use is natural water-buffalo manure, and they leave the pepper grains to mature in the sun, and it has this intense, almost fruity flavour. Here; try it.'

I crunched one of the wrinkly black grains in my mouth. It

was true: behind and beneath the fiery blast of heat was a pungency and complexity that have led to there being no other pepper permitted in my kitchen than Parameswaram's Special Wynad ever since.

In the spice rack I saw good Manchego saffron, star anise, fennel and pasilla chilli spice . . . If you're ever in north Cornwall and need to get hold of some hyssop, Middle Street is where you will need to come.

'Our *affineur* is Karine le Cointe in London, though we try to get as much of the good local cheeses as we can. D'you know Beenleigh Blue? Made from ewes' milk, you know, by Robin Congdon in Totnes. One of the best. All of our jams and marmalades and chutneys and pickles and tapenade and pesto and chilli sauces and mincemeat and tomato ketchup with celery leaves and all the rest of it . . .'

'. . . come from Mr Stein?'

'Yeah. Actually it's funny, but he very rarely comes in here nowadays,' she said a little wistfully.

There was a queue at the counter of the tiny shop, where lunchtime shoppers scanned the selection of homemade pies, fishcakes, pâtés, tarts, and ready-made dishes you could take away in a box as you would from any French traiteur. There were even some pasties up there at the back, but they looked rather rock-like and frumpy, as though they had sat there unwanted all morning. 'I'll have a chorizo and chilli bread, and a slice of your Devon apple cake,' said a well-groomed London voice, making me wonder for an instant why it was even well-groomed London people have such trouble with the word chorizo, when gnocchi and peperoncini and stracciatella seem to present no problem.

I followed a woman in a headscarf out of the shop and asked to see what she had in her bulging string bag. Somewhat dazed by my strange request, thinking perhaps I might be a plain-clothes store detective, she complied. The bag was full of elegantly packaged branded products: Stein's Cider Apple Chutney, Stein's Three Fruit Marmalade, Stein's Mincemeat, Stein's Extra Virgin Olive Oil – obviously made from olives grown and crushed by Rick's own hands – and a Stein's Christmas Pudding.

'To be honest I usually nip over to Tesco's in Bodmin for my basic stuff, and I do find the cheese in here's horribly expensive,' said the woman flusteredly. 'We have a holiday house along the coast, outside Port Isaac. Do you know it? It's terribly sweet. I daresay there are people who wouldn't *dream* of coming in here. The thing is, my daughter's turned into something of a "foodie", and actually *demands* extra virgin olive oil, would you believe.'

She was on her way down to the harbourside where she'd parked the car in front of the Seafood Restaurant, so I walked down with her and, after she'd roared off in her Land Cruiser, spent a happy quarter of an hour standing by the menu board picking up the comments of passers-by on chargrilled sea bass with tomato, butter and vanilla vinaigrette (£22.60) and fillet of wild salmon with a sorrel sauce (£21.60).

'Twenty-one pounds for a plate of fish! Daylight robbery!' cried one man.

'What on earth do you think he means with the vanilla?' complained a woman in a puffa jacket to her friend, who pulled a face and said, 'It sounds rather disgusting.'

'Horrid idea, isn't it? Give me the simpler things any day. See what he says: "A small lobster served either grilled or steamed would make a memorable first course for two."'

'Well at thirty-eight pounds I'm sure it would.'

'Yes. Well. Quite,' said the first woman, and the two of them stomped off.

'No, I'm afraid Mr Stein's not here at the minute. There's another series coming up, and he's filming like crazy,' said the maitre d' at the Seafood Restaurant. 'He'll be back next week for a day or two, but then he's off again.'

Behind him the dining room glowed with colour and life. I had eaten here ten years before, when it still seemed a wonderful provincial secret, with its gaudy yellow watercolours and its kitschy little conservatory tacked on the front, exactly like a posh restaurant might look in somewhere like Le Touquet. Now, from its glossy clientele and stratospheric prices, it seemed like a satellite of London chic. There was, needless to say, not a table to be had.

An hour and a half later, however, I was gratefully sinking into a bottomless sofa in the lounge of St Petroc's, the newest outpost of Steinland, having had a lunch that was perfect, it occurred to me, if the perfect meal is the one that comes closest to what you felt like eating beforehand without ever quite being aware of it. The lounge was a dream sitting room out of an interior design magazine special on seaside homes, all dark clumpy furniture and white fabrics and coir flooring. A young mother was just being brought an enormous chocolate birthday cake. She and the father were both red-faced and red-legged. They were from Chiswick, West London, down here for half-term with three children who were pleasantly ill behaved. (Is it part of the New British culture of laidbackness, learned perhaps from holidays in Southern Europe, that it is now thought acceptable for children to be seen and heard in restaurants, whereas before they were banished into outer darkness?)

There is a new fashionableness around in the once forlorn outskirts of Britain, and I appeared to have discovered a piece of it. Just the other day I'd sat on the terrace at Tresanton, the minimalist hotel in St Mawes, which outclasses all other hotels in Cornwall, and sipped a Negroni with my Ray-Bans on. The sea was sparkling, there were palm trees in terracotta pots, two grand Notting Hill ladies were flicking through *Women's Wear Daily* at the table next to me. For a moment it felt more like Capri, or at the very least Clerkenwell.

For little by little London style and London ideas of eating, ironically often based on a vague notion of Italian or French ruralism, are seeping inexorably out into the provinces. On the menu that day, for example, there was borlotti bean and pasta soup with bacon, rocket, chilli, Parmesan cheese and olive oil; sautéed squid with garlic and parsley; then steak with salsa verde and pommes frites; pan-fried salmon with white wine parsley and butter sauce; and roast Cornish chicken with balsamic vinegar, olive oil and thyme. For pudding there were then various simple things like strawberries and clotted cream, or Berkswell sheep's cheese with pear and rocket. I'd had the squid, the chicken and the cheese, and it was all so nourishing, so tasteful and nicely cooked and inexpensive, that I wondered, as I drifted off to sleep in the big Conran sofa, if I'd had a better Cornish meal in the whole of my life.

Picnics on clifftops, of course, notwithstanding.

5

to wales

glass eels, mountain mutton and glorious cheeses

I spent the winter in Spain, feasting on cardoons and fresh chorizo and wild asparagus and other delights of the out-of-season Mediterranean. In a bar next to the bullring in Ronda in early spring, I ate a dish of tiny elvers, baby eels so thin they are not much more, or less, than slivers of sublime fishiness coloured with a stripe of delicate grey.

They came sizzling to the table in a little terracotta dish, fired up with thick slices of garlic and a single, coruscating red chilli. And at that moment I remembered the existence of the British elver fishing industry – one of the oldest gastronomical occupations in the country, along with the samphire picker and the travelling pork butcher – and began looking at my diary. Two days later I caught a flight back to London: 5 March was the next 'top tide'; by then, the elvers would be rushing up the rivers from their birthplace in the Sargasso Sea, and there would be fishing.

I knew of at least two places where the tradition existed, though I also imagined there must be more. Dorothy Hartley mentions the Somerset Rhynes and their 'marsh folk'. 'These marsh people, who live in the lands around Wells Cathedral, all know elvers.' But there is also the area around Gloucester, another fine cathedral town, where the Severn begins suddenly to look less like a simple river and more like the mighty estuary it eventually becomes. The land around there is flat, low-lying and criss-crossed with a network of ditches that are flooded by the incoming tide, forming a paradise for the multitudinous offspring of the eel. The month or two when the tides are high enough, usually in March, April or May, is the window of opportunity for elvers, as it is for elver fishermen. The baby fish – 'glass eels' to use the professional term – swarm along the edges of the river and the fishermen, who take to the riverbank at night, simply wait for them to arrive in their strange-shaped elver nets.

'Why is it so important to fish at night?' I asked Mr Wood of UK Glass Eels, sitting in the kitchen of his home in a suburb of Gloucester.

'Because glass eels are negatively phototactic,' he said, which I think means that only an absence of light will bring them to the surface where they can easily be caught.

Mr Wood was flicking through the tide book. 'Now then. High tide tonight is at between 10 and 11 p.m. So if I were you I'd get down to Quedgeley or Epney, between Longney and Manor Farm. Or you could try Elmore Back, there's usually people down there. It's become rather a popular hobby. In fact there's barely room to move on the bank these days. Not surprising, when you consider these things can get one hundred pounds a kilo. Nice bit of pocket money.'

The phone rang. It was a business call for Mr Wood, who sells elvers from France, Portugal and Britain either to eel farmers, or to bodies concerned with building up existing wild eel stocks, or to those strange people in foreign countries who are excited by the idea of elvers as an edible delicacy.

'No, well, he's stuck with a load of fish in France from the last tide which he can't sell,' he was saying. 'A thousand how much? No, all our fish have gone, these are fish from two weeks ago. Asia is not going to take any of these French fish. I would definitely budget for ten per cent dying, ten per cent will die, I should think.'

'Have you ever eaten elvers?' I asked his daughter, who was doing her homework at the kitchen table.

She made a moue of disgust. 'Nah, I don't fancy it. When they're all fried up together, all gooey and . . . eeeurrghhh!'

'We do fish something like fifty tons a year in the whole UK. But the population is going down all the time,' said Mr Wood when he came off the phone. 'Two hundred years ago the tide pushed them into a huge area, into all these ditches for miles around. The tide would have flowed all the way up to Worcestershire. But the weirs on the river have destroyed their migration system. The elvers can't get into the ditches, so you're not getting that dispersion of population throughout the whole countryside. Add to that the pollution in the river, and it's a pretty grim picture.'

Before the sun went down I took a trip to Gloucester's

Eastgate Market, where one of the fish stalls occasionally had elvers for sale. It was a modest sort of workaday market with nothing from which to take your bearings in a gastronomic sense, unless you counted a bright orange block of mass-produced Double Gloucester at the butcher's stall alongside the brawn, the haslet and the chitterlings in their tight pink plaits.

'You must be joking,' said the man at Workman and Meadows. 'D'you know how dear those things are? Actually the price has come down a bit. Used to be three hundred pounds a kilo, now it's nearer a hundred. But you'd need at least a pound for a decent serving, and not many people round this way have got that kind of money, if you understand me. Would I eat them myself? Nah – wouldn't touch 'em.'

Down at the Elver Station, an industrial warehouse on the banks of the Severn Canal as it runs through Gloucester Docks, there was not an awful lot going on. The big holding tanks were sluiced down and empty, the polystyrene boxes piled high in readiness. On the wall I saw an elver net hung up to dry, a big, squarish structure reminiscent, in shape at least, of an old-fashioned box kite.

The fat friendly elver man was tucking into a Cadbury's Creme Egg. Well, it *was* nearly Easter. He had been up all night last night and it had been a poor night's fishing, perhaps because yesterday was a Thursday and most fishermen have normal jobs on Friday morning. But tomorrow was the weekend. Tonight, he assured me with a sticky grin, there would be no holds barred.

I found myself a place to stay, in a bungalow B&B on the muddy little hammer-shaped peninsula where the Severn almost doubles back on itself.

'When I was a girl, I could see out of my bedroom window, all along the riverbank. They had the old lanterns,' said my landlady. 'They make up the net themselves, you buy the fabric.'

'And what are they actually like, the elvers?'

'They look like little black worms. Eugh.'

'And what do they taste like?'

'My dear, they taste of nothing. Sort of watery.'

She shivered at the memory. It is odd, the British dislike of the slithery and gelatinous in food, especially when you consider that once upon a time as a nation we salivated over such things as brawn, tripe, aspic and blancmange. 'Don't talk to me about elvers, I can't stand 'em. I used to fry them up in bacon fat – and an egg in it. That was my husband's favourite. He used to go elvering every weekend in the season.'

In Gloucester and surrounding districts, 'to elver' is a much used local verb. Families and individuals enjoy what are known as 'prescriptive rights' whose origins are lost in time, though in point of fact the true rights may be restricted to local people from certain parishes along the Severn. Such is the demand for elvering sites that local landowners have been charging up to one hundred and fifty pounds a year for access to the river. Since the police have become interested in the possibilities that elvering offers for criminality, however – mainly in the shape of DSS benefit claimants making money on the side – the riverbank has resembled something of a battleground.

'Fishermen in Elvers Crisis' ran the headline in *The Citizen*. I saw the paper on the bar at the Anchor pub in Epney, unofficial headquarters of the elvering fraternity. It had been raining for days, the high tide had brought the river almost to flood levels, and it was a bitterly cold night. None of that seemed to constitute a problem for the dozen or so local blokes who were huddled conspiratorially in the corners of the pub, nursing their pints of Carling Black Label.

One of them, a fat man in a blue shell suit, lurched up to the bar with a girl at his side and said, 'I'll 'ave a steak, luv. Rare. With barbecue sauce on top. And chips. Lots of 'em.' He burped, at astonishing volume.

'Are you an animal, or something?' said his girlfriend, half amused.

While they waited for their drinks I asked her, 'Will there be any elvering tonight?'

'Well I've just sat beside this lout for half an hour with an elver net on his roof rack, so I reckon they'll all be out there, yeah,' she replied.

'Eh? What are you blatherin' about?' said the boyfriend.

'This guy wants to know about elvers.'

'Yeah, well, all I can tell you is, basically, all the fun's gone out of it, elverin'. Before, we used to do it for the crack, 'ave a bit of a laugh. You'd get killed out there, now, for a kilo of elvers.'

Out in the pub car park and along the bank, guys in vans and cars, sitting at the wheel chain-smoking nervously, seemed to be waiting for some kind of signal. Glimpsed through the rear doors of their vans were the ghostly shapes of elver nets.

The river was rushing higher and higher, powering past at sinister speed. Fall in, as my landlady said, and you'd be 'swep' away'. She'd been telling me earlier, as she showed me my room, about the Severn Bore, the strange annual phenomenon by which a miniature tidal wave comes racing up the river from the sea and tourists race to the spot to watch its progress.

I made my way to the edge of the river. A loose chain of feeble, flickering lights could already be seen along the waterfront as the fishermen began setting up their nets. I chose one at random and picked my way through the mud to the source of the light.

''Ere, give us a hand with this,' said Steve, who was struggling to manipulate his bulky elver-net into the water while keeping his torch focused on it. I took the torch from him and shone it at the water as the net descended into the murky depths. Immediately the river buffeted the net, and you could hear the water swirling within it.

'Fuckin' 'ell,' said Steve, taking a firmer hold.

We waited for a few minutes. Nothing seemed to be happening. Steve was a builder, currently unemployed, from the nearby village of Saul, where he would be taking his catch to the elver station tomorrow morning.

'Nah, they don't ask no questions,' he said. 'No problem. You can make a few hundred quid a night, if you're lucky. But it's not as easy as it used to be. The filth's got wind of it, for a start.

'Would I eat them? Nah. Rather have a nice saveloy and chips, me. Well, they're disgusting, aren't they? All slimy and nasty . . . Whoops, here they come. See 'em?'

He raised the net out of the water, and I shone the torch inside it. 'See that little wriggling stuff in there? That's them.'

A few elvers, no more than a generous tablespoonful, had made their way upriver and glistened in the corner of the dripping net, writhing in the torchlight. It was hardly enough to be celebrating over, but Steve knew there would be more as the night went on.

We waited in silence for another ten minutes, and this time a good handful came up. Another ten minutes, and there might have been a small plateful. By the time Steve had a pound or so in his plastic bucket I felt confident enough to ask him: could I possibly take a few off his hands? For my own consumption, as it were.

He sold me an amount a little less than a half-pint for a tenner. Next morning I took them downstairs to my landlady at the B&B, only to see her face light up with delight.

'Oh my gosh now, what are you bringing me them things for?' she complained, but cheerfully went into the kitchen and cooked up a plateful in the way she used to: fried in bacon fat, with an egg stirred in towards the end, so that the baby eels congeal into a sort of fishcake.

When an ingredient is truly at the height of its season it is always worth trying, and nothing could be more thoroughly seasonal than this. Mrs Thompson was wrong about one thing: the elvers didn't just taste of water, but had an exquisite subtle savoury fishiness and the mildest imaginable meatiness, which the salty bacon fat set off to perfection.

What made the dish even better, though, was its rarity. I was partaking here of a dead delicacy, a piece of culinary archaeology that will never again form part of our national cuisine – until tastes change, perhaps, and elvers are once again valued for something more than what the Continentals will pay for them.

Glass Eels à la Mode de Gloucester

Rinse 450g of fresh elvers in a big bowl of salty water. Drain and rinse again in more salty water. Drain once more, and dry in a clean cloth. Melt 2 tablespoons of lard in a frying pan, then fry 8 rashers of streaky bacon until crispy. Remove the bacon from the pan and arrange around the edge of a warm dish. Lower the heat, add the elvers, season, and stir fry for a few seconds until they turn white. Pour on 3 beaten eggs, and stir along with the elvers until the egg has set. Tip into the dish. Serve immediately – with a jug of cider on the side.

I drove into Wales over the Severn Bridge, thinking of all those elvers swimming for dear life beneath me, and headed westwards, towards the tip of the snout of the Welsh pig. The floods of the previous few days had turned to bitter cold, and a fall of unseasonal snow made the tops of the Brecon Beacons look like failed meringues.

I broke my journey in Ross-on-Wye in order to make a sad little pilgrimage. The town plays a pivotal role in British gastronomic history, though not, it must be said, for the most edifying of reasons.

In a hotel somewhere in Ross – it has never been established exactly which, and one can understand why – Elizabeth David stayed for a while during the bitterly cold winter of 1947. She had returned from Egypt not long before to an England in the grip of rationing and misery. In Cairo her cook, Suleiman, had served her such delights as lamb kebab, ful medames and apricot ice cream. At the hotel in Ross – could it have been the Pencraig Court, which has the gardens and the river views that she described? – she was offered 'flour and water soup seasoned solely with pepper; bread and gristle rissoles; dehydrated onions and carrots; corned beef toad-in-the-hole. I need not go on.'

When ice turned to flooding, she was stranded. 'I stuck it out. It was an effort. By this time I was finding it very difficult indeed to swallow the food provided in the hotel,' she wrote. 'It was worse than unpardonable, even for those days of desperation; and oddly, considering the kindly efforts made in other respects, produced with a kind of bleak triumph which amounted almost to a hatred of humanity and humanity's needs.' Mired in nostalgia for the Mediterranean world she had lost, she took up her pen. And it's to this precise moment, I think, that the social historians of the future will point as the source, the wellspring, of the waves of social change that came upon the British in the second half of the twentieth century.

'Hardly knowing what I was doing, I who had scarcely ever put pen to paper except to write memos to the heads of departments in the Ministry which employed me during the war, I sat down and . . . started to work out an agonized craving for the sun and furious revolt against that terrible cheerless, heartless food by writing descriptions of Mediterranean and Middle Eastern cooking. Even to write words like apricot, olives and butter, rice and lemons, oil and almonds, produced assuagement. Later I came to realize that in the England of 1947 those were dirty words that I was putting down.'*

* 'John Wesley's Eye', *The Spectator*, 1 February 1963.

Twenty miles further west, at Abergaven[illegible] having heard from a friend that one of the finest foo[illegible] the country was to be found there. In my Welsh Food file, among all the leaflets inviting tourists to visit the Celtic Corner tea rooms and the Famous Welsh Chocolate Farm, I found the catalogue Vin Sullivan had sent me the previous summer. This was a seventy-page document encompassing pretty much every ingredient the modern chef could possibly dream of, from dumpling skins to durians, zander fish to zampone. I counted thirty-six sausages, thirty-five types of mushroom, thirty-one vinegars. Here was further proof, if proof were needed, that if there is any deficiency in British food it is not the result of material scarcity, lack of variety, or problems of supply.

Vin Sullivan, the delicatessen, was indeed a good food shop, though there was little distinctively Welsh produce here apart from a few shelves of fudge, biscuits, cordials, jams and other stuff, all packaged up to the hilt under trademarks like Welsh Cottage, with bows and frills and fancy labels.

The sight of all this ethnic frippery made me go over in my head what I already knew about Welsh food. There was bara brith, the speckled fruit cake sometimes made with treacle and lard. I remembered having enjoyed that on occasion with a good strong cup of tea, and/or a glass of oloroso sherry. There was laver bread, the like-it-or-loathe-it seaweed speciality. I wasn't sure I had ever enjoyed that. And there was Welsh lamb, popularly supposed (especially by the Welsh) to be the best in the world.

A few traditional dishes sprang to mind. Welsh rarebit, which was originally something like a Swiss raclette, the cheese turned and browned on its bread slice in front of the fire. Glamorgan sausages, stuffed with leek, caerphilly cheese and herbs. Cawl,

… The eccentric Englishwoman … invented herself as a Welsh nationalist … servants wore Welsh costume, gave a recipe for the … 867 book *First Principles of Good Cookery*. Elizabeth David saw it, and quoted it in her *Spices, Salt and Aromatics in the English Kitchen*, recommending as an accompaniment, rather bizarrely, a cubed honeydew melon sprinkled with lemon juice.

SALT DUCK

In a large, deep pot, arrange a bed of sea salt. Lie on it a duck of about 2 kilos in weight. Rub the duck with more sea salt and then cover it as nearly as possible with salt and leave for three or four days, giving the duck a good salt rub at least once a day.

Take the duck out of the pot, brush off and rinse thoroughly. Simmer at the lowest possible heat, skimming occasionally, in a large pan with two leeks and two carrots, all thickly chopped. In 2–3 hours the duck meat should be meltingly tender. Allow to cool and carve the bird. Serve with a wine-based beurre blanc, as recommended in Marc and Kim Millon's The Tastes of Britain. *Or try Elizabeth David's melon.*

Above and beyond the particular dishes, however, it seems likely that the best Welsh cooking of the past was characterised by a certain pleasurable plainness, as we can discern from this description by the novelist Thomas Peacock, who married a woman from Caernarvon and lived in from 1810–12, of a hearty meal at Ap-Llymry Farm: 'In a few utes the whole party . . . were seating over a clean homespun tablecloth, ornamented with fowls and bacon, a pyramid of potatoes, another of cabbage . . . a bowl of milk for the children and an immense jug of foaming ale . . . The young lady made tea: and afterwards from time to time, at Mr C's request, delighted his ear with passages of ancient music. Then came a supper of lake trout, fried on the spot, and thrown, smoking hot, from the pan to the plate.'

Trout With Bacon

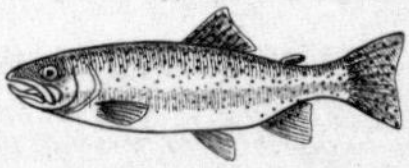

(serves 4)

Take four nice fresh trout, wild if possible, organically farmed if not, clean them, and rub inside and out with salt and pepper. Wrap each fish tightly from neck to tail with thin rashers of the best dry-cured bacon you can find, tucking fistfuls of parsley between bacon and fish. Place the fish together in a roasting pan and season with plenty of freshly ground black pepper. Bake the trout in a preheated hot oven for 15 minutes until the bacon is crisping up at the edges.

I bought a few packaged edibles from the shop: a pot of laver bread, slick and black as beach tar, a packet of Welsh cakes, and a slab of bara brith with a label that showed an old-fashioned

Welsh lady in a tall black h[illegible]ing by her hearth with a caul-dron of water ste[illegible] on the fire. It was a pretty meagre harvest of [illegible] food, all things considered, and I was ready to l[illegible] shop and feel disappointed for the rest of the day, [illegible] a shop assistant came out of the storeroom in a crisp white apron, pointed to me and said brightly to his colleague, 'Have you not shown him the cheeses?'

He had not shown me the cheeses, and I was keen to see them. Jane Grigson, writing in 1984, casts aspersions on the cheese-making ambitions of the Welsh, but I knew that since then there had been changes for the better. I peered into the glass cabinet. What was that one there, the one with all that heavy wrapping around it?

'That's Stinking Bishop. Actually not from Wales, but from Gloucestershire. They wash the rind with perry. It's a bit strong. In fact we keep it wrapped up like that for security reasons. Want to try a bit?'

Gingerly he removed the Stinking Bishop from its protective sheath, and immediately the shop was filled with an unbeliev-able ammonia-rancid stench. The Bishop, as its aficionados know it, is famous for its powerful aroma. If you are not well disposed towards these things, it may well remind you of some-thing between gasworks, socks and rotting fruit. I gather that at the cheese fair in Besançon in 1996 the French judges refused to believe that it was not made in France.

'Phwoah, God!' said the man, reeling backwards. 'A bit of an acquired one, that. We've also got some of the local gear. Let's see now. We've got Llanboidy, Llangloffan, Caws Cenarth, Pen-y-Bont, Pantsgawn, Pencarreg, Skirrid . . .'

The Welsh names came thick and fast, sounding guttural

and strange, more like characters from some cheap science fiction saga than cheeses. 'There's Cwm Tawe, that's a pecorino type, made by an Italian in the Brecon Beacons.' This was a hard, salty, tangy cheese, with a herby resonance in the mouth that was certainly more Sardinia than Swansea.

I tasted my way through Teifi Caerphilly (crumbly and creamy sweet), Caws Mangu (mild and grassy) and Pencarreg, an organic washed-rind cows' milk cheese from Aberystwyth, spectacularly rich and gooey like a good ripe raw-milk brie. And it soon became clear to me that there was in fact an enormous range of Welsh cheeses, even if most of their producers were non-Welsh incomers attracted by the Principality's glorious pasture and cheap land prices. Either way, it certainly seemed to me a strong possibility that cheese-making, and not tea rooms or chocolate farms, might be Wales' worthiest contribution to British gastronomy.

I munched on the bara brith as I walked through Abergavenny's little indoor market, where local ladies conspicuously lacking in tall black hats sold sponge cakes wrapped in clingfilm and jars of lemon curd. The brith was a good representative of its genre, a little bit granular with brown sugar, highly spiced and dense with citrus peel and cherries.

The reputation of the Welsh as bread-bakers and cake-makers goes before them. You would never have known it, however, from the high street bakery where I stopped to buy my picnic bread. The baked goods, here, were apparently closer to the British norm than the Welsh exception. As I stood in the queue my gaze wandered to the glass shelves of fancy cakes that lay in the window, alighting on the trays of elongated buns slathered in a slick of white sugar icing – kids used to call them

Sticky Willies – and the rock cakes and eclairs pustulent with fake-looking white foam and the mini Bakewell tarts with their luminous pink cherry sitting on a thick stratum of the same white icing.

The repertoire of British patisserie, at least as found in high street chains like this, is awful. Danish pastries from which any self-respecting Dane would recoil in horror: hard pastry, a mean ration of almonds and raisins, more white icing (do British bakers boil up vats of the stuff each morning?). Croissants whose acquaintance with the butter-pat has been brief or non-existent. Doughnuts with the squirt of strange red gunk deep within – the unspeakable at the heart of the uneatable. It is a terrible shame, because our national pastry heritage is richer than most, and a high street bakery chain that sold proper scones, crumpets, muffins, teacakes, lardy cakes, oatcakes, Eccles cakes with plenty of currants, Maids of Honour, macaroons, Chelsea buns, Bath buns and hot cross buns, would be the stuff that dreams are made of.

In the car park I nibbled a few sweet, sugary Welsh cakes with hunks of Llanboidy cheese, imprisoned the Stinking Bishop in plastic bags at the back of the glove compartment, and drove on towards Pembrokeshire. The snow was now churning in gusts across the landscape, making this Easter weekend, when we were supposed to be celebrating various kinds of rebirth, seem sunk in the barrenest winter.

Over the next twenty-four hours I was to eat two meals in which the two Welsh ingredients *sine qua non*, laver bread and lamb, figured prominently. If the truth be told, it is hard to eat a restaurant meal in Wales in which either laver bread, or Welsh lamb, or both, do not figure prominently. But I know which of the two I am only too happy to eat, and which I would be happy to banish for ever from my plate.

In the first meal – dinner at a country house hotel where the West Welsh bourgeoisie goes when it wants a slap-up Saturday dinner, and where the menus come in padded green plastic folders full of badly spelled French – the laver bread came *on top* of the Welsh lamb. This was a big mistake. The problem with laver bread is that it gives any sauce made with it a nasty brown sludgy appearance, masking with its muddy seaside flavour the true nature of whatever it's served with. The lamb underneath it was Welsh, but it could have been New Zealand frozen, or from Mars; the laver bread rendered it stateless and tasteless.

Tonight I was closer to Ireland – where, incidentally, most laver seaweed now comes from – than England, and light years away from London-born culinary modernism. Here there were fish knives for the prawn cocktail, in which the prawns, in traditional fashion, swam in a thick pink gloop, not so much on a bed as on a mattress of shredded iceberg lettuce. There were doilies for the wine glasses, and homosexual waiters in cute little waistcoats. Some of the dishes excitedly featured such ingredients as ginger and lemon-grass. It was the first time I had ever seen lemon-grass on a menu in Wales, suggesting that Thai spices had finally reached the westernmost point of Western Europe after an inexorable twenty-year march across the globe.

For the first time in Britain I felt a kind of culture shock, though it was hard to say precisely why. Perhaps it was the man at the bar ordering 'a Southern Comfort with a splash of lemonade' (try saying that with a Welsh accent). Or perhaps it was the way the waiter lifted the silver dome from my Fanned Melon with a triumphant 'ta-*da*!' At provincial restaurants, of course, the element of delighted surprise is precisely the element played down by minimalist London places, where a surly lack of emotion is thought to be correct.

The girls at the next table were trying out their holiday chat-up lines on each other.

'Here, get this. *Sei molto simpatica*.'

'Say what?'

Behind the wall a wedding party was in full swing, and the PA rattled away unrecognisably in Welsh. I felt suddenly depressed and ordered a plate of profiteroles, hoping they might cheer me up, only to find they were as awful as everything else. This was the kind of meal, I reflected sadly, that the so-called British Food Revolution was meant to expunge from the dining rooms of the nation.

A second meal: lunch at what I had heard was a candidate, along with the Italo-Gallic Walnut Tree Inn, for Wales's finest restaurant. The Farmhouse Kitchen in Mathry also made a big deal out of laver bread and lamb. The seaweed turned up in a sauce for two fat scallops in a filo purse. I remained, and remain, unconvinced. But the rack of lamb, a miniature crown constructed from the ribcage of something that tasted as if it had gambolled very recently, was a glorious thing. The meat was packed with sweet grassy flavour and roasted just this side of pinkness in a very fast oven that left the edges and corners of the meat a little seared and caramelly.

Ann Fitzgerald, chef-patronne, came out in kitchen whites, her hair up at the back. She was small and neat, spoke rather fast and poshly, and seemed to burst with a kind of fizzing energy – the sort of energy you'd need, presumably, to open a classy restaurant in the mid-1970s in the middle of rural Wales, which is what she did.

'All the fish comes from Milford Haven. Meat's all local,' she barked amiably. 'Everything else I get delivered. And if all else fails there's always the Tesco's in Fishguard. Cheeses? We've got twelve or thirteen, all Welsh of course. We could have thirty, forty. There are that many these days. We just picked the best of the bunch.'

And what about, er, any other good places to eat in Wales?

'Hmm. Standard's still pretty low, especially over this way. The Walnut Tree, bit of a classic, been going for years, lovely place, Franco and Ann, of course it's famous now. But round here . . . Pretty dismal. Someone I know told me they saw a couple in a restaurant being charged a tenner for a plate of chicken and chips. It was ten o'clock at night; kitchen was closed.'

Country people in Wales eat dinner between six and eight. None of the metropolitan lust for lateness, with its invidious effects on body and spirit.

'Point is, this was chicken and chips. And you won't believe it, but it actually came . . .' The chef glanced theatrically round the restaurant and lowered her voice to a whisper, '. . . *in a basket*.'

The further west I went the wilder and woollier the landscape and weather became. Notionally at least, this was farming country, though you couldn't see farmers around here having an easy time of it. 'Eat British Lamb!' suggested a sign in a snow-whipped field: '50,000 foxes can't be wrong!' Sheep and their lambs were everywhere, only visible now as dirty cream-coloured blots on the whiter-than-white hillsides.

By the time I crossed the county border into Dyfed, I was firmly into Cheese Country. The pasture in this part of the world is famous for its excellence. It was a shame that on a day like this neither I nor the animals could actually see it, but the fact remains that more than half a dozen of Britain's finest cheeses largely owe their existence to it. I got out the map and marked on it with red crosses the names to conjure with: Llanboidy and Penbryn, both cows' milk cheeses, and Pen-y-Bont, a goats' milk cheese, the three in a neat triangle around Carmarthen. Further north towards the Cardigan coast, two more cows': a superb on-farm Caerphilly in Caws Cenarth and the Dutch-influenced cheeses from Teifi in Llandysul. Sheep's cheese at Bethania, at the far edge of Dyfed on the road to Aberystwyth. Last but not least, at the final tip of the snout of the pig, where the ring in its nose might be, a magnificent couple of cows' milk cheeses at Llangloffan.

I went straight to the pig's mouth, and rolled up at Llangloffan just after midday.

'We've been up since six, I've just finished milking, the cows are out in the pasture now – what they can find of it under this snow, poor things,' said Leon Downey. 'I'm just making coffee – want some? Don't worry, it's not instant, it's the real stuff. We believe in real food here. *Everybody* needs real food!'

He sat down by the Aga to take a breath and fixed me with blue-grey eyes that seemed to glow and glint with evangelical energy.

'I've been preaching the Real Food gospel for years now.

Ever since we embarked on this new life. I used to play viola in the Hallé Orchestra for fifteen years, you know.'

Leon must have told his story hundreds of times, but seemed not to have tired of it.

'For a viola player, it was a good job. But I'd sort of begun to think that life was going past fast and furiously and I wasn't somehow feeling the full quality of it.'

That was when he and his wife sat down with a map and worked out which were the parts of the country furthest from motorways and conurbations. Having settled on Pembrokeshire, they had the local papers delivered to the home in Manchester, and eventually a farm came up for sale, and they bought it for £23,000. This was in 1977, with self-sufficiency at the forefront of the national subconscious thanks in large part to Felicity Kendal and her unforgettable performance as bubbly Barbara in *The Good Life*.

It is instructive to remember that at that time, astonishing though it may seem, there were no on-farm cheeses made in Wales, and probably no more than a handful in the whole of Great Britain. One Welsh cheese-maker I met told me he remembers his grandmother making cheese and butter at home, but not his mother. Of the Welsh tradition of cheese- and butter-making on-farm, there was nothing left. The Milk Marketing Board, which centralised and rigidly controlled milk production nationwide, plus the new interest in shop-bought produce, and who knows, perhaps also the new feminist impatience with household drudgery (since it was usually women who made the farmhouse cheese), were all partly to blame for the status quo.

The first few years for the Downeys were tough, what with

suspicious neighbours, a sudden loss of income and the general difficulty of making the change from the urban to the rural environment. Llangloffan Farm had its own traditional dairy, though it had lain idle for years.

Cheese-making came into the equation at an early stage.

'We bought a cow, we started milking it, we made a cheese, and we ate it, it was that simple,' said Leon, glaring at me happily. 'Then we made another cheese, which was slightly better than the first, and we ate that 'n' all.'

They bought their first cheese moulds, vats, presses and so on at local auctions of outmoded farm equipment. They kept pigs – Welsh/Large White cross for piglets and Gloucester Old Spot for bacon – and fed them on the whey left over from the cheese-making. A man came over from Mathry to kill them, one of the last of the area's travelling pig-stickers. They grew their own vegetables, and soon Joan was able to boast that she never opened a tin. She baked five loaves of bread every morning, made her own stocks, and had ducks and turkeys in the yard. One of her favourite kitchen tricks was to pinch a little curd from the cheese-making vat and make a Yorkshire curd tart with eggs, sultanas and syrup, baked in pastry.

Leon rummaged about in a drawer for a boxful of pictures of the early days, old snaps with the honeyed yellowish tints of twenty-year-old photographs that make the whole era look to modern eyes as if it were flooded with permanent sunshine. I could still catch a whiff of the 1970s in this kitchen with its dog-eared Elizabeth David cookbooks, its stripped pine and Portmeirion cups. Here was a nice one of Joan, a woman as hale and handsome as her husband, salting hams on a slate draining board. 'Look, those are our own hams, hanging in the kitchen there, wrapped in muslin – like they used to do!' cried Leon.

'I've got farmers on my mother's side, so I knew how to handle a cow. But I suppose you could say I'm adaptable. If I don't know how to do something, I just ask someone. Or I get hold of a book and find out. I'm a great one for learning from books, aren't I, Joan?'

She had just come in, her cheeks ruddy from the cold, bearing a basket of fresh brown rolls from the in-house bakery where their daughter now bakes the bread. She nodded and smiled.

Pleasing to discover that the notion of good food as pure food, produced on the spot by traditional and natural as opposed to modern and industrial means, was not some post-BSE fad but actually had a venerable history, especially in this part of the country. What Leon was saying made me look up again a passage from Smollett's *Humphry Clinker*, written in 1777, which has Matthew Bramble exiled in London and dreaming of the real food of West Wales, in terms which come strikingly close to modern eco-attitudes. At Brambleton Hall, he rhapsodises: 'I drink the virgin lymph, pure and crystalline, as it gushes from the rock, or the sparkling beverage home-brewed from malt of my own making . . . my bread is sweet and nourishing, made from my own wheat, ground in my own mill, and baked in my own oven; my table is, in a great measure, furnished from my own ground; my five-year-old mutton, fed on the fragrant herbage of the mountains, that might vie with venison in juice and flavour; my poultry from the barn door, that never knew confinement but when they were at roost . . . My salads, roots, and pot-herbs, my own garden yields in plenty and perfection; the produce of the natural soil, prepared by moderate cultivation . . . my dairy flows with nectareous tides of milk and cream; from whence we derive abundance of excellent butter, curds, and cheese; and the refuse fattens my pigs, that are destined for hams and bacon.'

Among the cheese-makers of West Wales, Leon and Joan are the pioneers. They were here first, and subsequent arrivals have tended to resemble them in their wide-eyed, back-to-the-land unconventionalism. The great majority of them are non-Welsh, and some of them, like Patrice Savage of Teifi and Andrea Gegen of Penbryn, are non-British. 'All the new cheesies have been here to pick our brains in the early days. We know 'em all, y' see.'

'Oi, Dad, I'm bringing 'em down again, okay?' came a call from the hallway.

'Okay, I'll be right out,' Leon called back, and then turned to me with a new idea.

'Why don't you go to see John Savage at Teifi? He's got some tales to tell about unpasteurised and pasteurised and all the political stuff. Now, do me a favour and come out and give us a hand with the cows.'

For the next half an hour I became an impromptu cowherd, co-opted to make sure none of the Llangloffan herd strayed into the Farm Shop, where the results of their labours were proudly displayed for sale, but instead lumbered placidly towards the milking shed to ensure the continued production of the same.

Along the north coast, the yellow gorse was out in big messy brushstrokes against a backcloth of deep green and black stippled with white where the snow had fallen and was now melting fast. It was an inhospitable chunk of coastline, craggy and almost treeless except for a few twisted thorn-bushes bent double by decades of ferocious Atlantic winds. A few holiday homes had appeared along the clifftop, mimicking in their simple shapes the whitewashed cottages that arrived here centuries before them. All the same, it did not look a very inviting, pleasurable or productive landscape.

A few miles inland, everything changed. The headquarters of Teifi cheese were to be found at the end of a dirt track in this corner of rural Wales, sitting squatly on a little hill looking down into a tranquil valley, green and luscious. The sense of quietness here was almost palpable. It seemed to make sense that the name of the farm, Glynhynod, means 'Remarkable Valley'.

Not everything round here was peace and love, though. The Savages were up in arms. Long-time militants for the cause of unpasteurised cheese, they had just received news of a proposed government ban on the sale of raw milk for drinking. If the ban on milk led eventually to a ban on raw-milk cheese, as they feared, their livelihood and that of hundreds of others like them across the United Kingdom would be seriously threatened. So they had been drafting carefully worded formal letters to the Ministry of Agriculture, Fisheries and Food and taking calls from worried colleagues, telling everyone who would listen that the on-farm cheese-maker's lot is not a happy one.

'The point is this,' began John Savage, a large pale man with a ring in his ear and a hint of a Dutch accent, with the air of one stating a creed, some basic point of belief, 'you can make a decent cheese from pasteurised milk. A decent, good cheese; but not a classic cheese, not a great cheese. In pasteurisation the milk sugars are slightly burnt, so that the finished cheese has this caramelised taint. The ban on unpasteurised milk does worry me, because it could be the thin end of the wedge.'

John was half-Irish/Scottish and half-Dutch, and his wife Patrice was completely Dutch. This may explain the similarity of Teifi cheese to a good Gouda, though their version of Gouda, tangy and three-dimensionally flavoured, was far better than any Dutch interpretation I have ever tasted. Perhaps it also partly explains the liberal, laissez-faire streak in their character. John began his cheese-making career on an organic co-operative in Holland, studying Gouda manufacture with a wonderful-sounding Mrs Vermeer. But high population density, pollution and the intense strip-grazing of pastures make Holland less good a site for wholesome cheese production than you might think, he explained.

'It's so different here. The cows graze hedges, wild flowers, and meadow grass . . . There's so much diversity here for them; the environment as a whole is just much cleaner too. The result is that the quality of Welsh organic cheese is probably higher overall,' said John.

Outside in the garden, meanwhile, the sun had come out and two children were sitting on a bench by the wall, babbling quietly to each other in Welsh.

John brought out a loaf of nutty brown bread and cut some slices. We sat there contentedly, munching away on his cheeses, savouring the differences, pondering the effects of age and the way Caerphilly seems to become saltier the older it gets.

'I like to eat,' said John suddenly. 'Do you like to eat?'

Oh yes, I said, scooping an avalanche of cheese crumbs back into my mouth.

'Well, when I came back to Britain there was something that surprised me. The way that eating sometimes seemed to be regarded just as an *inconvenience*. The way people just grabbed a plate, plonked themselves in front of the TV . . . The idea of sitting at the table, laying the table, taking pleasure in the food and the experience . . . That was something I'd found more on the other side of the channel. Did you know the Dutch eat twice as much cheese as the British? And the French eat three times as much?' he said finally, with a suggestion in his voice of having somehow proved a point.

He sat back in his chair, chewing energetically. His eyes were the same grey-blue, lit with the same bright flame of passionate conviction, as those of the other cheese-maker I had met that day.

I can't remember how I came by the number, but there it was in my notebook. Panteg: organic Welsh lamb and mutton. I called on the mobile as I left Teifi, and a woman's voice gave me directions to the farm, which was high in the mountains outside the town of Lampeter. Another passing snowstorm whipped in from nowhere, and the directions were those of a person who has forgotten quite how far off the beaten track she lives.

I stopped at a stone house where the farmer's wife let me use her phone. She was about to start cooking a roast dinner: potatoes were peeled and halved, and leeks lay chopped in a bowl on the edge of the dresser.

An hour later, after traversing a muddy track for miles through Wagnerian pine forests, I was sitting in another farmhouse kitchen looking out at a scene of mythical loveliness: a Highland cow, shaggy brown coat, long sinuous horns and all, with a calf of six hours' standing, mother and child marooned in a sea of swirling whiteness.

'They are next in toughness to the yak, apparently,' observed Annie. 'They can give birth in sub-zero temperatures, you know. A lamb would have been dead out there in a few minutes.'

Annie and her husband kept sheep as well as Highland cattle up above the treeline at Panteg Farm. She was a beaming, woolly-socked and woolly-jumpered lady wearing brown leggings whose original colour was mottled, today, with other more natural shades of brown.

'Well, it's a long way to come for a leg of lamb – and even longer for a leg of mutton,' she giggled as she made me a cup of tea. Annie and Jeff were among the few commercial producers of mutton in Britain, and they weren't sure how much longer the trade would last.

'There's about to be another food scare, y'see,' said Annie. 'Lamb older than twelve months. It'll send you crazy, it'll kill you. It's terribly, terribly dangerous.' Her mock-seriousness melted into a torrent of laughter.

These two were meat mavericks. They fed their animals organically, treated them for illnesses homoeopathically, and had nothing to fear from the diseases resulting either from industrial meat production systems or from the bureaucratic and financial repercussions.

Annie, a part-time teacher at a Welsh university, had glimpsed in her students something of the dark side of British eating habits. One boy, she remembered, once visited her at the farm.

'He said it was actually the first time he had ever sat down for a meal around a table. Poor boy, he looked terribly awkward. I even had the feeling he had forgotten how to handle a knife and fork, if he ever knew in the first place. Must be all those burgers and pizzas. Because you eat that sort of stuff with your *fingers*, don't you.'

On that occasion she had served up a sirloin steak from Panteg's very own Highland beef herd. She scrabbled around in her freezer to show me a packet of Highland stewing steak. Even in this solid state I could see the dark brownish-purplish hue of the meat, quite unlike the seamless scarlet of most beef as it languishes under the infra-red.

Jeff came in from the cold, shaking the snowflakes from his shoulder-length hair. 'It's not settling; it'll have melted in an hour,' he said. Seeing us examining this slab of frozen meat, he came over to point out the delicate tracery of fat lines running through the dark flesh.

'There's such a fetish for leanness these days. You just don't get naturally occurring fat like that,' he said as he pulled off his boots. 'What I have seen in supermarkets is these totally lean strips of meat on these styrofoam trays, and a slab of fat on the top – which of course is an admission of failure. 'Cause without this extra fat the meat will be virtually inedible. Hey, love, what have you done with those teabags?'

I took back to Sussex a big bag of that Highland steak and a fresh leg of spring lamb weighing just three pounds, a mini-leg of almost upsetting smallness.

With the steak I made a kind of no-frills bourguignon, using nothing more than half a bottle of red wine, some onions and carrots, and a handful of fresh thyme, sage and marjoram. The dish needed no stock, since the beef was so powerfully flavoured it created its own rich sauce, yet the meat was so tender it fell into juicy flakes, along the grain, under the fork.

The lamb met a very different end. I rubbed it with crushed garlic, sea salt and chopped fresh rosemary. Then, for lunch one cold sunny Sunday at Seven Sisters Beach, I wrapped it in tin-foil and roasted it slowly over a fire of pinewood and rosemary. There was certainly a thin layer of white fat along the surface of the leg, but that simply protected the tender meat from drying out or burning. It was a firmly textured, finely flavoured roast that reminded me that the best and freshest ingredients often have the virtue of tasting more truly of themselves than other examples of the same thing. A lemon more lemony, a potato more potatoey. And this Welsh spring lamb had a wilder, earthier taste, shot through with hints of the farmyard and wet wool – in short, a fuller range of 'lambiness' than I remembered finding in any of the many cuts of Welsh lamb I'd tasted recently. Happily, too, there was no laver bread anywhere in sight.

6

the north-west

in search of scouse, tripe and udder delights

Good food and transport are difficult things to combine. Think of the infamous British Rail bacon sandwich (white sliced bread, slimy bacon). Think of the institution of the transport café, with its menu of grease and more grease with extra grease on the side, and compare it with the French roadside routiers with the lorries parked in rows outside, where you can get a steak frites, a salad and a tarte aux pommes for a fiver all in.

Think, too, if you can bear to, of Little Chef, the best-known name in British roadside catering and, with four hundred branches, possibly the single most popular restaurant chain in the country. Little Chef and Happy Eater – that was the other major brand name I remember, though the two now seem practically indistinguishable – are places I associate indelibly with long and tedious car journeys as a child. Brightly lit, luridly coloured, teeth-grindingly cheerful places, they exercised a powerful attraction both over weary parents and their excitable offspring. After perusing the plasticated menu, I would usually order sausages and beans – my favourite childhood treat – and eat them in satisfied silence, the glutinous sweetness of the beans finding their aesthetic reflection in the candy-coloured glare of the decor.

I saw one on the A483 just outside Welshpool, as I sped northwards through the fogbound hills of Mid-Wales, and Proustian bells began ringing in my memory.

As I pulled into the forecourt of the red-brick building, my predominant feeling was not hunger but curiosity. In the twenty years since my last visit, would Little Chef have put aside childish things, as I had done, and taken account of changing times? Would the menu have succumbed to the influence of the TV cooks with their exciting ingredients and wizard ideas? How wonderful it would be, I fantasised, to find healthful, interesting, modern dishes to alleviate the tedium of long-distance driving and send you back on to the road with tastebuds tingling.

The decor was as before. So was the wipe-clean menu in its thick coat of plastic. When it came to the cooking, there were a few hints of fresh air: breast of chicken in a lemon and herb glaze and four-cheese ravioli with herb bread and a salad of carrots and courgettes sounded fine. With these 'Lighter Options' you could order red or white house wine – a daring novelty. Otherwise it was business as usual. Tuna salad was a standard 1970s salad, complete with canned sweetcorn and raw rings of red and green pepper. 'Farmhouse' chicken liver pâté would be better described as 'Industrial Warehouse' chicken liver pâté. The gammon steak, as if in accordance with some ancient law, still bore its coronet of tinned pineapple. Puddings featured such crabbed and miserable items as sundae, Sara Lee Danish pastry and pancakes with mapleen syrup, the neologism 'mapleen' implying that any resemblance to maple syrup is purely coincidental.

Some things in Britain never change, and the little chef could still knock out a plate of sausages and beans. The dish has a curious pedigree, I reflected, sipping a glass of Little Chef red. Tinned baked beans, originally marketed as 'pork 'n' beans', date from 1880, and arrived in Britain, sans pork, only in 1905, when the US company H.J. Heinz began exporting to a country at first highly suspicious of the product. Ironically of course, pork and beans in one form or another is classic rural food the world over, and one of the oldest of all British dishes. According to legend, King George III, sampling a pot of pork and beans prepared by the builders of Woolwich Arsenal, told the men that he would like to eat the dish 'as often as possible'. The beans would have been cooked in the slowest of ovens for twenty-four hours or more, together with honey, pepper, bayleaf and a nice bit of ham or bacon. I do not think that the beans I ate at the Little Chef outside Welshpool were prepared that way.

After weeks in the countryside, I was looking forward to a little big-city sophistication. Perfect produce is one thing, but I craved a little *cooking*. In most food-orientated societies the soul of good food is in the country and the city builds its dazzling edifice on that solid foundation. In Britain, to generalise wildly, the best and most interesting cooking is in the urban context.

Just before nightfall I arrived at Liverpool, a city that was once Britain's greatest port. Through it most of the available riches of the Empire customarily passed. In its booming heyday it would surely have paid host to a vast range of sensory pleasures, wine, women and song being only three. I cannot imagine there wasn't also a lot of good, hearty masculine food about, in the taverns and the company dining rooms and the great hotels of this famous city.

With this vision in mind, present-day Liverpool inevitably comes as something of a disappointment. Few places in Britain have less interest in cuisine or are so mean in their provision of it. I shall probably be upbraided by Liverpudlians furious at my misrepresentation of their city. As it seemed to me, however, central Liverpool has no proper food shop or delicatessen, no good bakery, no really good fishmonger (this in a port town), no decent market for fruit and veg. The latter particularly surprised me, because in the eighteenth century the market at Liverpool was regarded as excellent, its high quality, according to one contemporary source, owing to the exigencies of the French-Canadian immigrants of 1756, who demanded good and affordable vegetables for their soups.

As for restaurants, there is plenty of mediocre Chinese and Indian, but no affordable neighbourhood restaurant serving anything other than fish and chips and associated fried stuff. Oddly, there is no three-star flock-wallpapered Amex gastro-temple either, and no fancy tea room, more's the pity, since fancy tea rooms are the saving grace of many another Northern town.

I had come here partly to visit Rachel, who, hailing from San Francisco, has good cause to complain about the lack of decent food in Liverpool.

'It's like living in Eastern Europe,' she once told me miserably, showing me how the skin on her arm had turned a greyish shade of ivory from lack of sun and poor nutrition.

On my way up Castle Street there was a branch of Oddbins. Suddenly imagining the misery of an enforced exile from one of the world's most advanced gastronomic cultures – a place where even after the last earthquake the emergency soup kitchens set up in the street served black bean chilli with sour cream and rocket salad – I dived into the shop to find some Californian wine for Rachel.

There were shelvesful of every conceivable vintage and region, each wine with its little explanatory handwritten note, so youthfully cheery, so unforbidding, yet so unmistakably expert. 'This one's a cracker! Heaps of ripe cherries.' 'Gorgeous petrolly Riesling. Australia's hippest white variety. We love this one.' It has often seemed to me that British society is many times more advanced oenologically than gastronomically, and that expertise in wine, like horticulture, has been until recently at least a kind of substitute for, or displacement of, interest in food.

I walked back down towards Lime Street station, beside run down cinemas and shopfront hoardings plastered with posters advertising nightclubs. Ballistic, Uptight, Liquidation, Cream. Club life has, during the 1990s, become probably Liverpool's major cultural export, along with football mania and *Brookside*. Drinking and dancing certainly seem to have more of a claim on Liverpudlian hearts and wallets than dining out.

I racked my brains for the names of famous restaurants around these parts. The last time I was in Liverpool I remembered being taken by a friend to the dining room at the Adelphi, the grand hotel looming up like a tombstone at the top of Ranelagh Street, for Sunday lunch. If there was anything that would be impossible to mess up, we reasoned, it must be an old-fashioned Hotel Sunday Lunch. But the Adelphi managed it. The beef, lamb and pork were indistinguishable slabs of grey matter, borne on a squeaking trolley. My friend ordered the vegetarian option, and was presented with a plate of white rice dolloped with peas and diced carrots in a yellowish sauce, visually as well as culinarily, it seems to me, a most unadvisable combination.

Outwardly at least, there were few signs of innovation or excitement in the world of Liverpudlian food. On menus all over town the words that leapt most readily to the eye were that perennial double-act, pizza and pasta. It was as if they'd just arrived, a pair of exotic beauties just off the boat, bringing with them a breath of warm Mediterranean air. Have you met Pizza and Pasta, they've just arrived from Naples. Gorgeous, aren't they? Bella Pasta, Pizza Roma, Pizza Mia, Basta Pasta!

At a café in the city centre I asked for lobscouse, but they laughed in my face. Lobscouse – scouse for short – was once the Liverpudlian dish par excellence, a soup-stew of lamb or mutton, vegetables and pearl barley, with historical links to the Swedish *lapskojs* and the German *labskaus*. One would have thought the nickname Scouse, as applied to the inhabitants of Liverpool, meant that they ate an awful lot of this nourishing stew. Perhaps, historically, they did.

'You won't find that around much these days. There isn't

much call for it anymore,' said the big lady behind the tea-urn. 'You might get some scouse at one of the greasy spoon caffs up by the hospital. I can do you a nice plate of spaghetti instead, if you like . . .'

Lobscouse
(serves 6)

This old Liverpudlian dish is a kind of simple all-in stew making good use of the cheapest cuts of meat: neck of lamb and shin of beef. Cut up a kilo of the former and a half a kilo of the latter, and brown the pieces in butter or lard. Add enough stock or water to cover, bring to the boil and skim the surface. Add coarsely chopped root vegetables, the more varied the better (parsnip, turnip, leek, potato, swede and celeriac are all possibilities), and a few handfuls of pearl barley. Season generously. (Entirely inauthentic though it may be, I would also add handfuls of chopped parsley, thyme, marjoram and/or a bay leaf or two.) Cover and simmer for 2–3 hours. (If you can leave to stand overnight and reheat the next day, so much the better.)

'So where do you suggest we go tonight?' I asked my Californian friend, who bit on her thumb for a while and then said, with a great weariness at the heart of her voice, 'Oh, well, there's a balti place that's sort-of just about okay . . .' It was one of the least enthusiastic restaurant recommendations I have ever heard in my life.

They were Pakistanis at the balti place, but I could still see what Rachel had meant about Eastern Europe. Even the decor, the feel of the place, merely provided a fragile and unsatisfying sort of nicotine-stained comfort. On the next table were a dozen boozed-up Liverpool lads and, this being a culture in which curry follows beer as surely as night follows day, they were loudly restoring the balance between solids and liquids.

'Fookin' shite, Owen was way outside the penalty area, fookin' ref was nowhere in sight, fookin' prat.'

The food, as it is in most of the thousands of 'Indians' across this great United Kingdom, was curry-powdered slop, a succession of dishes each crowned with the same thick meniscus of dark orange or yellowish or greenish oil. The chicken tikka I'd ordered ill advisedly was unlike any other chicken I have eaten before or since: pyramidal chunks of meat, flavourless of itself, spongy and almost porous in texture, robed in a light brown gloop whose sweetness may have been owing to the ground almonds, but then again may not have been.

'Well, I did try to tell you, y'know?' said Rachel, pulling disconsolately at her garlic naan.

In Manchester, I reflected as I climbed back on to the M6, the situation surely can't be quite as bad. Manchester is after all England's biggest, brashest city after London and Birmingham, and culturally and economically much more muscular than Liverpool, which has turned into a sad caricature of itself. And where there is a strong culture and economy and plenty of self-assurance, there is usually some top nosh to be found.

There is not much of a tradition of good eating around these parts, it has to be said. Among the working classes there is barely a tradition of eating at all. In the early years of the twentieth century Robert Roberts, author of *The Classic Slum*, described the typical diet of the urban poor: 'The breakfasts that these children get are nominally bread and tea, if they get it at all. There is bread and margarine for lunch, and the dinner is normally nothing but what a copper can purchase at the local fried fish shops, where the most inferior kinds of fish such as skate are fried in unwholesome, reeking cottonseed oil. They frequently supplement this with rotten fruit, which they collect beneath barrows.' The furthest one might go in the direction of luxury was a sweet tea-leaf sandwich or 'sugar butty' – butty of course being the Northern term for anything served between slices of bread.

There may be people still alive in Manchester who remember this state of affairs, yet from the perspective of the early twenty-first century, when material poverty has been practically abolished even though other types of poverty – cultural, sensual, aesthetic – are still raging, it is hard to believe there was ever not enough to eat. Here, now, if you find a butty at all, it may well have mizuna and goats' cheese in it. If you want to eat skate, that most inferior kind of fish, be prepared for it to be pan-fried with a ginger and citrus butter on roasted garlic mash.

Design with a capital D – or rather design, in lower case – has arrived in Manchester with a vengeance. You only have to wander around the fashionable Canal Street district, epicentre of the new Manchester cuisine, to catch an eyeful of it. Along one side of the canal were prague five, mongolian barbecue, mash and air, manto and a few other lower-case establishments. Along the other were berlin and the slug and lettuce. The latter used to be a 1980s grub-pub with real ales and wheel-back chairs. It was now a frightfully trendy café/bar/food-space, with enormous glass windows affording views, from outside, of bald gay couples flicking through *The Pink Paper* over pints of Belgian beer.

An industrial past like that of Manchester does have its inconveniences, historically speaking, but the advantages in restaurant terms are plain to see. 'Post-industrial chic', meaning high ceilings, iron columns and vast amounts of cheap space, is par for the course. Everything else follows naturally: the chilly minimalism of the decor, the shouting youthful clientele and the faintly arch contemporariness of the menu, with its hip ingredients, its wry mix of traditions, its seared tuna with wasabi and roasted root vegetables with a cherry tomato salsa. (No one is ever going to serve Tournedos Rossini in a converted factory.) There are few other places I know where food is so closely determined by architecture.

Those in the know about the food scene here say there is both more and better than ever before. Fifteen years ago you could either go Chinese in Chinatown, Indian in Rusholme, or venture out with a bulging wallet to one of the frilly-doily posh places in the suburbs. In town there was the Market, still going strong, and sufficiently few other places that the restaurant critic at *City Life*, the main Manc magazine, had had a pretty easy time of it. This year was the first he'd felt the sheer number of new restaurants had made it impossible to keep tabs on them all. 'I recently feel my overview's started to get a bit blurred. There is an awful lot of food out there these days,' he told me on the phone, sounding, quite understandably, a little dyspeptic and jaded by it all.

I found a room at a hotel overlooking the canal, a green and tulgy strip of water adorned with a jetsam of upturned beer bottles and soggy nightclub flyers. It was Sunday morning, and there was a strong smell of disinfectant in the air. Across the way, a gigantic banner reading 'LOFTS AND APARTMENTS' fluttered in the cold wind from the side of a red-brick Victorian warehouse. Machinery rumbled somewhere. For a minute, as I stared out of the window, I entertained a pleasing fantasy of owning one of these post-industrial boltholes and flitting downstairs of an evening to eat in some post-industrial café-bar, rather as a Parisian might pop downstairs to his favourite *restaurant du coin*.

There are various theories as to how the current restaurant boom in Manchester began, but the one I like best is that it grew indirectly out of the club and gay scenes. It is all very well drinking and dancing all night long, but sooner or later you are going to want something to eat. At first it was simply that people wanted a drink and a bite to eat before hitting the dancefloor, somewhere that wasn't just a slimy old pub or a greasy old chip shop, and the morning after the night before they naturally wanted a delicious late breakfast and large amounts of good coffee. Before long, though, they were beginning to hanker after more sophisticated food and some of them were getting a little bit long in the tooth for full-on clubbing anyway and were happy to hang out after their supper and have a few drinks and a boogie on the nights a DJ was on. For all these reasons, the café-bar concept occupies a crucial place in the recent history of Manchester life. No one has ever bothered to count the number of such places currently trading in the city, but by now it must be into treble figures. They tend to have punchy, artful, resonant names like Velvet, Barça, Atlas or

Metz. Some of the food you get in some of them is actually better than in 'proper' restaurants. Or so they say.

At the Velvet, a ridiculously cool café-bar down by the canal where the walls and chairs were various shades of violet and deep purple and the floors were scrubbed pine, I contemplated pan-fried cod with chickpeas, lime, ginger and parsley oil, mushroom and ricotta pancakes with roast tomato sauce, and wild boar and apple sausages with leek mash and calvados gravy. It all seemed a little heavy and galumphing, however, for my frail Sunday constitution.

An unmistakable aroma was stealing over the city, making my nose twitch. A brewery somewhere was in full brew: was it Boddingtons, purveyors of the Cream of Manchester and a series of adverts celebrating the city's remarkable and healthy ability to take the mickey out of itself? I skirted Albert Square, peering in briefly at the Plaza Café, where the menu made a major feature of chips – you could have them with beans, peas, gravy or curry, or with an onion 'bargi' (as in argy) on the side. As I turned down Princess Street towards Chinatown I realised in a flash what it was that I craved: the opposite of soggy, mushy, greasy, bland, English food: the crunch and slither and intense savouriness, the perfect Sunday afternoon emotional pick-me-up of dim sum.

Before there were café-bars in Manchester, before there were architectonic brasseries, there were big Chinese restaurants. The four-floor Cantonese joints in the few blocks between Mosley Street and Portland Street that make up Chinatown were always some of the greatest stalwarts of Manchester restauration. Indeed, it was they, together with the Punjabi restaurants of Rusholme, that probably taught the city what good food was all about in the first place. In the alley between Faulkner Street and Portland Street, where the Moon Wah and the New Hong Kong and the San Lee Sing sit back to back with the Bei Jing and the Royal Orchid, there was a roaring concatenation of steel tubes of extractor fans, making nicely obvious the industrial vocation of these nineteenth-century buildings.

The Yang Sing, which I now looked for at its usual address at Princess Street, in a grand five-storey block formerly connected with the cotton trade, was and is one of the biggest feeding factories of them all. T.K. Yeung, the man who opened it back in 1977, had a reputation as the finest dim sum chef in the city, and his restaurant soon attracted a host of influential clients, both among the Chinese population and from the wider Greater Manchester community. The Yeungs can show you pictures of the old Princess Street restaurant in full sail, all 610 covers of it, at a gala night in October 1985, thronged with big-bellied business people, their wives in glittery dresses and full Northern war paint. After a fire at the Princess Street site in October 1997, the G-Mex Centre immediately offered the use of their restaurant. After that Yang 'Singe' – as it was known for a while by local wags – moved to another temporary home, a strange 1960s office block in Charlotte Street, and this was where I finally tracked it down.

I ate minced dace and sweetcorn fritters, prawn cheung fun with just the right sloppy white slipperiness of texture, barbecue pork buns, spicy meat and nut dumplings – a rare departure from Cantonese convention – and, as a small act of homage to the Lancashire love of offal, a plate of ox tripe with ginger and spring onion. The tripe had been sliced in small floppy fan shapes, perhaps to make it seem a more delicate morsel or perhaps, as with pasta, to allow for maximum absorption of the sauce. I followed all this with a whole plateful of sensational miniature custard tarts. It was exquisite, inexpensive and there was slightly too much of it. What more can you ask from a Sunday lunch?

I lurched out into the streets in the early afternoon. Wherever you looked, through whichever plate glass window you peered, Mancunians were still brunching and Sunday-lunching. The big brasseries had swung open their doors to catch the afternoon-after-the-night-before trade, and they were all packed and buzzing with life.

This was the last Manc eating trend the South ever got to hear about, fashions up here taking a good year sometimes to penetrate the Net Curtain that runs across Britain at a point just north of Coventry. The four big brasseries, as far as I could see, were Nico Central, Simply Heathcote's, Mash and Sarasota. What they had in common was floor space, ceiling height, window size and a certain commitment to modern design sensibility and modern urban cuisine. The decibel count seemed high in such places, partly because the modernist aesthetic shuns the kind of soft furnishings that might otherwise soak up the sound, but also because people tend to talk louder anyway in environments like that, as if in an attempt to fill the airily impersonal space above their heads with the maximum amount of humanity.

The sky was already turning a cold shade of orange at the edges when I got back to Canal Street, and the last of the customers at Sarasota were just pushing out through the heavy doors, pulling their jackets tighter around them and muttering,

'Fookin' 'ell.' I was standing on the pavement looking at the menu, wondering idly whether roast sea bass with chorizo and basil tasted as good as it sounded and whether sirloin steak in a black pudding, bacon and raspberry jus wasn't modern North-Western cuisine taken just a parsnip chip too far, when a crop-haired woman in kitchen whites came down to smoke a fag in the doorway and invited me up for a drink and a chat.

We sat at a table by the window overlooking the canal and a car park beyond it, in which a tramp was just now tucking in to his evening meal: a bag of chips.

There was no doubt about it, Sarasota was a beautiful and imaginatively conceived place. Beneath us was the Manto Bar, no, manto bar, which is thought by trend historians to be the very foundation-stone of the Canal Street bar scene. The building seems to jut forward like a sprinter on the blocks, and the overhanging roof conceals an awning that begs to be rolled back on summer nights, when manto puts its speakers outside on the cobbles and the party spills out on to the street.

Lisa was a Cheshire girl born and bred. She had witnessed the growth of Manchester Good Food at first hand and now, as kitchen supremo at one of the city's most fashionable restaurants, found herself in a position of active influence in its further development as a gastronomic centre.

Manchester's restaurant scene was finally approaching saturation point after a decade or more of boom-time, said Lisa. Already the signs were that diners were tiring of the Big Noisy Restaurant and craving a taste of something simultaneously more intimate and grander. Low-key places, such as The Lincoln, which had opened without fuss or fanfare the month before my visit, and Reform, with its swags of purple velvet, tiger-skin seating and opulent food to match, were currently the talk of the town. Meanwhile the brewery-owned chains and multiples had already started moving in on Canal Street, severely watering down the area's once predominantly gay clientele.

Lunch next day was at Air, part of Oliver Peyton's gastro-paradise on Sackville Street. The further up the building you go the more splendid the food and surroundings, until in Dantesque fashion you arrive, transported by a sky-blue painted proto-industrial lift, at the apogee of Manchester's unique adventure in combining food with other elements of modern style.

If you press the wrong button and the lift stops at Floor 3, as I did, the doors opens to reveal a sudden scene of chattering chic, all acrylic-bright colours and label-clad people, before closing again and whisking you up to your final destination. High ceilings, white walls flooded with light from the big factory windows; curvilinear, deep blue, organic, somewhat seventies-inspired furniture, with separate sofa units for extra-cosy groupings; flying-saucer lamps. It was like a scene from *Sleeper*. Blue lacquer tables, and an eau-de-nil acrylic floor that squeaked a little as the waitresses made their way towards your table.

Taking my place, then, in this simulacrum of twenty-first century glamorous living, I sat by the window and tittered to myself as I checked out the view. On the fourth floor of the building directly opposite, a few yards from my table, was a gym, full of perfect-bodied people straining away in energetic silence.

I ordered two starters, feeling that as an idea two starters was perhaps a little too eighties, and that the waitresses would be giggling at me behind their hands. While I waited, a dish of lamb rump with cumin polenta and confit of beetroot arrived at the table beside me, where a group of hipsters were talking about their plans to open a nightclub. I could see that the confit was not, as you might have expected, a pile of bleeding vegetable, but a delicate arc of tiny purple cubes stretching around the plate.

Terrine of smoked duck and foie gras came with a salad of endives and figs – the figs woefully, wilfully out of season – which included a crisp caramelised roundel of plum. There was thought in this cooking; it wasn't any sort of triumph of style over content. Plum tomato tarte Tatin was one of the few Tatins I hadn't seen and made a lot of sense. The thin slices of sweet tomato melded delectably into the pastry, and around the plate was a thin black skein of something that looked and tasted like a reduction of Worcestershire Sauce. If there is to be a renaissance of true British cooking, I suppose Worcestershire Sauce will have to come into it somewhere.

For the time being, then, Manchester was still a pretty good place to eat out in. How good was it, though, as a place to eat *in* in?

As usual, the question was a tough one to answer. Lisa had sworn her friends were adventurous cooks. As I searched the city next morning it was clear that an adventurous spirit was exactly what you'd need if you wanted to buy good ingredients in Manchester. Improbably yet scandalously enough, as far as I could see there was no specialist cheese shop, no delicatessen, no proper food shop in the centre of England's second city.

If further proof were needed that Britain is no longer really a food-market culture, it could be found at what is still Manchester's main public market. It was tiny, an apology for a food market, a few stalls shoved into a corner of an upper storey of the retail megalopolis of the Arndale Centre. At Gregg's, the only bakery of any consequence, there were barm-cakes, a sort of brown bap with grains on top – 'barm' being a medieval word for yeast – and Eccles cakes and Lancashire oven bottoms (another sort of large white bap, made with a small amount of fat, with a cross marked on the top – British food specialities are often less interesting than their names would have you believe). That, plus a range of meat and potato pies containing 10 per cent meat and 'flavour enhancer', made up the ethnic selection. I looked in vain for Manchester tarts, a custardy confection with a topping of meringue. 'Oooh no, loov, we don't bother wi' them,' said the lady.

Over the way at the butcher's – the only one in the market – the panorama was grim. Shiny piles of pre-sliced luncheon meat, corned beef, slimy pink ham, and the squared-off white stuff we have tacitly agreed to accept as turkey meat lay meekly in a neat parterre of plastic parsley. The cheese selection – two industrial slabs of generic Cheddar – was extraordinary when you consider that within an hour or two of Manchester are two of the finest cheese-making areas in the country, Lancashire and Cheshire.

Finally there was some good news: two impeccable fish stalls, the fish fresh and highly varied. If I'd wanted a trevally or a grouper for my tea, or a nice Manx kipper or some juicy-looking clams for a salsa alle vongole, I'd have been lucky. And the parsley was real. They were trying hard. But where were the keen-eyed shoppers? The place was empty, and the staff stood waiting. When an old lady tottered through they stood to attention, but all she wanted was a little bit of haddock. 'Mind you take out t'bones, loov . . .' A real fish market needs the slap and shiver of high turnover, not the occasional pensioner looking for half a pound of fillet. There is after all, no worse destiny for a fish than not to be sold.

I drove northwards into the wilds of Lancashire. Here were small towns like Clitheroe, Oswaldtwistle, Wigglesworth, names that, to a Southerner with little first-hand knowledge of his own country, conjure up all the hackneyed images of Lancastrian life that came to us via the TV when we were very young: fearsome women with curlers in their hair; tremendous busty barmaids with clanky earrings; a boy on a bike making his way up a steep cobbled street, to a soundtrack of Dvorak's New World Symphony played by a brass band.

I headed dutifully towards Accrington town market, and a few sights there made my mood lighten. The wonder of good British food is its uncanny ability to pop up at unexpected moments, in unexpected places. Common items on the greengrocers' stalls here were bags of ready-cut and washed cabbage, carrot and other seasonal vegetables, sold as 'broth mix'. It was good to see that Accrington still knows how to bubble up a nice soup. There were also ready-soaked split peas for pease pudding or homemade pea and ham soup.

'What should I do with them?' I asked.

'What should you do? You should boil 'em and boil 'em and boil 'em, till they're as soft as you like. And if you want mushy, you just keep on boiling till all the water's boiled off.'

At Len's, the butcher's, there was potted brawn and potted beef, 'potting' being a technique for preserving meat and fish, as old as the hills, which no one in the South of England bothers with nowadays. But where was all the famous Lancashire offal? Where the tripe, where the trotters, where the parts of the body so unmentionable that they can only be spoken of in hushed euphemisms? Where the black puddings?

It was all to be found at Bob's Tripe Stall, in one of the passageways leading out towards the open-air market with the dodgy trainers. There used to be two tripe stalls at Accrington Market. The competition had now dropped out of the race, but Bob's had sailed on regardless, ready to supply the bits of animal that no one else wanted to the few locals still willing to eat them.

My eye ranged greedily around the stall, aware that what we had here was one of the most tenacious British regional culinary traditions of all.

'Well, basically, y'see, there's three kinds of tripe,' said Bob, with the faint air of one explaining an elementary piece of knowledge to an idiot. 'This one here's black tripe. That has a beefier flavour.' It wasn't exactly black, more an interesting shade of greyish-brown. 'And this one's honeycomb tripe; see the honeycomb shapes there on the cow's stomach wall?'

Hmmm. Oh yes.

A lady in neat granny-wear, her hair hidden from view under a headscarf, joined me at the counter.

'I'll have a bit of that nice soft tripe, when y've a moment, Bob,' she said.

'I'll be right with you, loov. Now, what we're going to do, we're going to give this lady some white tripe. Take a look at that, would you.' He pulled up a small square of wobbling ivory-coloured flesh, brandishing it in mid-air. 'That all right for you, loov?'

'Aye, lovely,' said the lady, smiling quietly, in anticipation of a treat.

In addition to black, white and honeycomb, there is another kind of tripe, a type of soft squishy mess that is tripe that has been a little overcooked, and this is known as 'invalid' tripe, with the stress on the first syllable. It is popular with the old, toothless and infirm. It was also recommended to me by another of Bob's customers, a Mrs Brown of Darwen, who had just popped in for a half-pound of honeycomb for her husband's tea. Seeing that I was a beginner with tripe, Mrs Brown took me under her wing.

'Boil it up a bit, then put plenty of salt on it, and a bit of vinegar,' she advised. 'Do you like chips, loov? Well then, do yourself some chips, and you'll have yourself a proper meal. Or you could do tripe and onions, double the amount of tripe to onions, a bit of butter, cook it all in milk, gently, with a pinch of nutmeg and plenty of salt.' She smacked her lips and winked at me.

'Course, you could try it joos' like this, loov, as it comes. Eh, Bob, give 'im a bit, loov, joos' to try.'

Oh dear. It was only eleven o'clock in the morning, I still hadn't breakfasted, and the thought of that cold sliminess . . . To most people born after the Second World War, the texture and flavour of tripe are repulsive. Why this should be so, when tripe was once a delicacy and still is in Florence, Madrid and the Caen region of Normandy, remains one of those thorny cultural-historical questions I am quite unable to answer.

If any food can be said to taste of a bad smell, it is tripe. I tried to chew, watched all the time by an expectant Mrs Brown, feeling myself surfing a tidal wave of nausea. Who wouldn't prefer to eat Bernard Matthews's Extruded Turkey Meat Mini Kievs, I reflected bitterly as I gulped down the white rubbery mass, when traditional British food was so hard to swallow?

'See, that's lovely, eh?' said Mrs B.

The other items on offer at Bob's stall seemed to divide into two sections: those I would far rather eat than invalid tripe – into this category came the old-fashioned beef puddings, sold in a bag for boiling with suet, potato and salt, and the potted stews of pork, beef and lamb in single-serving pots – and those to which even invalid tripe would be preferable. Cow heel is an ivory-white object, uncannily preserving the shape of the foot. Pigs' mows, a part of the pig's anatomy I have not been able to identify, made a hideous sight: wrinkled and heaped-up greyish lumps, looking like lung cancers on a surgeon's slab. There was foot oil, a thick yellow by-product of the cow heel, sold in little plastic bottles for the use of hill-walkers, the elder, and folk wi' bad backs. A pile of dry white bones for dogs. Lancashire positively wrings the cow dry of all possible nourishment and usefulness.

But the most bizarre and mysterious item of all was something called dark roll, a long tube of meat with a grey, spongy, ill-defined interior.

What in God's name was *that*?

'Bull's wazzel,' said Bob.

It wasn't a word I had ever heard before, but I understood it.

Now, since we had unwittingly strayed into the realms of what you might call heavy offal, there was an important question I had to ask. Where was the udder? It was the one cut of offal absent from the display in front of me. I had been told in Yorkshire, which also has an old tradition of udder-eating, that a small Lancashire market town might be the only place in Britain still eating it these days. I imagined a slab of milky whiteness, a rasher of blancmange. How would the udder be sliced, I wondered – horizontally, or vertically? There would be a rubbery exterior, and a cool gelatinous fatty interior.

'Where's the udder? I'll tell you where the udder is. We can't sell it any more. Government regulations. But we can still sell milk,' said Bob drily. 'The cows they're killing now, they're all under two years old. Got no udder to speak of, y'see. For a tasty bit of udder you need a cow with . . . well, with big 'uns, if you know what I mean.'

If udder is now a nonexistent delicacy – and some might think this an occasion for rejoicing – black pudding is another story. Once a national speciality, it is true that its popularity has dramatically declined. An elderly lady I know says she once saw eight or nine different kinds of locally made black pudding at Bideford Market. I wonder how many she'd find today? But, as in other aspects of food and eating, the North keeps the flame alight, and Bob's Tripe Stall maintains a modest trade. They hung in curling bunches in a glass-fronted fridge, both the ordinary short sausage and the Bury pudding, which is longer and can be used in emergencies for whacking assailants over the head. Rather than being black, they were a dark mahogany brown in colour, glistening in their freshness with hints of deep red. These puddings were made by Ireland's, a small concern a few miles away at Waterfoot. 'He's down in the valley, on the border of Yorkshire and Lancashire. So I do speak to him occasionally,' said Bob wryly.

A 1600 cookbook declared: 'Small otemeale mixed with blood, and the liver of either sheep, calf or swine, maketh that pudden . . . whose goodness it is in vain to boast because there is hardly to be found a man that doth not affect them.' Four centuries later there is little change, except that liver is seldom added to black puddings these days, and that not everyone is probably quite so enthusiastic about them as I am.

I ordered a lean one to take away – you could choose between lean, medium and fatty – and Bob split it open into steaming quarters and handed it to me on a napkin, splashed with bright yellow mustard from a squirty bottle. I went out into the cold sunshine to watch a smooth-talking auctioneer offload kitsch ceramic figurines. The pudding had a clean, richly meaty taste, and a creamy texture flecked with chewy oats. It was not very generous with the spicing, but that's the British way. Still, it was delicious and, at 58p, cheaper and infinitely better and more nutritious than any of the fast foods that plague the high street. The renaissance of this particular Great British traditional food is long overdue.

Local dishes, local ingredients. People have always wanted these things, but the more globalised and impersonal the food industry has become, the more they seem to matter.

Next morning I meandered out into the countryside – the patch of old Lancashire that remains, wedged between the giant conurbations of Manchester, Leeds/Bradford, Blackburn and Preston – under a sky that had turned a miserable shade of mousy grey, like a cold cup of factory tea. I stopped the car outside the village of Goosnargh and walked along a footpath, hoping to resuscitate my faltering appetite. Streams played down the valley, bisecting the rich pasture into marshy peninsulas. The grass was a vibrant emerald green, the muddy corners of the fields the same encrusted blackish brown as a fresh black pudding. This was a landscape whose charge of nutrients one could almost feel, buzzing in the air above it, ready for transformation into delicious fats and proteins.

There is nothing very remarkable about Goosnargh, visually at least. But it wasn't by chance that I had made my way there. It happens to have a range of local foods that are not just tourist tat or twee bohemian hobby, but dignified and excellent.

I stopped first at the post office to pick up a packet of Goosnargh Cakes, sweet and crumbly buttery biscuits, delicately flavoured with caraway seed. A postman, just emptying the pillarbox as I walked by, directed me to the cheese shop in a little parade behind the main road that sells not one but two world-class unpasteurised local cheeses. And the man in the cheese shop told me about Reg Johnson, producer of some of the finest poultry in the realm, whose turkeys and ducks and chickens and geese are giving Goosnargh something of the same ring of gastronomic glamour as Bresse and Gressingham.

The farm was a little way outside the village. It had the reassuringly chaotic and grubby look that farms have before they are mechanised out of existence and turned into factories. But Reg, who had seen his corn-fed poultry business take off spectacularly in the last few years, had none of the gloom that I had seen attached, like a large black cloud, to the rest of the farming community. He was a born-again evangelist for Quality, buzzing with enthusiasm and sales figures.

'Now tek a look at these, will you. Just look at the colour on 'em. We've just sent off a hundred today, and another hundred tomorrow. Chefs go absolutely wild for these birds,' he said, whipping away a plastic cover to reveal a pile of duck carcasses. I could see what he meant about the colour, which was a creamy yellow I couldn't remember ever having seen on a duck. Reg would be the first to admit that it is largely thanks to chef Paul Heathcote, who has his eponymous restaurant in the nearby town of Longridge, that the idea of corn-feeding ducks and chickens occurred to him in the first place. Heathcote had been one of the first and most loyal customers for these Goosnargh birds, and some of the most famous chefs in Britain had followed in his footsteps. Reg's conversation was peppered with their names.

'See these chickens? Marco loves 'em. Albert Roux told me he thinks they're the best; you know he's even *exporting* them now, for the restaurant he's got in France. British Airways have been sniffing around too. They say they want to "regionalise" their in-flight menus. Whatever that means. See those turkeys? Mash and Air want four hundred of them next week.'

There is no enormous mystery to the success of Goosnargh poultry, as anyone who has ever noted the difference between a corn-fed bird and a battery broiler will be able to tell you. The secret is in the feed, and in letting the birds develop at a natural rate rather than pumping them full of hormones and leaving the lights on so that they eat more. Outside in one of the barns, a flock of geese stood quietly in the half-dark of their dry and sweet-smelling home. Heathcote wanted forty of them in a fortnight's time. I wondered, seeing them so smug and snug, whether they were conscious of their great good fortune.

Maybe there'd be Goosnargh gosling on the menu today. Driving into Longridge, I felt the faint prickles of excitement, the champagne bubbles in the blood, of arriving in an unfamiliar provincial town where a famous chef is working and you have a table booked for lunch. It felt like the kind of pilgrimage you might expect to undertake in France, where you can easily imagine driving into the middle of nowhere for the express purpose of lunching at the Moulin de Mougins or the Auberge de l'Ill in Illhausern, but for which it's hard to think of an equivalent in Blighty. Except for this.

If Lancashire is the Lyonnais of Britain, as someone once said, then Heathcote might very well be the Lancashire version of Paul Bocuse. No one else in the country does the rootsy *cuisine du terroir* that he does with such passion and imagination. He is very possibly the man who, by his application of French haute cuisine techniques to the products of his environment and culinary heritage, is doing most to bring classic English cookery back into fashion.

'My early diet was made up of things like beans on toast,' he told me smilingly, sitting in a chintz-covered chair in the restaurant sitting room. He is a local boy made good, still talking in a softened and sophisticated version of the delicious local burr.

'I had a fondness for Warburton's Potato Cakes; still do, as a matter of fact. It's something you see around here. Basically potato and flour, I suppose, put together and fried off. I was quite fussy as a child until the age of fourteen or fifteen, which was when I discovered I actually enjoyed cooking and I wanted to know a lot more about it.'

Behind his conventional career path – from Sharrow Bay to the Connaught Hotel and back up North to Broughton Hall outside Preston, before opening his own place in Longridge – lies a secret history, a hunt for that Snark-like entity, the essence of Englishness in food. At the Connaught he learned about oxtail, steak and kidney pudding, Irish stew and the other robust English dishes the restaurant served on a plat du jour basis week in, week out. There was no doubt that each was a splendid example of its type, but Heathcote came to realise that these dishes had a potential that had so far never been realised. They could be refined and transformed – 'highlighted' is his word – and given a new shine and elegance.

The repertoire he has built up over the years goes way beyond the proud simplicities of traditional English food to something at once richer, more complex and more personal. This is not Modern British Cooking, which I understand to be a kind of palimpsest of Oriental, Mediterranean and Californian styles predicated on the notion of catholicity and originality. This is something different: there are no dizzyingly exotic references, no artful nods towards Sicily or Thailand. The roots of Heathcote's cooking just keep showing through. The menu at Longridge takes in roast partridge, rack of lamb, pig's trotter, game 'tea', bread and butter pudding. There are few fancy sauces as such, unless you count the English-style use of 'juices', but plenty of delicious tracklements – a concept which is also central to the English culinary philosophy – such as candied onions, herb dumplings, coriander cream, pea purée and braised cabbage.

One of the things that anchors him most firmly to his Lancashire *terroir* is his respect for charcuterie and offal, notably in the form of black pudding. When he first served this dish it was very rarely seen in restaurants; if British chefs thought of it at all it was probably with scorn. It can now be found, as Heathcote observes wryly, on every third menu in the country.

It was midday – time for the chef to get back to the kitchen, and for me to use up an hour or two before lunch.

'Why don't you go and have a chat with my friend Ruth?' said Heathcote. So I drove through the drizzle to find another of Goosnargh's great contributions to British gastronomy, the Lancashire cheese made by Ruth Kirkham, though when I arrived at the farm, a few miles out of the village on a little back road, Mrs Kirkham had just popped out.

'She's just bobbed out,' said her son, a beefy lad with wrists as thick as thighs, who was just in the act of cutting the curds from the morning milk. 'But she won't be long. Come in and give us a hand, if you like.'

The dairy was a tiny room, cluttered with presses and moulds and a large steel vat at which Graham was slicing away through the cool white heaps of fresh curd. Though spotlessly clean, it was hardly the state-of-the-art laboratory you'd expect from a producer of raw-milk cheese in these unenlightened times. The glory of Kirkham's Lancashire is that it's absolutely not a modern, soulless, hygiene-obsessed product, but a farmhouse cheese in the true and literal sense of the word.

Lancashire is traditionally made with the curd from the milk of two or three consecutive days, which is supposed to impart an extra dimension of flavour to the finished cheese. The curds are milled and salted, moulded and pressed, and then either smeared with butter and wrapped in cloth or covered in a thin layer of white wax. At two or three months of age it is a fine, crumbly, ivory-coloured cheese, tasting creamy and flowery and pleasantly cool. A few months later it has more kick, more bite, more warmth. 'That's the stage we call "Tasty",' explained Graham. And within a year it has a glorious rich tanginess, but it still remains creamy and crumbly, because creaminess and crumble are what a proper farmhouse Lancashire like Kirkham's is all about.

Mrs Kirkham herself appeared at the dairy door wearing a green fleecy coat and cream-coloured Wellington boots, her hair done up in a neat old-fashioned perm.

'I've been making this cheese for twenty-two years,' she announced with a smile of pride. 'And that's every day for twenty-two years, mind, even Christmas Day. No slacking!'

She pulled on a mob cap over her perm and rolled up her sleeves.

When I got back to the restaurant the car park was full of executive cars and I was last to take my place in the hushed dining room. I was pleased to see that all the trappings of an expensive provincial restaurant were present and correct: the heavily patterned wallpaper, the nests of tables, the judicious touch of bare stonework providing a frisson of rusticity.

One of the beguiling things about Heathcote is the thorough-going Anglo-Saxon line it takes on menu language. The little bowl that arrived at my table, for example, was what in less fastidiously Francophobe places might be called an 'amuse-gueule' or 'amuse-bouche', but the waiter here described as a 'pre-lunch starter, with our compliments'. Call it what you will, it was memorable in the simplicity and the nonchalance of its construction: a few broad beans without their skins, some pieces of artichoke heart and wild mushrooms, cooked in their own juices, and spiked refreshingly with lemon and chives. With a basketful of breads – cheese, sage and onion, black pudding and poppyseed, and a plain milk roll – the English character of the meal was established from the start.

'All right?' said a husband on another table to his wife, who was happily devouring a braised pig's trotter filled with ham hock and sage with its tartlet of pea purée, foie gras, quail egg and shallot sauce.

'All right 'n' all,' she said.

The black pudding arrived. So this was it: a shimmering circle of black flecked with pink, sitting on potatoes that had been *crushed*, as the menu carefully put it, and not merely mashed. The pudding had an extraordinarily creamy texture, falling apart in the mouth to reveal a cunningly incorporated morsel of toothsome sweetbread. Alongside it on the big white plate came a modest pile of haricots in a sauce made unctuous, I would guess, by long reduction, and pungent with bay leaf. This, I realised with delight, was nothing more or less than baked beans, Mr Heathcote's childhood favourite, purged of their nursery associations and horrid Heinz tomatoey sweetness.

Paul Heathcote's Baked Beans with Black Pudding

Mr Heathcote makes his own black puddings. I don't recommend this, unless you have plenty of time on your hands and a good source of fresh pigs' blood. Look instead for

a good ready-made pudding in a natural casing. Lidgate's, the butcher's in Holland Park in London, does a nice one with plenty of oatmeal.

For the baked beans, soak a kilo of dried haricot beans in cold water overnight. Place in a pan with a peeled onion, a handful of fresh thyme and enough chicken stock to cover. Bring to the boil and simmer until the beans are properly tender, topping up with stock or water as required.

For the sauce, sweat 8 shallots and a garlic clove, all finely chopped, in butter in a pan over gentle heat. Add 100ml of port and 100ml of Madeira and reduce by two-thirds. Add 500ml of red wine and reduce by half again. Add 250ml of veal glaze and 2 bay leaves, bring to the boil, skim and cook till a thick sauce-like consistency is reached. Sieve finely and keep warm.

Boil 3 large baking potatoes and crush them into small pieces using a potato masher. Cut the black pudding into 2cm slices, brush with butter and heat under the grill. Place a pile of potato in the middle of each of four flat soup bowls, and put a slice of black pudding on top. Scatter the baked beans around the plate, garnish with chopped cooked carrot, and spoon over the sauce.

It was the apotheosis of sausage and beans, just as the Little Chef version on the A483 outside Welshpool had been the nadir.

The waiter took the plate away and my gaze wandered outside the window to a small rock garden, where a display of decorative cabbages lit up the grey day with their peculiar plumage of purple, pink, cream and green – another nice symbol, like the dish I'd just eaten, of homespun English values elevated to a new level of beauty.

7

cumbria

cured ham, addictive fudge

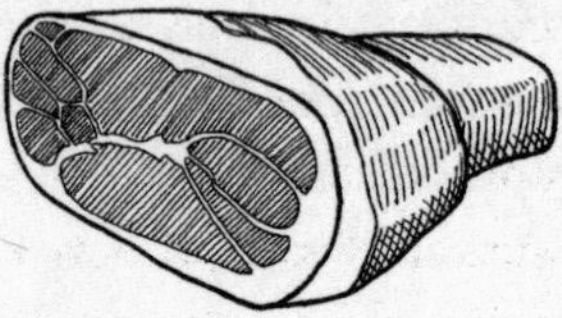

For anyone interested in the archaeology of post-war British catering and hotel-keeping, the Lake District ranks as a prime site for investigation.

A tourist destination ever since Wordsworth and his friends made it one, the area must have had hotels in country houses ever since the mid-nineteenth century. But the first country house hotel, in the sense in which the term is understood today (chintz furniture, four-poster beds, candlelit dinners) was undoubtedly Sharrow Bay, overlooking the lake at Ullswater.

When it opened in 1948 – the year after Elizabeth David had had her epiphany in Ross-on-Wye, remember – the price of a room at Sharrow Bay was a pound, which included breakfast, tea, dinner and hot chocolate in the bedroom.

The patron was Francis Coulson, a draper's son from

Bedfordshire who believed in the finer things of life: cuisine, flowers, fine art, decoration. With his partner Brian Sack, who gave up a career as an accountant in 1952 so they could run the hotel together, over the years he filled Sharrow Bay to bursting point with antique figurines, china, clocks, teapots, plants and pot-pourri. In the kitchen, his passion was for Edwardian richness and extravagance, difficult ideals to maintain, surely, in the hotel's early years, when rationing was still in force. Jane Grigson believed, controversially, that Coulson was the inventor of that now ubiquitous dessert, the sticky toffee pudding.

For him there were no short cuts to culinary success; it was all about treating the best possible ingredients with the greatest possible care. 'Cooking is an art,' he was known to declare, 'and all art is patience.' Food at Sharrow Bay was legendary, moreover, in its generous hand with the cream. A doctor once reported to one restaurant guide that the seven-course dinner there was 'the quickest and most pleasurable way to a coronary I know'.

Coulson sadly died in 1998, on the very day Sharrow Bay was celebrating its half-century, leaving the place to Brian Sack with whom he had run the place for forty-eight years.

And Sharrow Bay begat Miller Howe. John Tovey, a cook at Sharrow Bay, parted company with Coulson and Sack in 1971 and left to start another country house hotel and restaurant on the banks of another lake a few miles further south. Tovey had originally planned a career in the theatre, and there was a good deal of theatre in his food and hospitality. Spectacular multi-course dinners were staged nightly. The influence of Coulson had made its mark: this was proper fancy food, and there was to be no skimping on the luxury ingredients. 'He wouldn't use a pint of cream when he could use a quart,' remembers one frequent visitor to the hotel.

I sat in the lounge – there is no other word to describe it – contemplating the moss-green leather wing chairs, the smoked-glass coffee tables, the brown carpets and the Mozart G Minor Symphony on the PA. Indeed, this was the way that restaurants used to be – plush, comfortable, claustrophobic in their decorative excess. The lunch I ate was proof, however, that though decor may remain anchored in the past, the march of culinary fashion is relentless. Serrano ham, rosemary polenta and roasted pepper with truffled rocket leaves and toasted viennoise bread. Hake with chilli, sesame, soy and coriander pesto. Cannon of lamb with Dijon mustard and aubergine caviar wrapped in puff pastry; celeriac and wasabi purée; red wine sauce. I wondered whether Mr Tovey would have approved. There was, after all, not a drop of cream in sight.

'I took over in January as head chef when Mr Tovey retired,' said the chef, a small girl in her late twenties with glossy brown hair tied back in a bun. 'And the first thing I did was throw out all the heavy cream sauces.'

In my mind's eye I saw great vats, barrels, of heavy cream sauce being rolled out of some dark storeroom into the daylight.

I sat by the lake for a while to sober up, then drove a little northwards, losing myself on empty backroads that wound between moss-lined gorges and deep Romantic woodland. Good things come to those who have no idea what they're looking for, and before long I came upon a whitewashed farmhouse with a bed for the night.

'Beef and sheep, for our sins,' said the farmer's wife, briefly grim-faced as she pulled on the white lacy duvet cover. 'Still, mustn't grumble. We'll survive, we're *determined* to survive. Now, let's think about breakfast. Cumberland sausage, bacon, mushrooms, scrambled egg, fried bread all right for you?'

The thought alone was enough to give me heartburn. What I needed was fresh air and exercise. I bounded out of the house on to a green hillside bordered with oak trees, dark and soggily brown with last year's leaves. A few sheep scarpered as I loped down the slope into a misty, waterlogged valley. Behind me a waterfall emerged from the woodland and became a stream, snaking its way through rushes across the valley floor. Beside a fence where the crag began its near vertical ascent, something was moving – a huge brown stag with antlers like branches, lumberingly looking for food, much as I'd been doing these past few months. I stood rooted to the spot, a little intoxicated perhaps with the mountain air, as darkness fell and the stag moved like a ghost through the deep oak woods.

When I woke next morning the mist had cleared and a thin sunlight fought its way through the sodden undergrowth.

'You've been ever so lucky wi't weather, haven't you, loov?' beamed Mrs Nugent as I tucked in to a tranche of Cumberland sausage. I had certainly been lucky with Mrs Nugent. The sausage she served, coiled in the tight traditional spiral, was firm, peppery and delicious. And her bacon was a superbly meaty, fresh-flavoured example with the merest hint of sweetness, and none of the streaks of whiteness left by inferior 'crocodile' bacons that have been weeping inconsolably in the pan.

Both items had come from Woodall's, suppliers of some of the finest charcuterie in the realm, and the possessors of a Royal Appointment to prove Her Majesty's excellent taste. The coat of arms, gleaming with freshly painted colour, shines proudly above the lintel of the little shop in Waberthwaite on the west coast of Cumbria along the road to Egremont.

A small but important subsection of British gastronomy could be defined as 'traditional foods produced in village post offices'. Goosnargh biscuits, Jerrey's Suffolk hams, the Welsh bara brith from Capel Garmon and Woodall's all fall into this category. Why the category should exist at all is intriguing. Perhaps the sale of stamps and groceries allowed for production to continue, while other small-scale food producers in the area, lacking this useful economic support, were quietly driven to the wall.

Making my way to Waberthwaite along a near-deserted B road that followed the brief plain between the dramatically cloud-heaped mountains and the sea, I found the post office down a narrow lane off the main road and took my place in the queue behind a lady in a headscarf clutching a DSS form. While I waited, I cast my glance about the shelves of this little village shop with its packets of flavoured jellies and Bobby's Marsh Mallows, its tins of Bird's Custard, and its discreetly placed tree of 15-denier tights.

The shop was in two parts, like the business. At the front was the post office; at the back a miniature food hall, with ranks of old and wonky carved wooden shelving round the walls and, as if to emphasise that Woodall's moved with the times, a pair of shiny chill-cabinets with glass fronts. In these you could see the slabs of dark pink bacon, the curled Cumberland sausages, the packets of pre-sliced ham that make up the bulk of the turnover. The eyes were drawn skyward, however, to the hams hanging from the beamed ceiling, their surface crusted and black with age. What we had here was a product that people come from near and far, from Kendal and Kyoto, to admire and sample: the famous Cumbrian air-dried ham.

It had always seemed a mystery to me how one could possibly air-dry anything in an area that is often said to have the highest rainfall in the whole of the British Isles. I must have been giving off gamma-rays of doubt as I stood there staring at the roof, for, before long, a white-haired lady in a pink shop assistant's coat – June Woodall, wife of Richard Woodall, known to his family and friends as 'Bar' and the ham-meister hereabouts – came up to me and sweetly said, 'They do very nicely in here, you know. Are you surprised? I suppose a lot of people are. But they're up there for a year or so, to dry, you know, and we've never had a problem with a single one.'

June brought out a step-ladder, took down one of the precious black lumps of air-dried ham and, placing it on the marble surface of the counter, carefully pared away the skin and the nice thick casing of fat and cut a few fine slices especially for me.

June gave an indulgent smile as I chewed away at the tender ham with its delicious salty punch, a kind of shy English take on Parma.

Eight generations of the Woodall family had been making fine hams of one sort or another. They were once just one of the pig-owning families in the area. 'There used to be a slaughterhouse out the back. I've got relations as remember people queuing up with their pigs,' said June, her blue eyes bright.

In those days what is now a humble village shop was a big grocery store, supplying all the farmers and their wives between Seascale and Millom, a distance of roughly twenty-five miles.

June's mother-in-law was from Suffolk, and Bar found in an old book of hers a recipe for the famous 'Suffolk cure', which involves steeping the ham in a mixture of black molasses and usually beer, though in this case vinegar. The ham spends a month in this sticky black pungent tar-barrel, and is then hung for a year and sold as Cumbria Mature Royal Ham. As you'd expect from its contact with the molasses, it packs a punch of salty sweetness that to me is inexplicably a British taste and one that is completely beguiling. Not a ham for every day, perhaps. But I can imagine that, served thinly sliced as a first course with ripe figs, dressed with a little olive oil and black pepper, it would certainly make the odd Chelsea dinner party, bored into insouciance by the old combination of Parma ham and melon, sit up and take notice.

That evening I took up *The Good Food Guide* again, losing myself a little as usual in the glorious illusory world it creates, in which there is no disappointment, no crippling expense, only the most ambrosial tastes and sights. The language of the *Guide* owes its peculiar pompous tone to its 'inspectors'. I have often fantasised about the gilded life of these wondrous beings, who seem to flit from restaurant to restaurant like hummingbirds from flower to flower, penning comments that they are careful to make sound as highbrow as possible in the hope of seeing themselves in print.

'Nicolas Le Roux displays enormous potential. His pressed

terrine of sea bass with a coriander, saffron and mussel *nage* was beyond reproach,' suggests one.

'The show-stopping *assiette gourmandise des desserts de chez Henri* brought our meal to a magnificent climax,' pronounces another.

'The warm tian of haggis and neeps in a ginger and Bailey's *jus* was bloody marvellous!' raves a third. (Okay, I made up the last one.)

I looked up the places in Lakeland that the *Guide* said were worth the detour, dithering between Underscar Manor in Ambleside, where you dress for dinner and 'luxuries are given an airing', and the more casual-sounding Borrowdale Gates Hotel, where the chef's repertoire 'touches on aubergine piedmontese, oriental spring roll, and ceviche of salmon and monkfish'. Suddenly filled with dread at the idea of another five-course dinner in some sit-up-and-beg restaurant, and equally reluctant to brave the gloomy chasm of Windermere's Chinese, Indian, and pasta/pizza joints, I decided to look for a middle way. Tonight I would do what thousands upon thousands of Britons do on a regular basis, spending £4 billion a year between them. I would have dinner in a country pub.

Casting my mind back over my previous experience of eating in public houses I remembered a wonderful shoulder of lamb, perfectly roasted and unfeasibly huge, at the Halfway Bridge in Sussex, a grilled fillet of brill with Puy lentils at the Crooked Billet in Oxfordshire, and a memorable fish and chips, memorable not just because it was served in newspaper, at the Moody Cow in Herefordshire. One of the best food pubs I know is the Crabtree in Lower Beeding, where the pub Sunday lunch is reinvented as a luxurious eating-event (linen cloths, candles, big chiming glasses) and the basic elements of the roast are reorganised and refined. Slices of braised pork with a stuffing of nuts and berries were piled up with parsnip chips and sweet turnip and surrounded by a shallow pool of sauce.

By the same token, there had been some hideous moments. Like the time I found a four-inch nail in my spinach and flourished it in the face of the landlord, who thought I was playing a practical joke and bundled me out of the front door. Or the time I and a group of friends turned up at a lovely old flagstoned Dorset pub and asked what there was to eat. The grumpy old chef-patronne said she had five servings left of asparagus soup. Oh dear, we said, but there are seven of us.

'No matter,' she barked. 'I'll water it down.'

Whoever it was who said that the pub could become the 'bistro of British catering' had a point but, as usual in the universe of Britfood, reality and possibility are two different things. If only pubs could have the laidback, open-all-hours quality of the true French bistro. Too often, still, the kitchen clangs shut at 2 p.m. The furniture is still the same brown-glazed brewery standard-issue stuff. Service is often slapdash; shy local girls who can't quite keep up. The food is sometimes pretentious beyond belief, cooked up by some overstretched dinner-party cook who has been reading too many recipe books. One should also be aware that commercial catering firms have cottoned on to the pub food boom and are busy supplying 'instant' cook-chill dishes that sound and look as if they've been freshly prepared by a real live chef.

I left the car outside Hawkshead, which, being the most ridiculously pretty of all the Lake District's pretty little towns, has no intention of allowing traffic to spoil its tourist appeal.

A torrential downpour was just beginning, and I ran straight for the Red Lion, a pub whose carved lintel showed a naif figure of a man taking his pig to market. I took one look at the menu here – everything was smothered, drenched, sprinkled, napped with a seafood sauce, or laced with a minted pan jue (sic) – and ran on, sprinkled, smothered, drenched, to the Queen's Head around the corner. A smell of deep-frying in cheap oil emanated from the back of the pub. Inside, among the panelled walls and timbered ceilings (the historical atmosphere spoiled slightly by the pink-tinged glass double wall-lamps that look like something out of a New Orleans brothel), one could eat grilled goats' cheese, sweet and spicy chicken wings, followed by a meringue nest with fruits of the forest. Even the most adventurous dishes, served on Big White Plates in the London style, had an obstinate sort of pubbiness about them, a kind of dowdiness that clung to them like cigarette-smoke to velvet curtains.

So I moved on again, hungry by now, to my third attempt at a pub supper. The King's Arms was much more to my liking: they had liver and onion, turkey and ham pie, roast quail, and Westmorland pie, a curious concoction of ham, potatoes, onion, cheese and herbs. I dried out in front of the log fire (all good country pubs must have one) and ate a plate of meaty faggots, a dish I hadn't had for years, with the life-enhancing caul fat still visible in delicate trails on their surface. I swilled them all down with a couple of pints of Robinson's and fell into a bit of a reverie beside the fire, thinking that there was really nothing much wrong with bangers and mash, bubble and squeak, and faggots as a sideline to the noble business of serving fine bitter.

FAGGOTS
(serves 4–6)

Roughly chop 250g of pork liver and 250g of pork or lamb hearts. Briefly mince together in a food processor and combine with 500g of minced lean pork in a large bowl. Core and peel two Bramley apples and grate them into the bowl. Add a finely chopped large onion, plenty of salt and pepper and a generous handful of chopped fresh herbs (thyme, sage and chives as well as garlic, for example). Preheat the oven to 180 °C/Gas Mark 4.

Caul fat, though hard to find these days, is essential for this dish. When you locate some, it is worth buying a good lump and freezing it.

Pulling off squares of the lacy caul fat, shape the meat mixture into balls the size of satsumas and wrap each one with the fat. Place the faggots in a roasting tin and cook in a hot oven for 40 minutes.

Remove them from the pan to a warmed serving dish. The scrapings and liquid left in the pan will form the basis for a delicious gravy. Serve with peas and mashed potatoes.

Bright and early the following day, with the mist lying in a thick eiderdown over Coniston Water, my route lay northwards again, through a network of villages whose names were an odd combination of the quaint (Blindcrake, Plumbland, Papcastle) and the outright bizarre (Pica, Lowca, Pelutho, Blennerhasset).

From the pier at Maryport, where I stopped for a walk along the sea before turning inland, I could see across the Solway Firth to the south coast of Dumfries and Galloway, a misty green ghost in the afternoon sunlight. I could only wonder what culinary pleasures awaited me in Scotland, and whether the border, just a few miles further north, would mark any sort of gastronomic as well as cultural frontier.

Before I crossed over, however, there was one place left in England I had underlined on my road map, a small town that I'd sworn to visit ever since the previous summer, when I was staying the weekend at a big house in the South-East.

It was late on a Saturday night, and after several bottles of fine claret, an enormous dinner and a glass or two of some digestif or other, my hosts and the other guests had long since retired to their rooms. I, too, was just about to do so, when I was seized by a desire to nibble something. Groping clumsily inside the drinks cupboard, from which I remembered that cashews and pistachios had emerged with the gin and tonics, my hand fell on a small white box with gold trim and lined with fine greaseproof paper.

I can still smell the buttery-caramelly aroma of the contents of that box; still taste the explosion of rich milky sweetness. It was fudge, but it was not the ordinary sugary crunchy stuff that you can take or leave. This had a warmth, a reverberance and an aftertaste that stayed with me as I climbed the stairs to bed.

Remember the name on that box, I said to myself. In copperplate writing, like a smart invitation to a society wedding. The Toffee Shop, Penrith.

For an establishment that has been described as 'England's

finest sweet shop' and counts among its eminent supporters Lord Lichfield, who first ate its fudge as a child at his ancestral home in Shropshire and has sung its praises ever since, there is something almost disappointingly modest about the Toffee Shop's premises, stuck in a sidestreet at the unfashionable end of Penrith town centre. It was a busy Saturday afternoon and there was a queue out of the door of the tiny shop, under the blue awning, alongside the window with its display of blue and white china plates piled with Toffee Shop boxes of various sizes. At the counter, two jolly ladies in white pinafores packed up the orders. You could have plain fudge, or fudge flavoured with mint oil, or proper toffee made with butter, sugar and black treacle. I decided on a big box of the plain fudge, and leaned on the window and looked at the landscape, the pine-covered hills around this cordial, prosperous little mountain town.

At the back of the shop were eight brass pans, polished to a red gleaming shine. In one of them the day's batch of plain fudge was bubbling, a velvety and sublime-smelling mixture of butter, sugar, milk and nothing else. I stood by the pan for a while, watching the staff fuss and fret over it, stirring it from time to time on their way through to the shop to stop it 'catching' on the bottom and ruining the delicate flavour, and then pouring the thick steaming fudge into cooling trays.

As I walked back down the main street I could stand it no longer. I ripped open the box and ate a few rough squares of the fudge. It was just as I remembered it: intensely buttery, but not cloyingly so, and almost like wine in the way its flavour rolled around the mouth. The oddest thing was that, among the billows of creaminess that went on and on, there were aromas of flowers and fruit, a tanginess that reminded me by turns of oranges, apples, pineapple and apricot jam.

Quite how a product that contains only milk, sugar and butter could offer such a kaleidoscope of flavour was a conundrum. For now, though, there could be no further detective work. I had to drive, and think about Scots food, and keep hold of the last few shreds of my fading appetite. I stowed the box at the back of the glove compartment and slammed it firmly shut.

8

edinburgh and glasgow

la nouvelle cuisine écossaise?

I raced across the echoing landscapes of the Borders in early June, as summer struggled into life. Hawthorn bushes had started to flower; the primroses were small and undernourished-looking. The cuckoos were only just tuning up. But the gorse blazed yellow on the hillsides, the sun came out in response, and the air was as crisp as a fresh apple.

My preconceptions about Scottish food were several. One was the belief that Scotland still maintained a traditional national cuisine, whereas England's was in danger of extinction. Were you to invade a Scottish home at suppertime, you might find any number of homely Scots dishes being prepared and served, from cock-a-leekie to cullen skink to cranachan and clootie dumpling – or so I hoped and imagined. For me at least, the survival of a culinary tradition, however rudimentary, is always a consummation devoutly to be wished.

I knew about the high reputation of Scottish raw materials – beef of course, salmon of course, wonderful shellfish and seafood in general, smoked food, cheese, soft fruit, and so on – and I was aware that a growing constellation of fine restaurants was making intelligent use of these riches: the Peat Inn, La Potinière, the Ubiquitous Chip in Glasgow, the Creel in Orkney and a host of others. I had even heard there was something called Modern Scottish Cooking, scoffed at by some, talked up by others, but which, notionally at least, was blowing a cool breeze of modernity into Scottish kitchens.

For long periods of their history the Scots have eaten, if not sophisticatedly, at least nourishingly and well. The staple dish until the eighteenth century was barley broth, which was apparently much appreciated by visitors to the country. James Boswell was surprised to see Dr Johnson lapping it up. 'You never ate it before?' he asked. Johnson said that he had not, 'adding that he did not mind how soon he ate it again'. During the mid-nineteenth century, when most labourers in England survived on the modern régime of bread, potatoes, tea and beer, their counterparts in Scotland still followed a traditional diet, far superior in nutritional value, consisting mainly of oatmeal, milk and root vegetable broths. Frank Buckland, medical officer to the Guards, commented in 1863 on the fact that English recruits tended to be puny and undernourished, whereas the Scots were healthy and of fine physique.

For all its virtues, however, Scots food also has its dark side – its *leyenda negra*, as the Spanish say. I knew from hearsay before I arrived in Scotland that certain parts of the country had the worst diet in Europe, impossibly high in saturated fat, starch and sugar and suicidally low in vitamin C. Heart disease was rampant. What you might call the *Trainspotting* side of Scots cuisine consisted largely of things encased in batter and deep-fried in bad oil. Cod and haddock and sausages were only the beginning. There were deep-fried Mars Bars, served with chips and sprinkled with salt and vinegar ('salt 'n' sauce' in the Scots vernacular), and deep-fried haggises. Pies filled with a meat slurry imported from Belgium under the official category of industrial waste. Chips with curry sauce. All washed down with Irn-Bru, the unearthly orange fizz that may have a better claim than whisky to be called the Scottish national drink.

At a service station outside Galashiels I glanced at the menu. It was an inauspicious start. Fish and chips, pie and chips, chicken and chips: the usual sad litany. The All-Day Scottish Breakfast, a token stab at ethnicity, featured various fried 'puddings' – black, white, red, fruity – and a fried slab of the sausage meat called lorne. Coffee culture, which was meant to have bequeathed to southern England the strange new argot of tall skinny lattes and extra shots, didn't seem to have made it yet to southern Scotland. What I was served under the description of 'filter coffee' put me in mind of the eighteenth-century Swiss traveller Charles Moritz, who advised those who wished to drink coffee in Britain to 'mention beforehand, how many cups are to be made with half an ounce, or else the people will probably bring them a prodigious quantity of brown fluid'.

'Not too keen on fry-ups, then?' said a voice by my side as I stood by the counter.

'Depends, doesn't it?' I replied glumly.

'Well, let me tell you, this isn't as bad as it gets.'

'What is as bad as it gets, then?'

'As bad as it gets is a wee hamburger, inside a bun, the whole thing covered in batter, deep-fried, and all that served inside another bun.'

I had to laugh, if only at the sheer diabolical genius of the idea.

Donald was that rarest of things, a bronzed Scot, tanned by the sun in some oil-producing corner of the old Soviet empire. We sat down with a bottle of Highland Spring at the same Formica table and I told him what I was about was really good Scottish eating, not the kind of hellish junk he'd just amusingly described.

'Really good Scottish eatin', eh? I've had a lot of that in my time. Let's see . . . Well, my mum's a superb baker; she made bannocks and pancakes and girdle cakes and butteries and shortbread. She made a wonderful soup. You know the Scots are big on soups. My favourite was Cullen Skink – that's haddock and potato. It always had this rich creamy yellow colour, the way she made it. Pies, meat pies, casseroles . . .'

Cullen Skink

(serves 6)

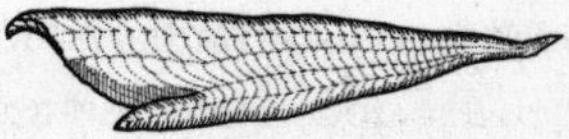

In a heavy-based saucepan, gently fry a chopped onion in butter. Cut up a kilo of smoked haddock into large pieces – properly smoked Finnan haddock, if possible, without yellow dyes and artificial smoke flavouring – and add the pieces to

the pan along with half a litre of water. Bring to the boil and simmer for 20–25 minutes.

Remove the fish from the pan, discard the skin and bones and separate the flesh into flakes. Stir 250g of mashed potato into the remaining water, along with 750ml of milk, and return the flaked haddock to the pan. Allow to cook for a minute or two; season with salt and pepper. Just before serving, stir in 150ml of cream and a tablespoonful of chopped chives.

There is no journalistic proposition more readily assented to than an interview about what someone ate as a child, partly because what you put in your mouth seems at first to be a wonderfully uncontentious issue, and partly because food is simply the best of all possible vehicles for nostalgia.

'Just by the sandbar at Nairn, at low tide, there used to be cockle beds. They called it the cockle shore,' said Donald, sliding forward with both elbows on the Formica. His eyes were taking on a dark greedy glint. 'Five years ago now, commercial harvesters came up from the South and raped the beds, left almost nothing, but that's another story. As kids we'd go cocklin' down by the sands. We had proper puddings. And summer fruit: raspberry, currants and loganberry, sometimes strawberry.'

The Macleods lived and ate in the country Scottish style. It was a solid diet of fresh, slow food, long on starch and protein and short on green vegetables, since Scotland, for reasons of climate and geography, has never been strong on those. When Donald married a busy young woman, impatient with the time-consuming stodge her mother-in-law made, it was goodbye to all that and hello to the pasta and salad, the margarine on his toast and no porridge in the morning.

'I could bring her a pheasant, but my wife wouldn't thank me for it. She'd probably prefer a chicken breast, if the truth be known,' said Donald ruefully.

There was a great rugby match on at Murrayfield, and the centre of Edinburgh was officially Full Up. But there is so much more to this great city than its centre, and by leaving my car in the New Street car park and jumping on the first bus to Leith I found a fascinating satellite, or rather a star in its own right, of the rapidly expanding Edinburgh food scene.

Latterly around the world, aesthetic revolutions happen mainly in converted docks. Leith, once the grotty Piraeus to the Athens of the North, was one of the original heartlands of Edinburgh's recent gastro-boom, though it was hard to believe so from the sleaze of Leith Walk, where the Caprice Lounge and Greedyguts Takeaway were the limits of gastronomy. The main action, as I soon discovered, happens not in crummy inland Leith, but on the harbourside itself, which had turned in the space of twenty years into a restaurant quarter of surprising excellence. I found my way down to the dockside past the 1960s housing blocks behind Shore Place, with their soundscape of screaming children and clattering pots and pans. It was seven o'clock in the evening, just after Scottish tea and washing-up time, but the stilettos were only just beginning to click out of taxis into the fashionable restaurants of the harbourside.

Nearest to the housing blocks – within spitting distance, if their inhabitants were to lean far enough out of the window – was one of the chicest of all Edinburgh restaurants, 'fitzHenry:

a brasserie', whose peculiar name made it sound like an avant-garde novel. Behind the grimy granite walls and the big black double doors – it looked like it had once been a prison, or at least something dirty and functional – this was an identikit 'trendy restaurant' of the type that has sprung up in every major city in Britain, in which the clientele occupies an age range of twenty-five to forty and the menu reads like a check-list of modish ingredients and techniques, to the point where you almost detect an element of irony among all the jus, confit, sabayon, polenta gnocchi and Crottin filo parcels on grilled vegetables with a balsamic reduction.

Further up Shore Place there were more and greater possibilities: three panelled, comfortable fish restaurants almost one after another, in increasing order of quality. The Ship was a food pub trying to be something more; the Shore seemed to have got there without trying too hard; and Fishers, where I ate a soulful meal of roast marinated crevettes and a steamed seabass with wild garlic, smoked mussels and Pernod, with a delectable pea and tarragon risotto on the side, had the clear-eyed firm-jawed feel of a place with serious culinary ambitions. Everywhere was packed and buzzing, and for the first time since Manchester I had a sense of hunger and pleasure and understanding combined in a nice sort of urban mélange. The dining classes here had no chips on their shoulder nor chips on their plate. So much for the traditional image of Edinburgh as dour, mean and puritanical. It bore out a memorable passage in William Harrison's *Description of England*, written in 1577, where the author discusses the Scottish propensity for high living: 'In Scotland likewise they haue given themselues (late yeares to speake of) vnto verie ample and large diet, wherein as for some respect nature dooth make it equall with vs; so otherwise they far exceed vs in ouer much and distemperate gormandize, and so ingrosse their bodies that diuerse of them doo oft become vnapt to anie other purpose than to spend their times in large tabling and bellie cheere.'

In search of more bellie cheere, next morning I turned my mind to produce. Food shopping in Edinburgh turned out to be more fun than in any other British city I had yet seen. My first port of call, as is only right and proper, was Valvona and Crolla on Leith Walk, the mythical and marvellous Italian delicatessen, established in the 1860s, that rises effortlessly above all other Italian delis in the country. V&C seems to be saying, with a certain proud and haughty air, that the usual run of such places, in which musty old packets of pasta sit hugger-mugger with industrial salamis and dried-up parmesan, is just not good enough.

Before you can think of something they might not have, you realise they already have it. Vast selections of rices, flours, oils and vinegars, dried and fresh wild mushrooms, wines; fresh Italian fruits and vegetables ('we have a direct refrigerated link from Milano market to Edinburgh'); hams and sausages hanging in ranks from high ceilings flooded with light . . . I wandered as one in a dream through corridors lined with beautiful food, managing to restrict my purchases to a slab of torrone, a pot of preserved candied mostarda di frutta, a pack of gnocchetti sardi allo zafferano – tight wrinkled little pasta shapes, coloured a rich golden yellow with saffron – and a big slice of succulent, suppurating gorgonzola, caught in the act of collapsing decadently on to its wooden board like a courtesan on to a sofa.

Next, remembering that one of Britain's great cheese emporia is based in Edinburgh, I made my way uptown to the headquarters of Iain Mellis Cheesemonger's in Victoria Street, where I tasted my way through a dozen Scottish cheeses under the guidance of a small girl with a glittery stud through her nose. The British cheese-making renaissance has made great waves in Scotland, where a new cheese is created seemingly every other month. Scotland has produced some of the cheese world's great battlers against bureaucracy and interference, men like Humphrey Errington, whose heroic struggle to save his Lanark Blue from extinction – after the local council declared it so heavily contaminated with *Listeria monocytogenes* that it might have caused a national outbreak with a fatality rate of 40 per cent (false accusations, needless to say) – was unique among the food scandals of the 1990s in having a happy ending. And John Curtis of Easter Weens, makers of the glorious unpasteurised washed-rind Bonchester, the British answer to Camembert, much-mourned since it ceased production in 1998. This particular ending was not so happy. Harassed for years by the Food Police, Curtis's dairy manager eventually fell sick as a result of constant stress. During the writing of this book, I received by fax a press release from Curtis informing anyone who would listen of the sad fact that there could be 'no resumption of cheese production at Easter Weens until there is definite evidence of a more sympathetic attitude to raw milk cheese production by the British government'.

I piled into my basket a series of fragrant paper-wrapped lumps, a quarter each of unpasteurised Cheddar from the Isle of Mull, Cairnsmore sheep from Galloway, Criffel from the Camphill Village community near Dumfries and Sweet Milk from Wester Lawrenceton near Inverness. I took the whole lot, plus some Adamson's oatcakes – coarse, nutty, crumbly, toasty and rich – up to the top of Arthur's Seat, there to gorge and gaze at my leisure.

There is such variety in the new Scottish cheeses, and each of these four was quite different from the next. The Isle of Mull was paler than Southern Cheddars, but fruity-tasting and tangy; the Cairnsmore strongly sheepy, salty and resonant; the Criffel soft, smooth and buttery under its orangish rind thickly spattered with blue mould; and the Sweet Milk, mild and soft, lived up to its name. It was blustery cold up there on that strange urban mountain-top, but I pulled my jacket up around my ears and feasted on a view with all the scale and drama of somewhere ten times quieter, ten times more remote, the city sprawling like a thick grey forest over its various hills and the Firth of Forth ahead of me, a wide sleeve of Wedgwood blue, fringed at its eastern, estuary end with a feathery skein of mist.

Then I made my way down the hill and took a cab, via Holyrood Park Road and Melville Drive, to Bruntsfield Place. In the absence of a proper public market – markets being the great missing link, the great missed opportunity, in British eating – I'd been told by more than one Scots gastronome that this part of the city was the best place in Edinburgh to shop for food. In terms of sheer variety, they weren't wrong: between Tollcross and Morningside there were bakeries and pastry shops, butchers, greengrocers, fishmongers, wholefood shops and delis, and, not least, a second branch of Iain Mellis's cheese heaven.

For quality too, this was good stuff. Sanderson's butchers, a nice old white-and-blue-tiled shop, had been in the family for three generations. They sold fine steak pies and sausages and black puddings with plenty of oatmeal, and there was a queue out of the door on this bright Saturday afternoon. A few hundred yards away, however, they had a rival in Wm Christie, who specialised in Ardrossan pork and a huge, delicious-looking homemade haggis. 'Fresh Wild Haggis, from the Hills of Glencoe' read the card in the window.

Further up the street, there were freshly made juices at Mango and Stone, biodynamic bread at the Engine Shed, waffles at À La Bonne Gaufre, Scots bannocks, morning rolls, drop scones and crumpets at the Breadwinner . . . Two fine fishmongers, G. Hughes and Robert Main, stood almost opposite each other. To have one good fishmonger in a single street, or even in a single town, is remarkable enough in pisciphobic Britain. To have two seems like the height of good fortune.

From the beginning of Bruntsfield Place, down the slope of Leamington Terrace, you could see the gaunt shape of McEwan's brewery and the grey hills beyond. I was heading back into town, and at Tollcross, right by the King's Theatre, I found a place I'd missed on the way out. Lupe Pintos delicatessen, the Hispanic version of Valvona and Crolla, was colourful and crammed with Latin-American loot: jars of *mole* and hot banana wax peppers, and chillies hanging in a glossy curtain above the counter: chipotle, cascabel, pequin, mulato, ancho and chilhualle negro, with its deep rich overtones of plum and liquorice. The shop smelled of spice and heat.

'We do a wee bit o' a lot o' things,' said Doug, the owner, in his black beeny hat. 'We've got probably the best range of tequilas in the Western world. We've got *loads* of hot pepper sauces. We've got Jamaican jerk seasonings, Spanish cheeses, American pickles, bagels, masa harina, Brazilian stuff, you name it. Edinburgh's an international city, ken? Always has been. The reason I like living here is the way we adapt and adopt.'

He was right, of course. Scottish culture has always been receptive to influences from abroad – rather more so, perhaps, than the English. Jane Grigson makes the point that the Auld Alliance with France left its mark on a number of traditional Scots dishes: tartan purry, a mixture of chopped kail (i.e. cabbage) and oatmeal, began life as *tarte en purée*, and sooty bannock, which sounds like someone burned the cakes, is actually *sauté* bannock, meaning a pancake. (Mrs Grigson also claims with a straight face that the call of the Scottish dairymaid, 'Proochy-moo, proochy-moo,' derives from the French '*Approchez-moi*,' but here I suspect her of a mischievous little joke at her readers' expense.)

Anyone concerned with the history of Edinburgh eating should take a trip to Henderson's Salad Table in the New Town. When it opened in the early 1960s, there was nowhere like it north of Carnaby Street. Janet Henderson, the founder, wore long flowery skirts and was considered by the prim and priggish standards of the time to be a 'crank'. This was where the Mediterranean flavours, the casual Mediterranean way of eating, first disembarked in Scotland. Janet's helper in the early days was a Spanish girl called Covadonga, whose culinary style brought new colour and warmth to the stodgy puritanism of early wholefood cookery. Henderson's is still remembered by many Edinburgh diners as the first place they ever saw an aubergine. The day the place got its first primitive coffee machine in 1963 was a major event: it was only the second to arrive in Scotland.

They were ahead of their time; perhaps inevitably, they have since fallen behind. When I visited, the restaurant, which was full of bespectacled refugees from the rugby final, seemed more like an unreconstructed old-fashioned healthfood joint – there was red wine and cashew nut pâté followed by lentil and butterbean bake; timewarp veggie food – than the trendsetting haven of exotica it had been once upon a time.

Food fashion has moved on, and in some surprising new directions. Nowadays the ethnic influence everyone wants their menu to reflect is not Italian, or Thai, or Moroccan or Creole, but Scottish. Whether or not the New Scottish Cuisine, as some have called it, genuinely represents a resurgence of Scottish cooking or is more about a generalised hankering for ethnic identity is a moot point. In the hours before dinner I strolled about the New Town, peering in windows and picking up menus. Within a caber's toss of Henderson's I came upon Stac Polly, named after a mountain, one of the stars of the renaissance, if renaissance there be. 'THE SCOTTISH RESTAURANT' said a sign, as if to make things clear from the start. Inside I could see tartan-covered chairs and emerald green tablecloths and purple curtains – colours that, according to the blurb in the window, 'reflect the heather-clad hills'. The menu featured haggis in filo pastry, which had become a signature dish, and shortly afterwards almost a cliché, of the New Scottish Cooking. Thereafter you could have fillet of Scottish beef, sautéed parsnips and dauphinoise potatoes with shallot and tarragon game jus. Hardly very *typique*. Perhaps it was Scottish only in the sense of being hearty, honest and substantial. But then came the surprise: the menu *also* featured roasted red and green pepper salad with mozzarella cheese, endive leaves, toasted pine kernels and an olive oil and balsamic dressing. I think it was at that moment that I decided not to take the New Scottish Cooking too seriously any more.

The weather had changed overnight, and in the morning light Edinburgh suddenly looked cold and unfriendly. So I picked up the car and drove west for an hour or so, watching the clouds roll back and the sky turn blue. And then I remembered what I think I'd always known – that Edinburgh under rain can be the grimmest horror-movie backdrop imaginable, whereas Glasgow with the sun gleaming on it, bringing out the variegated colours of its grimy stonework, can be the most exhilarating, grandest, smilingest city in Britain.

I found a room opposite the School of Art, Rennie Mackintosh's fascinating masterpiece of whimsical severity, and went straight down to Sauchiehall Street for a Scotch pie at Bradfords the bakers – Scotch pies have, or should have, and do have at Bradfords, a thin pastry casing filled with good lean meat and suet – followed by a cup of coffee in another Mackintosh masterpiece, the Willow Tea Rooms. To get to the Willow, you have to go through a high street jeweller's shop full of pseudo-Mackintosh jewellery, climb a staircase or two and there it is, the jewel-like Room de Luxe, as it was known, with its odd grey and lilac colour-scheme, its high-backed torture-chamber chairs. On the walls up the staircase are early photographs of founder Kate Cranston, who had four tea rooms in Glasgow at the turn of the last century and commissioned Mackintosh to design the Willow. An Edwardian lady in a multi-tiered Edwardian dress and an 'artistic' feathered hat, she hardly looks like a harbinger of modernism in the pictures. Most fascinating to me, however, were the framed original menus from the Willow. For such an elegant and exclusive venue, what it offered was very dowdy fare: you could have a basin of cream soup and bread, a mutton pie, sausage and chips or a savoury meat rissole, tomato sauce and chips (4d), followed by curds and cream, Devonshire junket, or calf's foot jelly.

Like Barcelona, and Manchester, and Sydney, and the other cities it is spiritually twinned with, Glasgow is big on Design, and the visitor is never allowed to forget that fact for long. Restaurants here are sometimes almost more interesting for their interiors than for what they put on your plate; such as Rogano's in Exchange Place, after the Criterion on Piccadilly Circus surely the most luxurious and loveliest dining room in Britain. I sat on a banquette among the gold art deco ocean-liner splendour and drank a glass of Joseph Perrier champagne while Rogano's maitre d' gave me a crash course in the recent history of Glaswegian eating.

Until five years earlier, the city had boasted no more than half a dozen really good places to eat. Now there were twenty or so, and it was getting hard to keep up. There were the classic, grand, or sedate places like the Ubiquitous Chip, One Devonshire Gardens and Rogano's itself. But the buzz was all about the cutting-edge Designed places like Yes, and the Bouzy Rouge, and Gamba, and Malmaison, and Nairn's, run by TV chef Nick Nairn.

'How do we compare to Edinburgh? Och, Edinburgh food's a wee bit *staid* compared to Glasgow. Stuck in a late eighties timewarp, Edinburgh is,' said the maitre d' disdainfully. He wore a black tie, a black shirt and an expensive-looking black suit.

Unlike London, which now shrugs its shoulders at modernism generally, there is still a discernible sense of surprised pride in Glasgow at just how chic and up-to-date Scotland is capable of being.

Armed with a list of the city's coolest food venues, I set off to follow the trail. At Air Organic in Sauchiehall Street, shaven-headed clubbers nibbled quietly from their bento boxes, as if stunned into silence by the curvilinear grooviness of the decor. At Tun Ton in Hope Street, recently made over by Graven Images, the *ne plus ultra* of Glasgow design teams, the food was par-for-the-course modern brasserie stuff: the pâté was served with ciabatta, the lemons Moorishly preserved. This was not so much comfort food as confit food.

'Tinderbox: a coffee house on Byres Road with a fabulous interior,' raved *Harpers & Queen*. I jumped in a cab and we threaded through the gridded city streets, the cab driver rabbiting away about the changes for the better in Glaswegian life. As we passed Yes, a frantically trendy plate-glass-fronted eaterie on West Nile Street where you could choose between Thai spiced breast of chicken or gateau of haggis, neeps and tatties, he said nonchalantly, 'Och, aye, that one's been aroond for a while. These new rai-strents, they're popping up all the time.'

I sipped on a cappuccino in the shiny zinc splendour of Tinderbox. And then, feeling that all this coolness had struck some kind of a chill in my bones, I took out the mobile and called up a friend of mine who cares little for trendy food and plenty for proper Glaswegian scran. I should make first, he said, for the Grosvenor Café, where the Full Scottish Breakfast is a feed of frightening proportions, featuring bacon, eggs, fried bread, sausage and puddings black, white and fruity, all gently oozing their warm grease on to your plate. 'For the full effect, you should wash all that down with a bottle of Irn Bru,' suggested Larry. Or there was the Horseshoe Bar in the city centre, which does the quickest and cheapest three-course lunch possibly in the whole of the United Kingdom for the outrageous price of £2.20. Failing all that, there was always the University Café on Byres Road, the Tour d'Argent of greasy spoons, founded in 1918, where the signature dishes are black pudding, tattie scone and knickerbocker glory.

Since I was just around the corner I popped in to the University and ordered a couple of scones to take away. At twenty pence the pair, I reflected, it would be hard to fill yourself up more cheaply with anything, anywhere, at any time. 'Salt 'n' sauce?' asked the man behind the counter, and before I'd had time to stop him he was coating the triangular potato cakes in a thin brown liquid from a plastic squeezy bottle. This 'sauce', a vinegary chemical substance splurted on to every sort of takeaway food from fish and chips to pies and peas, is probably Scottish popular food's greatest single obstacle to excellence.

Chomping on my tasty tattie scone, wincing occasionally from the gaseous blast of industrial acetic acid in the sauce, I sauntered further up Byres Road. In the stretch around the university there were health food shops, a good greengrocer called Roots and Fruits, a bakery or two and a cheese shop. But the further I walked out of the city the grubbier the streets and the nastier the edibles became. There were fry-shops every few hundred yards, and the air was full of the pervasive, nauseating smell of cheap corn oil that has spent too many weeks at boiling point for its own good.

I was slipping once more into the dreadful morass of white trash Scots cooking, where everything that can possibly be battered and deep-fried is battered and deep-fried. I saw meat pies encased in batter. I saw slabs of chicken meat covered with a scrofulous yellow crust of slimy batter, dripping with grease. And, just when I thought I had seen the worst, I hit rock bottom. A whole haggis, robed in batter, being eaten with great enthusiasm by a man striding along the street. With every lunge of his jaws at the haggis, it spurted a small torrent of greyish grease into the paper receptacle he carried beneath it. I could not remember having seen anything so distressing in a long time.

A thin rain was falling on the coagulated spaghetti junction of the Clydeside Expressway as I made my way back towards the centre. But before nightfall I was sitting comfortably in the midnight blue dining room at Nairn's, having already worked my way through a voluptuous dinner of foie gras and scrambled egg with pea purée, pan-fried red mullet with spinach, white bean and truffle sauce, and a superb cider crème brûlée with confit of apples and Calvados custard, and Glasgow and Glasgow food didn't seem quite such dismal prospects.

Nick Nairn, whose TV show had all of Scotland glued to the box – probably scoffing pizza and chips as they watched – is as passionate an advocate of fine Scottish food as you could hope to find. He is under no illusions, however, about the eating habits of his countrymen.

I told Nick what I'd seen that afternoon and he didn't flinch.

'Look, Scotland does have the most atrocious diet, still,' he said as he stood by my table. 'People have no real understanding of food, no culture of food. Listen, there are kids out there who think that chips come from supermarkets, not from potatoes. The problem is, how do you create a food culture from nothing? We need to teach food as a social thing, as sitting round a table, sharing. Food is not to be eaten while you're playing Nintendo. People in this country stuff their faces while they're walking down the street, like your guy with the haggis.'

He gave a graphic display of face-stuffing and I nodded my disapproval, and we both laughed at the irony of someone who has just eaten a vast and opulent meal, as I had, criticising anyone else for greed.

'Did you enjoy it, by the way?' said Nick, removing my plate. 'The mullet was good tonight, wasn't it? Have you had any cheese? Listen, I've got a fantastic Isle of Mull Cheddar, just in today from Iain Mellis. Can I tempt you with a slice? Or would Monsieur prefer a waffeur-thin mint?'

9

the highland larder

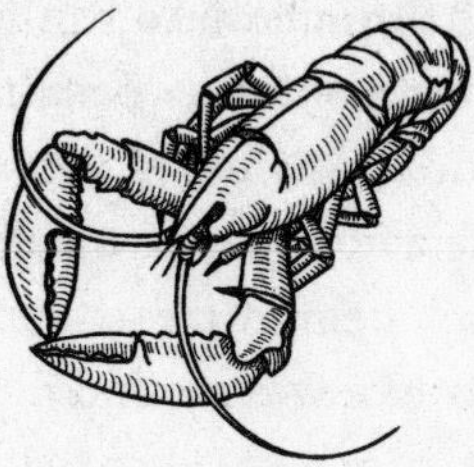

It was Donald's hot tip for Highland food. And, having no better one to follow, I followed it.

A smallish town outside Inverness, with the upright sensible look that granite architecture gives smallish Scottish towns. A proud little shop, gleamingly clean, and a big, blue-eyed young woman behind the counter who bristled and upbraided me when I unthinkingly asked for 'whoever's in charge'. Louisa McLean had taken on the family business out of loyalty to her father and was fiercely committed to making a success of it.

'You may have heard about our haggis,' said Louisa. I had, but it was also painted in large letters on the outside wall of the building: 'PRIZE-WINNING HAGGIS, NO. 1 IN SCOTLAND'. The fame of this haggis was the reason half a dozen coaches turned up at the shop every day in summer; the reason the Dingwall tourist brochure featured it as one of the town's major tourist attractions; and the reason that at certain times of year more than a ton of lights, pluck and other euphemistically titled items of sheep-meat continued to be processed at Geo Cockburn's in a single week.

'Hang on a sec.' She nipped into the back room and called out, 'How much did we make between St Andrew's and Burns Night last year?'

'Fifteen tons,' came a voice from within.

Louisa stepped back behind the counter. 'Fifteen tons,' she said to me. 'Christmas Eve was madness.'

'People don't make it at home. It must be the smell. We boil the meat overnight. When I come in in the mornings, I do think: urrrggh.'

Highland housewives came in while we talked, and Louisa broke off to serve them their pound of sausages, their brace of beefburgers.

'Hi there, how're yu? He's asked for a Mealy Jimmie tonight, can yu give me fae that?' asked one. A Mealy Jimmie was a dish popular in Dingwall, combining mince and tatties and the sultana-laden slicing sausage that the Scots call 'fruity pudding'.

On the floor by the door was a box lined with black plastic, full of fat turnips in their surprising livery of green, grey and purple. A clever idea, since haggis and 'bashed neeps' still go together like a horse and carriage. But there are other ideas afoot, Louisa explained, as the haggis takes its place in the world of haute cuisine. You can take some of the filling out of its bag and spread it on toast for a delicate starter. You can stuff a roast chicken with it. You can even flash-fry roundels of sliced haggis and serve them on a bed of rocket salad with a balsamic vinegar and olive oil dressing; though that's not the way they do it in Dingwall.

Louisa brought out a haggis she happened to have, cooked but cold, out the back. 'It's all mixed by hand, so you'll find there's a wee bite to it,' she said as I nibbled on the grey crumbly mass. There was a sort of spiciness that caught me on the back of the throat and made me cough.

'It's a bit of a secret recipe. All I'm allowed to tell you is there's no spices in there; just salt and pepper.'

Lady Login's Haggis Receipt (1856)

(serves 12)

1 cleaned sheep or lamb's stomach bag
1kg dry oatmeal
500g chopped mutton suet
500g lamb or deer liver, boiled and minced
2 cups stock
the heart and lights of the sheep, boiled and minced
1 large chopped onion
half a teaspoon each of cayenne pepper, Jamaica pepper, salt and black pepper

Toast the oatmeal slowly until it is crisp, then mix all the ingredients (except the stomach bag) together, and add the stock. Fill the bag just over half full, press out the air and sew up securely. Have ready a large pot of boiling water, prick the haggis all over with a large needle so it does not burst and boil slowly for 4–5 hours.

Within the memory of all but the very young, the Highlands of Scotland had a reputation for a cuisine as miserable and dispiriting as the local weather. The idea of a restaurant like the Peat Inn near St Andrews, where practically everything is locally produced, from honey to herbs, from venison to organic vegetables, would have been inconceivable. In the old days before the Food Revolution, Scottish salmon, grouse, scallops and whisky, all went abroad, to England or elsewhere. The population ate packet soups and tinned luncheon meat instead. Chanterelles were left to rot in the woods; button mushrooms in brine were the only admissible fungi. 'The coastal fringe and patches by the lochs that splash the grim slopes with the clear tones of cultivation offer little hope of a good meal,' wrote Jane Grigson in 1984. 'Bread is sliced. Vegetables may include potatoes and cabbages, and carrots with luck. Fish is frozen. Cheese is enveloped in plastic.'

Times appear to have changed, at least as far as the middle class is concerned; and not a moment too soon. The Revolution, of which Grigson herself was a kind of genial Robespierre, has swept northwards from the South of England into the furthest Highland glens. Nick Nairn has been on the telly, encouraging the Scots to think more highly, and to make better use, of the produce of their own back yard. Green-mindedness has brought people round to the idea of small-scale, organic production, which is also the way food was traditionally produced in these northernmost outposts of the United Kingdom. Ethnic – Scottish – food is fashionable. For all these reasons, the days when 'soup and a pie' at a country pub meant Baxters and Fray Bentos are practically over and gone.

For a whole week I ransacked the Highlands of their finest comestibles, until the car resembled a rolling, pungent warehouse of cheeses, oatcakes, shortcakes, marmalades and more smoked salmon, smoked venison, smoked mussels, bacon and kippers than seemed either credible or sensible. Halfway through the week I began to succumb to the condition known to food-loving visitors to Scotland as Smokehouse Blues, the symptoms of which – a heavy heart and a heavier stomach – tend to manifest themselves at the moment when the car turns a corner and yet another smokehouse hoves into view. I began to have strange dreams, the Scots equivalents of the dreadful West Country food nightmares of last autumn with their hellish, bubbling vats of clotted cream. In one, salmon leaped from the weirs directly into tar-blackened smokehouses where they died a choking death. In another a giant deep-fried haggis turned into a bomb, only to explode and shower me with boiling fat.

The odd thing was that these night-time horrors were not at all reflected in daytime reality. The sun was out, amazingly, and the lush countryside buzzed with summer. I drove along breathing the musky, invigorating scents of hawthorn and elderflower. Fields of oilseed rape shone with their preternatural saffron yellowness, and above them the hillsides wore a wispy garb of pinkish heather.

There was so much to eat and drink round here, I hardly knew where to start. At Moniack Castle the sign said 'Scottish

Wines', which sounded like a contradiction in terms but was not. They were country wines made from wild fruits and flowers – a great British tradition, and largely undersung by the sippers of Sauvignon Blanc – and I came away with a case of Silver Birch, a crisp, lipsmacking aperitif wine one could drink like a fino sherry. This was an area rich in delicious fragrances, of wild flowers and hedgerow blossoms. By Conon Bridge, I dropped in at Struan Apiaries, Scotland's premier honey producers, and bought some pots of raspberry-flower, lime tree, sycamore, and, best of all, thick, dark ling heather honey with aromas of mahogany and black treacle.

'They've been on the rape, aye. Any minute now, they'll be back on the raspberry,' said a tall thin affable young Scot.

I had found him in the warehouse, tending the centrifuges where the honey drips from its combs.

'Do you get stung much?' I asked him.

'Nae, we've all this protective gear, so it's not very likely you'll get *stang*,' he replied.

I so enjoyed hearing the Scots past participle of sting that I tried to see if I could make him say it again.

'How many times has it happened? You know . . .'

'What, me being *stang*? Och, I should think a hundred times.'

There were still old foods around here, made by old people to old recipes. I stopped in Tain to buy a loaf of bread at Grant's – they were still using the old oven, made by J. Cruickshank, Edinburgh, in the 1870s, and a wooden spade with which to take the loaves out – and the baker suggested I try a slice of his bread with a thick spreading of crowdie, the Scots fresh cheese, and a spoonful of honey. There was a lady up the road who still made crowdie, he said, anticipating my question. And I sped out of town to the red sandstone mansion in its own scrap of woodland off the main road, the headquarters of Susannah Stone and her Highland Fine Cheeses.

Susannah was a frightfully nice Englishwoman of a certain age who had married a Scot and stumbled into crowdie-making almost by accident.

She brought out a couple of old coats from the entrance hall and laid them on the grass and invited me to sprawl there in the sun and listen to her story of the Stones and their tentative beginnings as cheese-makers.

'Everyone made crowdie before the war. I'd watched my mother-in-law make it. We lived by the sea then,' said this lovely, smiling, faintly eccentric lady. 'But after the war you just couldn't find it, and my husband did hanker after it so.'

They had a few dairy cows on their small farm. Traditionally the milk would have been left to curdle naturally in the sun, the curds would have been scalded on the stove, mashed, salted and hung up in a muslin bag under the rowan tree.

The first time Susannah tried it, she stood the milk in a warm bathtub. 'After three days it still hadn't curdled, you see, and Reggie wanted to use the bath. So he popped down to Shake-the-Bottle, as the man was known, the chemist in Tain, and bought some lactophilic acid pills, and that seemed to work very nicely. Then I hung up the sixteen pounds of crowdie in a pillowcase. It was quite delicious, with a lemony tang, you know, as crowdie should be. We took some down to the grocer's and asked him to sell some. He was very suspicious of it. Nobody wants crowdie any more, he said. Anyway, he sold out in record time, and we duly made some more crowdie. Before long we had three churns in the bath. We used to deliver off the back of a tractor.'

Susannah ran back into the house for some cheese and oatcakes and I brought out bread and smoked salmon from the car, and we ate a fine little Highland *déjeuner sur l'herbe*, accompanied by thimblefuls of Balblair whisky from the little distillery a few miles further up the Dornoch Firth.

'It was my husband's absolute favourite,' said Susannah. 'I used to make his porridge with a lump of cream and a tot of Balblair.'

Since the early days the Stones had branched out into various sophistications of fresh cheese, including a crowdie mixed with chopped wild garlic from nearby Black Rock Gorge, and a wonderful double-cream cheese rolled in toasted oatmeal. Where the simple Highland crowdie had a lightness of texture and that beguiling lemon tang, the caboc was splendidly rich and sticky, with something both of the look and taste of butter.

'It's another ancient cheese; a chieftain's cheese, you know,' Susannah was saying. 'There's a bit of a tale attached to it, by the way. Mariota de l'Ile, she was an ancestor of mine, was hidden by her family in a cheese barrel at the age of twelve. But she was found, and dragged orf to Cawdor Castle to be married. Frightful story, isn't it? But the point is, the cheese they were making was probably caboc. I say, do have another tot of Balblair . . . Isn't this fun!'

Crowdie

This is the most basic cheese recipe of all, and so simple to make you wonder why no one bothers. I have found that full-cream Jersey or Guernsey milk produces the best result.

Pour the milk into a wide china bowl, cover with a clean cloth and leave it on a very, very slow heat – the hotplate of a Rayburn or Aga is ideal – overnight.

When you peer under the cloth in the morning the milk should have separated into curds and whey, the curds floating in a single lump on the surface of the whey. When cool, the curds will have set a little more and can be drained off the whey through a colander lined with muslin set over a pan.

Leave the curds to rest in the muslin for an hour or two until they take on a more solid appearance, then gather up the muslin and squeeze out any remaining moisture. Remove the curds into a bowl, mix with a fork, add a little salt. Roll the crowdie into a ball and leave in the fridge for a day or so before eating. It is wonderful for breakfast, with honey and toasted almonds.

In the course of my gastronomic travels in Britain I have thought a great deal, possibly more than is desirable, about Bed and Breakfast. I have pored over Bed and Breakfast guides and wondered why anyone in their right mind would call their establishment 'Nessun Dorma' and whether 'Highland hospitality at its best' means that you are woken by a piper at dawn and served devilled grouse for breakfast. I have lain in bed at 7.30 a.m. having been woken by the smell of frying vegetable oil, and wondered why it is that B&Bs never seem to serve what I would like – a cup of good, strong coffee, a glass of fresh orange juice and a basket of buttery croissants – at the time that I would like it. I have marvelled at the persistence in the national culinary repertoire of that monstrous invention, fried bread. (You can imagine a croûton, a hunk of good bread crisped up in the drippings of a pan of butter, olive oil or duck fat, as being a rather delicious sort of late-breakfast-on-a-Sunday food. But not a slice of Mother's Pride deep-fried in old Mazola at eight in the morning.) And I have felt the wonderful uplifting sense of freedom that comes when you have paid your cheque, climbed in the car, cranked up the music and roared away from all that doily-covered, swirly-carpeted claustrophobia.

The Highlands of Scotland must harbour more guest houses than anywhere on the planet. Along the roadsides of Loch Ness and the Great Glen, every other converted cow-byre and brick-built bungalow seems to have the B&B sign outside it, often with the curious addition that reads 'NO VACANCIES' unless the NO bit happens to be covered up, in which case you're in luck.

At my first Highland B&B the granny, a former crofter, lived next door in the old dwelling house. She had once kept a couple of cows, a field of potatoes and a boat on the shore of the loch. Now, at age ninety, she was reduced to squinting through net curtains at her son and daughter-in-law in their modern bungalow.

I remember a dark dining room with a shagpile carpet. It was a musical family: there was a clarsach harp in the corner, and the music on the piano was the pipe tune 'Morag of Dunvegan'. And, sure enough, in the next room I could hear someone practising the pipe-chanter: a muted, weedy sound; the genie trapped inside the bottle. The head of the household, who had worked most of his life on a salmon farm, told me his great uncle once piped for Queen Victoria, and that he and his wife were hoping the genes came through in their little girl.

'What would you like, then, for your tea tonight, dearie? Chicken tikka, or salmon?' his wife called through the dining-room door, while I peered at a photo on the mantelpiece of a brawny man in a kilt undergoing some kind of physical strain at a Highland games.

My next night's hosts could not have been more different. Fred and Celia had moved up from Purley to a former stables on the edge of the Great Glen, realising that here at least they would never be short of business, since the Glen attracts stag hunts from all over the world.

'There are four and a half thousand deer on this estate,' said Fred as he showed me to my table in a dining room that in a few weeks' time would echo with chattering Japanese and German voices.

Celia was a good cook and a friendly woman who, rather than abandon me to ponder in silence her collection of porcelain dogs, leaned against the doorjamb instead and chatted about the good life and food she had found on escaping from Purley. Serving me a mushroom soup, creamy and strongly fungal, set her off on a misty-eyed recollection of that moment towards the end of summer when a friend comes by with a shopping bag full of chanterelles for her.

'I always think of Harvey Nicks, the amount you shell out for a few tiny chanterelles, a couple of ceps. And here I am getting them by the bagful. Heavenly.'

Scotland's great strength gastronomically speaking was always its first-class raw material. There were always certain things you couldn't get easily, though: most of the shellfish was grabbed as it came off the boats by Spanish and French fishmongers who knew a good thing when they saw it, so paradoxically locals found it a rare and expensive commodity. Vegetables used to be hard to come by. 'I shop at Tesco's and Sainsbury's in Inverness. Everything's available these days, up here,' said Celia. The salmon steak she gave me next came from a farmed fish, but it was none the worse for that, in its rich hollandaise with tiny prawns. 'Game I get from Letterfinlay, down the road. You could try talking to them. There's a smokehouse there too, right on the edge of the loch. Terribly picturesque.'

As I polished off the last of a sticky toffee pudding with cream, the pink and white Dresden china clock on the mantelpiece showed it was just before seven o'clock. Never in my life had I eaten dinner quite so early; it would still be light for another three hours. I set off on a sheep path up the mountainside. At first the air was full of the medicine-sweet aroma of gorse. Then there was nothing but stubbly brown heather and water drip-drip-dripping, filtering down through sodden moss and green-grey rock faces. I put my face under a miniature waterfall; it was icy cold and zingy with minerals.

Back down the valley, where I had come from, sheep looked

like maggots against the dark-green river plain. At my feet were parties of glossy black slugs, gleefully awaiting the terrific summer rainstorm I could see beginning to power its way towards me along the Glen. If I raised my eyes in that direction, I saw Ansel Adams skylines mixing mist, cloud and sun rays in spectacular chiaroscuro, with mountains operatically draped in grey mist. It was a landscape so big, old and silent that lone cars on the loch road seemed to roar like aircraft.

As the first fat drops hit the back of my neck, I ran down the hill in the fading light.

Fred and Celia were what is known in Scotland as 'white settlers'. I first heard the term from the mouth of the lady at Letterfinlay as she clumped around her kitchen fixing me a cup of instant. She was born in Orkney and as a child remembered hearing stories about the Clearances, the barbaric English crime, tantamount to ethnic cleansing, by which Highlanders were uprooted from their land in the eighteenth century.

'People were just rounded up and moved, like animals,' she said, anger tinting the edges of her voice. I almost felt I should apologise. 'Even now there's still prejudice. People think we've got haithair in our ears!'

I looked around the kitchen. It was a real live country kitchen, neon-lit and un-designed and messy. Four large dog bowls were in position around the cooker, as if staking their claim. Country kitchens have changed, however, even this far from the centres of gastro-fashion; this one had lemon grass in a pot and sherry vinegar among the Lea & Perrins and Angostura bitters. On the wall was a scroll with a recipe for Stuffed Camel ('Serve on a bed of rice').

Roy, a man with a hairy, red-white-and-grey complicated face, sat me down in the living room. Out of the window was the loch, a few yards away, and behind it a staggering wall of mountain splashily coloured in brown and green and foamed on top with billowing cloud.

'I used to hunt that hillside,' he said, gazing at it. 'I used to have a small game dealership, took Germans out to stalk. Everything's changed now; there's much cheaper stalking in Russia. Here there are too many deer and not enough space, with so much forestry going on their natural habitat's being eroded. There's a glut, basically. We also do cakes, Scottish cheeses, smoked food, chocolates. And seafood of course. We only buy from traditional creel operators. The creel is a basket they put down. It's more humane. It means that undersized cod, for example, gets thrown back. Not like the Spanish, they use a dredging technique. It just sweeps up everything in its path.'

Letterfinlay might claim to supply everything from the castle to the croft, but what, I wondered aloud, do ordinary people in the Highlands actually eat? If I barged into a cottage one teatime, what would I find on the table?

Roy chuckled at this idea. 'Probably Findus. Frozen vegetables. There's still a lot of it aboot. I'm not trying to suggest everyone's eating like kings.

'If you want to know how people used to eat, take a look at that,' he said, pointing to a picture on the wall.

It was a print dated 1856 entitled *Weighing the Deer*, and it showed a chaotic scene of rural Scottish life, dead animals draped over tables in a hall full of milling people, many wearing grins suggestive of drunkenness, lust and/or sheer delight at the sight of so much food. In the middle of it all, a giant stag with fearsome antlers lolled on an enormous balance. It seemed a less than realistic picture of food habits either then or now. Most of the game caught on Scottish estates would have gone straight to the laird's pantry, or been sent South to London; proportionately little would have filtered down the class system locally, unless it were to estate workers who might be granted the odd brace of pheasant from time to time. The historical problem of Scottish food, then and now, is that little of the best of it is eaten by those who have a natural right to do so.

The ferry to Skye had been cancelled; the summer sky loured suddenly dark, the sea whipping up into peaks. I doubled back a little way along the west coast, stopping every so often to take in the complicated views. The main road shrank to a single track, but every few yards swelled up into a passing place with a white diamond sign, giving rise to a delicate ritual of thanks (a slight raising of the hand from the steering wheel, a smile, a mouthed 'thank you') every time one car stopped for another.

For a while the road skirted the foreshore, where the terrain was green and boggy; there were clumps of iris among the marsh grasses and a soft saltiness to the air. Then it wound up among straggly beeches, frothing up briefly into mossy woods of ash and oak, and up further into pine forest and heather-clad moorland and sinister miniature lochs fringed with slimy rushes. Between the woods and the water, there were big grey houses, little grey churches, and small white modern croft-houses offering 'en suite facilities'.

Waiting in Mallaig for the next boat, I wandered round a supermarket, picking up the usual ironies: Findus fish fingers,

Norwegian salmon and prawns from the South China Sea. In the chill cabinet, alongside squares of Canadian Cheddar and roundels of St Ivel, lurked a solitary haggis. And there were fried-breakfast kits in polystyrene trays featuring slices of white pudding, black pudding, fruity pudding, lorne. There was no bread of any real edibility, except for some white morning rolls, so called because they are made to be eaten in the morning and, like the French baguette, aren't supposed to last until the afternoon, though in fact most commercial morning rolls are so full of preservatives they stay fresh for days.

I looked in on Andy Race, seafood king of the West Coast, and talked with him for a while, about the cunning Norwegians with their inferior salmon, which, since it began to flood the British market in the 1980s, had pushed prices and profit margins as low as they would go. And the dastardly Spaniards: 'They've been poking around here begging for fish,' he said, making them sound like alley cats.

All at once the sea was startlingly blue again and the waves whipped up by the retreating storm were startlingly white – such is the whimsical nature of the Highland climate – and in the distance I could see the abrupt shapes of what some people call the Advocaat islands: Eigg, Rhum and Muck. In the waters of the harbour a family of seals was peacefully lolling, rolling, gyrating in the water with the self-satisfied air of animals or people when they have just eaten their fill of the freshest fish imaginable. It was nice to think that the Spanish had competition.

I was the only passenger on the rusty old boat as it cranked and creaked into a thick humid fog, the island invisible but ominously present ahead of me. The fog gave way to summer stormclouds, and then to rain. Sheltering under the dripping metal of the overhanging upper deck, I listened to the rainfall combine with the spattering spitting of a frying pan in the tiny galley alongside me, where a young crewman was cooking up a couple of eggs, slapping them finally between two slices of Mother's Pride and disappearing up to the bridge to help speed my bonny boat like a bird on the wing.

There was certainly no lack of choice for places to stay on Skye. It was simply a question of randomly turning off the road from Dunvegan with its Passing Places, and inquiring of Mrs Macleod or McInnes or MacKinnon or indeed Ms Kozikowska or Mr Van der Vliet whether a room could be had for the night at their little white Skye crofthouse – take your choice of old and whitewash-crumbly or modern and bungaloid. Once more I had cause to thank St Lawrence (the patron saint of cooks and foodies, since he was grilled to death) because Murdo Grant, B&B proprietor by Glendale, had a mother who, as a crofting woman all her life, knew more about the old ways of Highland food than most grannies in the vicinity had had hot dinners.

Through her daughter, she invited me in for a cup of tea and a chat. The old lady lived on her own in a cottage that had once been the village post office, and I walked there from Murdo's house along a winding road with the loch to one side and a complicated landscape of purple-green-brown hillsides, dotted with houses and sheep, both white, beyond it. Every few hundred yards a burn came innocently burbling down towards the sea, filling the silence with its sound. The air smelled crisp with iodine and sea ozone.

There was someone at home, talking on the phone in a Gaelic oddly interspersed with English. The talk all over the island was of a carful of kids killed on the road the previous week, and of the funeral the day before – a solemn affair, when cars jammed the country roads near Armadale and sad young people in ill-fitting black suits streamed along the hedgerows towards a barn of a Kirk with high windows. I heard the voice wind up the conversation and footsteps come to the door and hands open it. Inside was a dark, tiny sitting room with a ticking clock and a dresser adorned with mementoes of the Algarve.

'Och, dreadful, a shocking thing,' said Mrs Mackie, shaking her head as she hobbled to the kitchen to freshen up the pot. She was a short solid lady, slowing down and rusty of limb, but her eyes sparkled merrily. She was born on the tiny island of Raasay, a sliver of land falling away from the right-hand claw of Skye, and talked about 'moving over here' as though they were two different continents.

'When I was a child there was quite a lot of cultivated land over here. There was hay and oats. At home we lived quite well, quite well. We had three milking cows. And we planted potatoes, turnips, rhubarb, gooseberry, blackcurrants . . .' She stopped, concentrating. The jams her mother made . . . 'We had a rowan tree. She used to make rowan and apple jelly, and crab apple.'

Crofting is subsistence farming. When you realise what a tough life it must be, all those B&Bs suddenly make a lot of sense. Yet all the ingredients were there for what seems a good, if monotonous diet. Hebridean soil being wafer-thin – basically a skein of rotted matter fastened by grass to the rock beneath – most food was grown in special patches of deeper earth called lazybeds. The cows were the mainstay of life. From their milk came crowdie.

'This is how we did it,' said Mrs Mackie, enthusiasm making her twist and fidget in her armchair. 'You set the milk in basins. In the winter you put it by the stove. And in July and August, if the weather was a bit thundery, the milk would go thick by itself. You poured off the whey – you could use that instead of cream of tartar for girdle scones. And what was left was crowdie.' Girdle scones are griddle scones, a kind of flatbread cooked directly on top of the stove.

A staple dish was brose: oatmeal boiled up with salt, water or milk, and 'a wee lump of butter'. There was plenty of fish on the Isle of Raasay, but very little meat in summer. Once a week the family ate a good mutton broth. Prime cuts of meat were salted and put away. 'We made little cuts and rubbed in coarse salt. That way it might last two months. But it wouldn't always last that long, dear me noo, not in our family,' she chuckled.

She cast a glance at my untouched cup of tea. 'Is it a bit strong, dear? Fetch the milk, would you, dear, from the kitchen? I think I'll have a drop more myself.'

In Mrs Mackie's fridge, I saw, were a lump of cheddar, a packet of industrial ham, some small tomatoes and half a pan of something that could have been vegetable soup.

She had been peering at the *West Highland Free Press* with her thick reading glasses on. She was all of a jitter because the previous week the *Press* had carried a recipe for curing mackerel, and she had tried it.

'I've proved it a delicacy,' she said triumphantly. 'I believe it comes from the isle of Barra. The recipe says take the mackerel and split them down the back; of course you've cleaned them well. Then you cover them with salt and brown sugar overnight. Then, in July and August – the weather *must* be sunny – it wouldn't do if a shower got to it – you hang them on the clothesline. You cover them with a fine net. Sprinkle the net with black pepper, for the flies. And that'll keep one whole winter. With new potatoes alongside, believe me, it's really a delicacy.'

Since Mrs M. was born in the 1920s, the population of Skye has declined from 11,500 to 7,000.

As a young woman, when she moved 'over here', Mrs M. worked in what would now be called the catering industry, making ice cream for the schoolchildren in Portree, capital of Skye. Thereafter she went to one of the great houses on the island, where the food was both grander and more varied than that of the crofthouse. There were vegetables and herbs in abundance, since the house had a big walled garden and a full-time gardener. There was plenty of beef and lamb, and game from the estate. She knew few recipes at the start, but increased her repertoire with the help of Mrs Beeton's famous book.

'There's no doubt we had a healthy life,' she told me. Grannies like her are the backbone of Scottish life, the hidden battery that drives the starter motor of the country.

Her daughter was right: once she started on the subject of food and the old days, there was no stopping her.

She sounded off furiously on the subject of the young and their dreadful diet. 'The black stuff that comes in a tin. What's it called? Heaven only knows what's in that rubbish. And they drink it by the gallon.'

Mrs Mackie must be the last person in Britain not to know that the black stuff that comes in a tin is called Coca-Cola.

There is no doubt that dining at the Altnaharrie Inn is a bit of a performance. You will have had to make your reservation several weeks ahead, because Altnaharrie is now firmly inscribed in the itinerary of the International Three Star Dining Club, which means that gastro-pilgrims from London, America and Japan book it solid.

You will have to drive a long way north (from wherever you are coming, it's a long way north) and along Loch Broom to the small and somewhat grubby harbour town of Ullapool. You will turn up at the dockside in the early afternoon, from where a canopied launch chugs out across the calm water. To your left is the fjord-like expanse of the loch, to your right the open sea. And in a few minutes the boat has left behind the little port with its harbour smell of engine oil and chip shops, and all eyes swivel towards the sight ahead: a white speck on the rim of loch and land which gradually becomes a little white house by the waterside in a miniature valley of green that stands out from the starkness of the hillside beyond.

The story of the Altnaharrie Inn has many of the ingredients of a familiar narrative. A husband and wife without any previous experience of catering and hotel-keeping take over a run-down house in the country and begin offering meals and accommodation when they realise their idyll has got to pay its way.

For a restaurant with rooms in one of the remotest locations in Great Britain, run by two people who have never had a day's training in their life, the Inn hasn't done badly. Food cognoscenti I spoke to about it before my visit lowered their voices reverentially, suggesting we were referring to one of the very few places in the British Isles where cooking reaches the status of a true art form.

'People say, "Oh, we went with such high expectations,"' said the editor of *The Good Food Guide*. 'But, interestingly, what many of them then say is that those expectations were actually exceeded. Yet, as with all the great chefs, Gunn's cooking is highly focused, rather straightforward in some ways. So there is, yes, a kind of magic about the place.'

When they settled in the Highlands in the early 1980s Fred Brown and Gunn Eriksen can have had no very precise idea of where the course of their lives would take them. Fred is a vet by profession and a seaman by persuasion who had spent several years pottering on his yacht before meeting Gunn, from Norway, and bringing her back to his native Scotland.

There had always been an inn on the site, originally for drovers bringing cattle to and from Inverness. It had been insensitively modernised, so Fred and Gunn set about recapturing its original architectural character as a Highland crofthouse, leaving interior walls white and uneven, before decorating the place in their own unique style, adding richly coloured rugs, tapestried chairs, heavy swags of curtain and a multitude of small paintings, engravings and quirky *objets*. Brown and Eriksen were passionate nature-lovers, and created only a small formal garden around the hotel while leaving the rest of its wild surroundings intact.

On the boat-trip over, training my eyes on the vision in front of me, I was surprised to discover that I was slightly nervous, a state I had only ever been in before a meal when arriving at some extremely grand and serious restaurant in France. Would this be the sort of place, I wondered, where gastronomic skills such as ability to pair wine with food, identify rare species of mushroom and pronounce correctly the names of obscure cheeses were to be tested to the limit?

Nothing could have been further from the truth: the Altnaharrie's atmosphere was relaxed and relaxing. From the moment I was met at the jetty by Fred Brown, a quiet smiling grey-haired Scottish gentleman in a Nehru jacket, I was in safe hands. Fred took me through the menu for the evening and handed me a copy of the wine list, a tome-like document of impressive range and quality with a notable slant towards Burgundy, as Fred feels this is the wine that best suits Gunn's voluptuous cooking.

I nibbled on a strawberry from the fruit bowl and gazed out over the loch, where a group of porpoises played amazingly near the shore. I began to take in the details of my room and its decor. A yellow and blue colour scheme meticulously observed, right down to the blue glass beakers and the tiny still-life of two yellow pears on a Cornish blue-striped dish.

In the dining room, big enough for a maximum of eighteen diners, we gathered in a shy silence, the evening's fortunate few. There was no music in the room. The only extraneous sound was the quiet rhythmical plashing of the waves on the loch.

When the first course arrived, the room went into a stunned, deeper silence. On an enormous plate with gold edging was a composition of forms and vibrant colours worthy of Matisse. The meat of a whole lobster claw, miraculously extracted whole, slices of lobster meat, shavings of white truffle and a tiny salad of lambs lettuce, rocket, coriander and dill were arranged around an intermingling of two sauces – one an intense lobster-pink, made with the roe of the beast, and another ivory white, conjured from the cooking juices and champagne, frothed up slightly with a little Beaufort cheese.

There followed a sublime asparagus soup with an intense purée of fresh asparagus slaked into it and a scoop of asparagus mousse at its centre. Eriksen seemed fond of these triple concertos on the same basic flavour-theme. I saw that one dish was linked subtly to another, so that the meal began to take on a kind of overarching logic. Sitting in the soup was a morsel of squat lobster tail meat, taking us back to the previous course. And underneath the mousse was a succulent little chunk of foie gras, which duly referred us forward to the next dish: the legs and breast of a squab, perfectly roasted, upon a more substantial slab of foie gras and alongside a finely sliced, hauntingly flavoured piece of roasted kohl rabi. A few morels and chanterelles were scattered about on a delicious reduction sauce made with red Burgundy. And as a garnish, a final brushstroke, to the far left of the plate I spied a few brilliant green stalks of something that appeared to be, yes it was, wild asparagus. *Et voilá*.

So far, so very good. Now it was Fred's turn to take centre stage. He glided around the small dining room reciting from memory in his gravelly Scots voice the names of two dozen cheeses, hailing from France, Scotland, England and Norway. I chose Epoisse, Bonchester, Jarlsberg and Beaufort (now where had I tasted that one recently?).

Then it was on to the puddings. Three separate dishes, each a set of variations on a theme. Tonight there was pineapple (sorbet, sauce, a baked thin slice of the fruit); chocolate (a tear-shaped box filled with mousse, ice cream, thickly dribbled chocolate-and-cassis sauce); and caramel (ice cream, caramelised pear, spun sugar), all three components of the meal's second act as fastidiously thought out and presented as those of the first.

This was Event Cuisine at its most sensuous and refined, yet it seemed an entirely personal creation, eschewing completely the modish ingredients, the pseudo-Mediterranean and pseudo-Oriental clichés of the 1990s. The dinner I ate at the Altnaharrie Inn made most British restaurant food look like the product of an assembly-line.

Next morning, after a breakfast which at last attained my ideal – a good café au lait, a glass of orange juice and a meltingly buttery homemade croissant – Fred had arranged for me to meet Ms Eriksen. It was a rare privilege, because Gunn is rarely glimpsed out of her kitchen, leaving even longstanding fans of her cooking to speculate on her appearance and personality.

I had always had a mental picture of a thin, wiry middle-aged woman, greying hair scraped back from a face wearied by years of work and concentration, so what emerged from the kitchen door and strode across the lawn into the summer morning was a complete surprise. She was a robustly pretty Nordic woman in her late thirties, with colour in her cheeks and a mane of blonde hair that she wore loosely tied up on her head. She had taken a quick break from the morning's baking, and squinted in the unaccustomed sunlight.

Visitors to the Altnaharrie often go away wondering about the culinary genius of this remarkable woman, who is rumoured never to have had a day's training in her life. Did she ever have a model, a guru, a pattern to follow?

She shrugged and smiled. 'No, I wouldn't say so. I know that I have a very forgiving mother who would let us cook and make a mess and involved us from a very early age, standing on chairs making bread and cakes and cookies and black puddings. It was purely because I wanted to learn. The freedom to do things and the freedom to think, and not to be knocked down for it – that's very important.'

Gunn is perpetually inspired by the world around her, both in Scotland and at their farmhouse in the Norwegian countryside, where she and Fred spend a few months every year. 'Inspiration comes in many guises, doesn't it?' she mused. 'But the scenery here matters a lot to me – the wildness of it, together with the softness of Altnaharrie. The hills are very stark, yet there's a certain lushness too. For me, inspiration comes in visual forms as well as flavours.'

It is a logical extension of her love of landscape that she tries to use local produce whenever possible. Fish, shellfish and meat are all sourced in the Highlands. Smoked seafood comes from Summer Isles Foods, along the coast at Achiltibuie. Wild mushrooms, garlic, hawthorn flowers and asparagus are gathered from the hills behind the house. Everything else comes rumbling up from Edinburgh, London and France and has to be 'brought across', which has in the past created some terrible logistical problems. Even as we spoke, a young guy was running ashore with a crate full of live local scallops, doubtless intended for this evening's daily remake of Babette's Feast.

'This is probably the craziest place in the world to have a restaurant!' said Gunn, grinning, shaking out her mane of golden hair and letting it fall down her back. 'To have opened in London would have been heaven in comparison. But I do love Scotland, and I adore the Highlands, and it was something I was simply determined to do. As for this place in particular . . . well, it just does something very special for me. I mean, look at that.'

She flung out her hand towards the loch, a passionate

gesture, and my gaze followed her fingers across the waters as calm as mercury, the pale blue sky reflected perfectly in them and, beyond, the wild hillsides, their bolts of deep pink heather and bottle-green woodland and, scattered on the forest floor, their secret cache of chanterelles. I made a mental note to pick up a bagful before setting out on my long journey to the South.

'I mean, honestly, have you ever seen anything more delicious in your life?' asked Gunn.

10

east anglia

back to cambridge on the oyster trail

In a single day and night I drove the country top to bottom, stopping off for a few hours in a Stygian service station on the A1 to sip a chaste mineral water and nibble an apple, feeling bloated and cross-eyed and miserable.

For the last three months I'd done little but eat and drive, eat and drive, and the combination was taking its toll. My skin had completely lost whatever pH balance it might once have had; my palms were sweaty, my nose was shiny. The psychological effects of so much gourmandise were alarming. I was so accustomed to thinking about food all day long, even when I was not actually consuming the stuff, that I now found it hard to make brain-space for any other subject.

Worst of all, I was developing a paunch. To anyone else it

might have looked small; to me, who had always thought of myself as trim and wiry, it was a dreadful aberration. I pulled in my stomach using all the force of my diaphragm, but the too sullied flesh refused to melt. For the first time in my life I understood something of the agonising mental distortions of anorexia. When I looked at myself in the mirror, I saw Bernard Manning.

I resolved to punish myself, in true Protestant style, for the excesses of the past year. For a fortnight I would follow the notorious cabbage soup diet, the quick-fix, seven-day cult diet supposedly promulgated by the coronary department of the Sacred Heart Memorial Hospital, though in fact no such establishment actually exists. In one of the most efficacious and unpleasant food régimes ever devised, the patient must eat almost nothing but cabbage soup. The soup may be garnished with the occasional banana or potato, but – and this is the real cruelty of the thing – he can eat as much of it as he likes.

Chris Patten, former Governor of Hong Kong, was an early celebrity convert to the diet. 'I have to say my love of cabbage soup has somewhat diminished,' he was quoted as saying after losing ten pounds by following it for a week. 'You can have it mashed down, shredded and spiced, but there is still a relentlessness about it which makes me understand central European history more clearly.'

I invested in a sackful of organic Savoy cabbages at Middle Farm, holed myself up in the granny flat at Filtington Hall and set to boiling up great pans of the vegetable, until the flat smelled like a prison kitchen.

For the first few days it was fine. It was a blessed relief, in a way, to know that from one meal to the next there was never any doubt about what you would be eating; no need to peruse a menu. I felt vigorous and healthy and slightly exhilarated by my own increased self-esteem. I even imagined, ridiculously, that I was already losing a little weight around the waist.

As the days wore on, however, I understood the bitter reaction of that foreign traveller in Britain who once wrote: 'The British have three vegetables, and two of them are cabbage.' Though I tried not to cook the cabbage more than al dente, the intolerable, unalterable *cabbageyness* of the soup drove me to distraction. On day four, bubbles began to appear on its surface. I dared not even step out of the flat, fearing that my pores had begun to exude the same methane reek that surrounded me all day long.

In a week I had indeed lost a few pounds, but I now longed to gain a few more. I needed to be on the road again, to taste variety and pleasure, to experience again the excitement of eating in a country where a little effort can bring such rich and unpredictable rewards.

I had eaten my way up the west coast of Britain; now I would see how much I could stomach of the east. One of the few agreeable effects of the fast had been that, having had little actual eating to do, I had had plenty of time to catch up on some gastronomic literature. According to all the authorities, East Anglia was famous for fine seafood, poultry, vegetables and fruit. There was little cheese, since dairy farming had never been widely practised, but there were Lincolnshire potatoes, Norfolk apples, Cambridgeshire asparagus, Essex bacons . . . I was alarmed to note the widespread agricultural importance in the Eastern counties of the brassica family, source of my recent woes, but I would steer clear of that. I would eat brown shrimps, and slices of sweet Suffolk ham. I would feast on oysters. 'The coasts most celebrated, in England, for them, are those of Essex and Suffolk,' pronounces Isabella Beeton in her great manual for life, *The Book of Household Management*. I would have to go gently for a while, to allow my metabolism time to get back up to speed. But I might as well start as I meant to go on, at one of the most famous restaurants on the East Coast: the Royal Native Oyster Stores in Whitstable, Kent.

I showered off the cabbage and drove there, swinging hungrily around the M25, and arrived at midday under a late summer sun that had done nothing to improve the colour of the Thames estuary, which was its usual unappetising shade of beige.

If you had no idea about Whitstable's major claim to fame you might get an inkling of it from the names of some of the businesses in the town: there is the Oyster Dry Cleaning Company, the Oyster Bed and Breakfast, even the Imperial Oyster Cinema, housed in part of an old warehouse belonging to the Royal Native Oyster Stores, the ground floor of which is now a simple restaurant with views out across the slimy estuary.

I needed a pick-me-up: what better than a dozen oysters to soothe the mind and refresh the body? The waitress brought me bread and fine French butter from the Charente firm of Lescure, and halfway into my first glass of chilled Alsace Tokay Pinot Gris I felt better already.

The oysters arrived on a bed of ice in a round aluminium tray decorated with dark strands of seaweed and bright chunks of lemon, a pot of pink shallot vinegar at its centre. The Native Oyster, *Ostrea edulis*, is a more highly prized and expensive variety than its cousin the Pacific, *Crassostrea gigas*. Its shell is smoother, paler, rounder; its body smaller, paler and slightly fatter. Being relatively feeble and disease-prone, the Native has had a hard time recently thanks to pollution, over-fishing and the parasite bonamia, which has decimated stocks. It also takes five years to reach maturity, compared to the Pacific's two or three. It is well worth the wait, however, since the flesh of the Native has a delicate sweetness and a reverberant flavour that the coarser, stronger Pacific lacks. When it comes to shellfish, a certain amount of racial prejudice is inevitable.

My oysters were slipping down in thick fleshy mouthfuls, leaving a slightly chalky dryness on the tongue, which coincided with a definite rush as the iodine and sea-salt hit the bloodstream like champagne. Oysters are less about taste than pure sensation, chemistry working hand in hand with biology, so that when I left the restaurant and crunched down the shingle past the boats pulled up out of the mud, I barely noticed that the sun had disappeared and the sky was now the same colour as the thick brown Thames; I was still in the grip of my twelve-oyster high.

The oyster was the Big Mac of the nineteenth century. Along the sea wall at Whitstable you can read the figures in black and white as you brave the spray whipping up off the water: in the course of the year 1862 the Company of Free Fishers and Dredgers, still the main purveyors around these parts, sent no less than 60 million oysters to the London market. These days it is rich people's food, but in Victorian London you could buy two hundred for four shillings, causing Sam Weller in Dickens's *Pickwick Papers* to exclaim, much quotedly, that 'poverty and oysters always seem to go together . . . the poorer the place is, the greater call there seems to be for oysters . . . here's a oyster stall to every half-dozen houses. The street's lined vit 'em. Blessed if I don't think that ven a man's wery poor, he rushes out of his lodgings, and eats oysters in reg'lar desperation.'

Around the coast of Britain there is a series of places where you can sit and gorge on locally caught oysters and drink white wine. If this were France it would probably be talked up into a fully fledged Route des Huîtres. This being Britain, it isn't. But one could almost put together a guidebook entitled *Humble But Endearing Oyster Places*, into which slim volume would go the Loch Fyne Oyster Bar on the west coast of Scotland, Carew's in West Wales, the Duchy of Cornwall Oyster Farm, the Company Shed in West Mersea in the tulgy Essex marshland south of Colchester, and the Butley Orford Oysterage in Suffolk in the heart of East Coast bivalve country.

I had been to the Oysterage once about ten years before, and it didn't appear to have changed a jot. The restaurant was more or less a single room looking like a 1960s waiting room, with a bright green stripe around the walls and schoolroom chairs. The sugar was still kept in stainless steel bowls and the menu in one of those padded plastic folders with MENU in swirly writing on the front. Even the waitresses, shuffling local girls with believable smiles, seemed the same. One of them kept mixing up the orders.

'Your scallops, sir, madam,' she announced cautiously, putting them down in front of a surprised couple.

'Oh, but that's not what we ordered,' said the woman.

'I think they're ours, love,' called a grey-permed lady who had popped out for a late tea with her grey-permed friend.

And the waitress gratefully deposited the plates on their table and the ladies tucked in. I could see that the scallops had a frill of mashed potato piped around the edge. Fanny Cradock would have approved.

The same girl then brought me pre-sliced Hovis and a saucer of margarine, quickly followed by a dozen oysters. The oysters they served here were enormous Pacifics, the shells almost as big as my hand and the mollusc itself a full-to-bursting juicy mouthful of delicately flavoured tender oyster meat. To accompany them I took care to drink a local wine, Shawsgate 1991 Muller-Thurgau, from just around the corner near Framlingham, where Mary Tudor was crowned Queen. It was an aromatic and crisp wine, full of vitality, tasting of Bramley apples and lemon peel with a drop or two of honey as the tartness receded. It was a gunshot marriage, this Suffolk seafood and this Suffolk wine, but it worked out perfectly. It was clear to me the British now have what the French have in Gros Plant du Pays Nantais and the Spanish in manzanilla: white wines to drink with our own seafood *in situ*, at a table no more than a few miles from where fish was caught and wine was made.

Such a decadent high tea had to be compensated for, so I set off out of the village and along the coast, through boggy farmland beside the sluggish River Alde, which meanders almost parallel to the sea for a while before eventually deciding, what the hell, that it might as well meet the ocean now, can't put off the moment for ever.

This was the Suffolk of myth, memory and Britten operas: flat, wide-skied, faintly sinister in its visual confusion of sea and land with marsh, creek, sandbank, inlet and everything else that is neither one nor the other. Beside Orford Creek was a bedraggled-looking cottage and outbuildings and I walked towards them, making certain this was the house of Mr William

Pinney, owner of Suffolk's premier seafood empire, by the oyster shell I saw poking out of the mud-slicked driveway.

It has to be said there is not much sport in oyster fishing. They just lie there in the mud and wait. We crunched over a heap of their shells, scrambled up the earth dike and down a muddy path towards the creek. The sudden view, peaceful and free of mankind, made me sigh happily. The tide was low, leaving the river bed a curving arm of pale mud lined with the lush green of marsh grasses. A few seabirds, no doubt used to the occasional free oyster, wheeled expectantly overhead.

In the foreground a few grimy little boats lay sprawled on the mud. One of these was Mr Pinney's oyster boat, which when fishing is in progress serves to pull the dredger along the bottom of the creek.

The dredger was a rusted old iron contraption looking rather like the head of a very large prongless rake, with a kind of rope bag at the back into which the oysters tumble as they are scooped from their gooey beds. The babies, known as spats, come up from Whitstable, and Mr Pinney puts them in at different points of the creek to begin their three-year sojourn.

Beneath their duvet of mud, then, the oysters pass their comfortable lives, rocked by the rise and fall of the tide. In many ways it seems an enviable existence. Enviable, that is, until the moment of rude awakening by a big-armed Suffolk lady armed with a knife, who prises off your clothing and offers you on a bed of ice to ravenous decadents, to be sprinkled with Tabasco and swallowed alive.

Does culture bring affluence, or is it the other way round? Are Britten and Pears indirectly responsible for the surprising number of good restaurants in the Aldeburgh area, or did they come to the Suffolk coast because there was good eating to be done? The answer is surely the former. This is how it goes: *artistes* value places for their low-rent housing, aesthetic beauty and simple traditional inhabitants who don't beat them up. They bring their artistic friends for the weekends; they bring *their* friends, and the new bohemian and middle-class elements in the area import their metropolitan ideas of food. And so, in the case of Aldeburgh, you have Regatta, the Lighthouse and the Café 152: three restaurants that would be almost as much at home in Soho as in Southwold, in Farringdon as in Framlingham.

It is the decor that takes longest to catch up. At 152, the walls were a provincial Provençal shade of terracotta that Londoners would have sneered at; there were plasticated tablecloths and candles stuck in wine bottles. The food, on the other hand, was immaculately up-to-date.

This was the first meal I'd ever eaten in East Anglia that had anything resembling style about it. The robust terrine of pheasant and pigeon, irregularly marbled pink white and green, like the crazy paving in provincial back gardens, came with a fresh garlicky-gingery pickle of pear and fig. To my surprise the cod fillet on Puy lentils with salsa verde actually worked, the lentils smoky and intensely savoury with the fish providing the texture and solidity of flavour and the very un-Mexican *salsa* of capers, garlic and parsley giving both a generous lift.

Woodbridge had once been a vibrant little Suffolk market town, with crowds coming in from the surrounding villages to sell and be sold to. Now, following a pattern replicating itself all over Britain, the two big Tescos, a Sainsbury's and an Asda outside the town were leaching the commercial life from its heart. Fifty thousand small grocers closed their doors in Britain between 1986 and 1996, while food superstores multiplied from 432 to 1,034. Research has shown that sales in traditional grocers fall by between 13 and 50 per cent when a superstore opens on the outskirts.

In Woodbridge's one and only proper food shop, the delicatessen Loaves and Fishes, I stood with the owner as he filled the wooden shelves with tastefully packaged wholefoods, and we railed enjoyably against the supermarkets and the terrible uniformity they impose on us all, eventually agreeing that in fact there are very few things in the world that come as close to pure, naked evil as an out-of-town Tesco.

He led me out of the front door to the little display of local produce, a golden cache of quinces, a basket of bletted medlars, a box of Norfolk Royal apples and a sack of the handsomest walnuts I had ever seen. The nuts were a deep and beautiful brown colour, fatter than most walnuts and much more deeply ribbed and wrinkled on the surface. The shell had two very distinct and bulbous halves to it, reminding me of the medieval theory that walnuts had to be good for the brain because they resembled it so uncannily. Inside there was a much greater ratio of shell to flesh than is usually the case, but the luscious, haunting creaminess of the nut itself was a revelation.

I bought some unctuous local sheep's cheese, as oozy as a good Brie, a slab of tangy, deep yellow, mature Lincolnshire Poacher, surely East Anglia's greatest cheese, and a bag of D'Arcy Spice apples, a variety first found growing in an Essex garden in the eighteenth century.

Now all my Anglian picnic needed was a few slices of good ham. Fortunately for me, as it happened, two of the best ham producers in the region were to be found in the inland village of Peasenhall. Suffolk is one of the handful of British counties to have its name attached to a particular recipe or cure for ham. 'Wiltshire', for example, means that the meat is brined rather than dry-cured in salt, and for Suffolk ham the gammons are left to stew for several weeks in a mixture of treacle and beer, the finished product possessing a halo of pungent sweetness and a dark hue from the inky blackness of the marinade.

At Creasey's the butcher's, they took me backstage to see the vats of black stuff with the hams bobbing in them pale as corpses.

'The Suffolk name . . . I reckon that comes from Delia, 'cause she mentioned it on one of her shows,' said the butcher boy affectionately.

A little further up the main street, at Emmett's Stores, the man with the ponytail gave a snort of derision when I mentioned La Smith. Unsurprisingly, since it was his grandfather who started curing with the sweet pickle and the technique was well known in the area before that. The only morsel I was able to add to the controversy was that, East Anglia being a massive producer of sugar beet and molasses being a by-product of the beet industry, the Suffolk cure might perhaps have originated in a clever piece of recycling.

Emmett's Stores was a chaotic mélange of post office, minimarket and display case for Mr Jerrey's range of pork products, which included hams marinated in treacle and Guinness, in cider and brandy, and in Guinness and port, and a sweet pickled bacon with the same dark brown tint around the edges of the meat.

When I arrived Mr Jerrey, a Dickensian character with a scraggy white beard, a grubby blue smock and a pungent Suffolk accent, was busy in his pickle shed. He sloped out of his lair to tell me the hams were pickled for four to five weeks and then hot-smoked over oak sawdust in the smokehouse behind the shop.

I bought a few slices from the counter at the front of the Stores. The meat was an unusual but absolutely normal grey, not the porky pink of supermarket hams where the colour comes from the addition of preservative. Neither in terms of flavour, texture nor general eating quality did it have anything in common with the slippery-slimy fatless skinless plastic-coated substance eaten by the British in barely believable quantities, which is described as ham but has no real right to the use of the word. It was chewy yet yielding to the teeth, satisfyingly meaty, with a good salty punch giving way to a subtle, not cloying or artificial, honeyed sweetness on the aftertaste.

It was time to move on: there was so much eating to do, and so little time. I drove directly westwards, crossing into Cambridge, the realisation dawning on me that official county boundaries in East Anglia have less real meaning than do the fiefdoms of local breweries. When the pubs stop serving Adnams and start serving Greene King, then you know you're leaving Suffolk and approaching Cambridgeshire. Anyone asking for a pint of Abbot Ale in a Norfolk pub risks one of those 'American Werewolf' moments, dreaded by all travellers in the backwoods of Britain, when cloth-capped heads swivel and a terrible silence falls.

The city of Cambridge never had much of a reputation for gastronomic excellence. Unlike Oxford, which always seemed to me a pleasure-loving sort of place, Cambridge citizens never struck me as having much interest in food. Though there have been certain honourable exceptions. In *Remembrances of Cambridge* (1854) by Henry Gunning, the Reverend William Collier – clearly a charming fellow who took the Christian injunction against gluttony with a pinch of salt – provides one of the nicest examples of food love, or rather food *lust*, in the whole of English literature:

> 'When I was last in town,' said he, 'I was going to dine with a friend and passed through a small court [*I often imagined this to be the courtyard of the old Eagle pub*], just as a lad was hanging up a board, on which was this tempting inscription:
>
> "A roast pig this instant set upon the table!"
>
> The invitation was irresistible – I ordered a quarter; it was very delicate and very delicious. I despatched a second and a third portion, but was constrained to leave one quarter behind, as my dinner hour was approaching, and my friend was remarkably punctual.'

My own culinary reminiscences of a three-year stay at Cambridge are none too rosy. In my college we were encouraged to eat in a subterranean canteen mysteriously known as the Buttery (had butter ever been made or stored there? I doubt it). Down here the food was of the chicken and chips, macaroni cheese variety, and was mainly just edible, though it sometimes descended to positively Gothic depths of nastiness.

I still suffer from recurring nightmares caused by one particular dish of tongue in sauce. The meat was grey and hard, and you could feel the tastebuds of the cow in question rasping horribly against your own. But the worst thing about these meals was having to eat them at 6.15 in the evening, regardless of the season. Since a large number of students at the college were Northerners, the snotty Southerners among us always assumed this timetable – and the ribsticking food – were part of a general effort to make them feel at home.

As a concession to South-Eastern and feminine tastes, there was a lunchtime salad bar in the eighteenth-century great hall, and here you could crunch your way through walnut and red cabbage, three-bean, and rice, raisin and (tinned) sweetcorn. As I remember there were also cold cuts, wrinkled and leathery chicken legs (left over from yesterday's Buttery tea, perhaps), and slabs of rather good pork and game pies, and afterwards there was fruit or Ski yogurt.

Faced with such a panorama, we took matters into our own hands: we cooked up our own food. One friend made her own noodles and produced Chinese banquets, piling bamboo steamers in teetering towers on the single ring of her Baby Belling. Another friend, an effete young man from Trinity who was an admirer of Wagner and Wilde, once produced a memorable feast in his sixteenth-century rooms, the menu for which I still have somewhere. It consisted of Sevruga caviar, breast of mutton with caper sauce, and Burnt Cream, a classic dish which some food historians, though not all, believe was invented in the kitchens of Trinity College and subsequently frenchified to crème brûlée.

MUTTON WITH CAPER SAUCE

(serves 6)

Place a leg of mutton in a casserole dish and surround it with a coarsely chopped swede, 6 turnips, 6 small onions and a whole head of celery (cut into pieces). Add a teaspoon of black peppercorns and plenty of sea salt. Cover everything with cold water and bring slowly to the boil. Simmer until the mutton is tender, allowing 40 minutes per kilo.

To make the caper sauce, melt 2 tablespoons of unsalted butter in a heavy-based saucepan. Add the same amount of flour, stirring constantly. Allow to cook for a few seconds, then add enough milk and lamb stock to make a thick sauce. Add a dash of white wine vinegar and a handful of chopped capers. Season if necessary. Simmer, stirring, for a few minutes. Serve with the mutton.

BURNT CREAM

(serves 6)

Peel and roughly chop the zest of half a lemon. Add the zest, a stick of cinnamon and a vanilla pod (remove the seeds) to 600ml of double cream. Briefly scald (but do not boil) the cream with the lemon and spices. Pour the cream through a sieve.

Make a rich custard: beat 7 yolks and 1 whole egg with 2 tablespoons of caster sugar in a deep bowl, and slowly add the warm cream, stirring gently. Set the bowl above a bain-marie over a low heat, stirring constantly with a wooden spoon, until the custard is thick enough to coat the back of the spoon. Bake at 170 °C/Gas Mark 3 for 10 minutes in a shallow 10-inch dish set within a wider dish half full of cold water. Remove, leave to cool – a skin will have formed on top of the custard – and chill thoroughly in the fridge.

Thickly sprinkle the custard with caster sugar (you can also experiment with various types of sugar, granulated, soft brown, demerara, etc.) and place under a grill pre-heated to maximum. (Or you can use a blowtorch à la Marco Pierre White.) Watch it like a hawk until the sugar melts and begins to caramelise and brown. Turn the dish to ensure an even colour. Swiftly remove and chill again before serving.

For my part, I raided the tented stalls of the market place and spent whole afternoons cooking over-ambitious three-course meals. Since my kitchen and my rooms were in different buildings, I would carry the hot food along one of the city's major exit roads, often in darkness. Roasting a duck with fresh limes in an oven not much bigger than a toaster then seeing the steam and glimmer of the bird in the headlights and smelling the aroma of meat and citrus fruit through the exhaust fumes as I rushed it to table is a culinary experience not easily forgotten.

And when we tired of self-catering, you could always eat out – though as we soon found out, Cambridge in those days was a virtual desert for really good restaurants. The year I matriculated, Jane Grigson wrote, in some exasperation, that she would 'only be convinced that this well-endowed region is not just destined to become the freezer centre of the country or its sugar beet capital, when Cambridge manages to support a first-class restaurant or even a good plain restaurant – but perhaps that requires the blazing skill of a Frenchman, like Raymond Blanc at Oxford.'

A considerable percentage of my student grant was spent at establishments that were neither first-class nor even good and plain, such as Charlie Chan's, a Cantonese place on Regent Street. There was a cluster of cheap Indians up on Mill Road: my favourite was the Meghna, affectionately known as the Smegma. And when rich uncles or old headmasters came to see you, there was always Don Pasquale, then an old-fashioned trattoria serving the traditional repertoire of avocado prawns, cannelloni, vitello alla marsala and cassata. *The River Café Cook Book* having revolutionised the way a certain sector of the British population thinks about Italian food, that sort of straw-covered Chianti-bottle menu seems to come from a land that time forgot.

I started at the centre of things, the market with its red and blue striped awnings, probably a longer-standing fixture in the town than King's College Chapel itself. There were more cheap clothes-and-trainers stalls than I remembered, but the veg was the same as ever. Run-of-the-mill imported stuff, exotica we never saw in my day, and a few jewels of East Anglian agriculture that gave me the old itch to skip lectures: pickling onions hanging in huge string bags, Lincolnshire cauliflower, Kentish cobnuts and quinces, and field mushrooms as wide as dinner-plates. I still had a slice or two of that Suffolk-cure ham left in the car and a drying lump of that multi-grain, multi-everything Suffolk bread. Together with a bunch of flat-leaved parsley and some garlic and butter, I could whip up a nourishing student-friendly dish of stuffed mushrooms if I could only find a Baby Belling somewhere.

The most common complaint among my food-loving Cambridge friends was that there was no half-decent deli counter in the city, nowhere to buy Kalamata olives and slices of *coppa di Parma* and *dulce de membrillo*, simple things you could nibble on as you settled down with a glass of fino sherry to write that long postponed essay on the role of irony in *The Rape of the Lock*.

In St Mary's Passage, a gloomy alley opposite St John's College, next to a tiny public garden, there was now an excellent deli counter in the shape of the Cambridge Cheese Company. I am glad, nevertheless, that it never existed in my time or I would certainly have sunk even further than I did into the mire of student debt.

It was a smallish shop, crammed to the gunwales, but not in the disorderly and unappetising manner of some delis that makes you suspect that some of the produce has been on the shelves gathering dust for years. There was something about this place that gave you confidence, which is what matters in a business that depends entirely on the good taste of the proprietor. The cheeses alone were worth the journey. This was a man who understood that cheese is a continuum, not a lump of dead matter, and that like any living thing it must be treated carefully if you are to get the best of it.

In a matter of minutes I'd made a mental wish-list of the following: (1) Tins of tuna, or rather the superior *bonito del norte*, from Ortiz El Velero, one of the best fish canners on the Atlantic coast of northern Spain, with a covetable retro packaging design of yellow, red and blue sails with silvery bits of the tin showing through. (2) Sea salts, exotically flavoured, from Hanbury Foods in King's Lynn, including Australian Scented Salt and Outback Salt, the latter boasting one of the most extraordinary ingredient lists of any product I know ('Ground Bush Tomato, Mountain Pepperleaf, Wattleseed, Native Pepperberry'). (3) Portuguese Miscute de Couve pickle, in a jar with a picture of a cabbage on the label, its contents flecked with orange chilli and – I knew from experience as well as from the manufacturer's warning – '*muito picante*'.

British delicatessens used to be and still are largely places where delicate eating went no further than a quarter of floury pink taramasalata, another quarter of floury pink hummus, a few desiccated olives and a small lump of prehistoric Parmesan.

The exotica available here seemed to indicate that this city had taken a giant leap forward in gastronomic terms, though it was hard to imagine prim, puritanical Cambridge providing much of a market for some of the products at the back of the shop, where they occupied their own special rack, like adult magazines at the newsagent. Bad Girls in Heat. Scorned Woman. Hot Bitch at the Beach and Hot Buns at the Beach. The labels on the little bottles bore gaudy fifties-style designs showing gorgeous girls with long legs and enormous Pamela Anderson breasts, the subtext being, as an English student might put it, that chilli sauce this hot is very much a macho thing. Apart from sex, the other major thematic strands were fire, death, madness and apocalypse. It seems a little extreme for a mere table condiment, but some of the newest chilli sauces on the market really are frighteningly strong. Hence Ultimate Burn, Dave's Total Insanity, Last Rites, Nuclear Hell, Tongues of Fire (The Unspeakable Hot Sauce) and, my favourite, Blair's After Death Sauce. The cult for hot sauce comes mainly from America, where they are evolving them so intense that only a single drop is needed to spice up an entire cauldron of stew. Endorphin Rush, one of the highest concentrations of capsaicin to be found anywhere on the planet, probably ought to have a health warning attached to it.

There must have been fifty different pepper sauces on those shelves, all individually sourced from America, Africa, and the Caribbean. Was there really a demand in Cambridge, I asked the owner of the Cheese Company, for such a magnificent range of pleasure-poison?

'Not really,' said Paul with a devilish grin. 'It's just that I love chillies and I want other people to love them too. They're actually very different, there are some subtle distinctions of flavour. Some are proper sauces, and others are simply pure liquid essences of heat. You know, when you make some sort of soup or stew, and you put in maybe half a teaspoon, and as you're eating it you think, oh my Gawd, this is *hot*.'

He gulped theatrically, clutching his throat. 'But then you just get this fantastic buzz of endorphin. Chilli is addictive, I tell you. And my evil plan is to turn as many Cambridgeans into addicts as I possibly can.'

That week had seen the start of two major international conferences in Cambridge – one on Packaging Design for the New Millennium and the other on Nutrition and Disease Prevention in the Developing World (the Developing World clearly not quite being ready for packaging design) – and on the day I arrived every hotel in the centre of the city was full. Every hotel except one, that is. What happened to me that night is every travel-writer's nightmare. It is the antithesis of everything that is romantic and exciting about being away from familiar haunts and reminds you that there are people in the world – perhaps the majority – who have no interest in the notion of cultural difference, let alone exotica like Outback Salt and *miscute de couve*. That night I had no alternative but to stay in the Holiday Inn.

I tried bravely to look on the bright side. It would be a kitsch experience I might be able to write about in a witty and diverting manner. There would be CNN and MTV, no landladies listening at the door and no morning stench of fried bread. There would in all probability be a Corby trouser press. There might even be room service, surely one of the most exquisite pleasures of modern life.

Ensconced in my room with its view of students sobbing into their books in some dusty Victorian library, I pondered the dull pink and mushroom decor, wondering what sort of genius interior designer could have come up with a scheme so entirely free of cultural signifiers, so inoffensive that by paradox it became an insult to the sensibility. Some day, I reflected glumly as I peered into the mini-bar, when all national barriers fall away and the planet coalesces into one homogeneous mass, all hotels will be made this way. There will be no more little family *pensions*, no more characterful converted mansions in the English countryside, and everything we eat in every hotel will be taken from the Holiday Inn Room Service menu: choose from tropical fruit medley, Norwegian prawn Marie Rose, followed by tuna and pasta bake, pizza marguerita or olde-fashioned fish and chips. And for dessert, why not treat yourself to our toffee and banana crumble?

I took one look at that menu and decided to try my luck in the town instead. My spirits were low as I walked out into the streets, where Cambridge's famous Siberian wind was beginning to make its presence felt on what was supposed to be a late summer night. Up by the Grafton Centre, a 1960s blot on the historic city centre, various dining options were available: I decided against the Bengal Tandoori, where I had an obstinate memory of a fellow student throwing up all over the flock wallpaper, and resolved to avoid the encyclopaedic Footlights, which described itself as a 'Mexican American and European Café Bar and Restaurant'. It was getting to the point where, if my old college Buttery hadn't closed two hours ago, I might almost be prepared to give it a go for old time's sake.

Across the dark expanse of parkland common was a line of low shapes – the university boathouses crouching beside the river. There were a few feeble lights from a riverside pub, and I strode across the damp grass thinking I would slurp a pint of Greene King IPA while considering my next move. But as I got near the Fort St George there were other lights nearby – a warm glow of garden lamps and curtained windows belonging to a townhouse on its own in the midst of the common that had the look of a grand family home, perhaps that of some rich local businessman whose wife had gone a little mad on the fabrics and fittings.

All at once it came back to me: the hype about the half-Spanish chef who was rumoured to have opened the first decent restaurant in Cambridge since records began. Steering away from the pub I made for its welcoming lights, and they happened to have a table for one next to the conservatory, not too close to the men from Tetra-Pak. And I allowed myself to savour a delectable dinner of lamb sweetbreads in a salad with Parma ham and almonds, followed by sea bass with a tomato butter sauce, 'ratatouille' and 'tempura' of sage leaves. I was still a little tender from my cabbage fast, and told myself to stop there. In the selfless spirit of research, however, I went on to try the pudding of roasted pears with pain perdu and raspberry sorbet; and then, of course, I had to finish with a little cheese. It was Jean-Anthelme Brillat-Savarin in his *Physiologie du Goût* (1825) who compared a meal without cheese to a beautiful woman with only one eye.

It was a nearly perfect meal, except that the tempura had the texture of a doughnut and sage leaves are inedible at the best of times. There was nothing in the least East Anglian about this meal, of course, because despite all the excellences of East Anglian produce there are no recipes to follow, no culinary repertoire from which to take your bearings. But one mustn't be churlish. The main thing was that it seemed possible that Jane Grigson's prayer for a first-class Cambridge restaurant may actually have been answered at last. Even if it had taken the blazing skill of a half-Spaniard to do it.

11

north-east anglia

meeting millers and catching crabs

When you mention to a person from Cambridge that you intend to travel north of the city into the flat and monotonous land known as the Fens, they tend to register the same expression of horror as if you'd said you were going to paddle a canoe alone across the Okavango Swamps.

The Fens are not quite as bad as all that, but as I drove towards Ely one dark morning the countryside was even balder and boggier than I remembered it, the range of colours it offered an even meaner selection of greys and browns. The names of the villages – Shippea, Mappea, Eye – looked even odder, and the few people out on the streets even more dwarf-like and suspicious-faced. This bleak black country is one of the few landscapes in Britain that can actually inspire a sense of supernatural fear.

Here and there, across the featureless expanse of farmland crosshatched with the dikes and canals that cause some people to call this South Holland, the Ordnance Survey maps of northern East Anglia show dozens of windmills. Most of these mills are now either demolished, converted into bijou dwellings or simply abandoned to their fate, a pepperpot tower with no sails and gaping holes where the windows once were. But a very few remain in active use, and the flour they produce is one of East Anglia's gastronomic glories.

Downfield Windmill, in the village of Soham near Ely, was all set for demolition when a housing estate went up around it, until it was rescued in the nick of time by miller Nigel Moon, who now works another mill in Rutland. When Moon arrived in 1974 it had been dormant for nine years, and before that was only used for milling animal feeds, driven not by the wind but by a prosaic tractor motor.

When I drove up Mrs Ina Kite and her son were in the mobile home beside the mill, huddling in front of a two-bar electric fire. The wind had been low and the mill still all day. Mrs Kite came out in an old coat, moth-eaten woollen socks and sandals, a fine grey stubble of moustache around her lips.

Her son shook my hand and slouched away. His hooded gaze seemed directed mostly at the floor.

Were there many windmills around here still operating that they knew of, I wondered?

'Nuh,' said Andrew.

'Well, there is one round the corner at Swaffham Prior, isn't there, love? It's run by a man who works, I think in a recruitment office, during the day and only mills really at weekends. There's Haddenham Mill, that's almost capable of working.

There's Wicken. That's being restored. It'll work in a year's time, all being well,' said Mrs Kite.

She smiled indulgently at her son. He was currently living in a caravan next door to Wicken Mill, so that his unique expertise in windmill technology would no doubt be called into play by the consortium of people who had undertaken to restore it.

In the mid-nineteenth century there were eight working windmills and a watermill in the village of Soham. Downfield is the only one left, and even the casual observer could tell that it has seen better days. Only two of the original four 'sails' were still in place, and there were broken windows and a general slight air of decrepitude. Mrs Kite wrung her hands and bemoaned the lack of money, and timidly offered to sell me a kilo of flour made up in a nice paper package with a windmill block-printed on the front. This organic stoneground English wheat flour is some of the best flour money can buy.

Andrew Kite had been obsessed with mills all his life. At six years old he first announced his desire to be a miller – wind or water – when he grew up. In the school holidays, while other boys went fishing in the canals or sailing on the Broads, he went to work on the restoration of a nearby mill. During Mr Moon's last two years at Downfield he worked alongside him, picking up the final arcane secrets that he would need when he took over Downfield on his own.

We stood in the ground floor of the mill amidst the great beamed oak machinery turned white by centuries of wind and wheat flour, and I tried to remember some of the words used to describe the mill's various moving parts, like the cap (being the top or lid of the pepperpot, which moves round freely according to the wind), the fantail (the small wheel that turns the cap), the governor (which determines the gap between the millstones) and the monumental wheel at the very top of the mill, known as the wallower.

We climbed the tower by a series of rickety staircases. 'Do be careful, there's a hole in the floor up here,' said Mrs Kite. Sure enough, there were gaping holes in all the floorboards, and various missing panes of glass in the windows through which came a bone-chilling draught.

We reached the top, or at least as far as non-millers were permitted to go, and I peered out of the window, puffing from the exercise, at the view over dark dreary fenland. Below us sprawled the housing estate, built on what was once the mill field. It made an odd counterpoint, these neat earthbound bungalows inhabited by earthbound people, and this romantic edifice caught in among them, existing in and governed by the movements of the atmosphere.

'See that little church over there on the horizon? Next to it, that's Wicken Mill,' cried Mrs Kite.

The wind came up of a sudden, and the eyes of the miller and his mother took on a sparkle. These were people who were used to listening to the wind, used to judging its direction and power.

The mill creaked and strained against its wooden brake, but with only two sails to go on, there wasn't yet enough force and constancy in the gusts for the millstones to turn with sufficient speed. Would they turn today, if the conditions were right?

'Yeh,' said Andrew as he climbed out of sight to where the millstones lay motionless, thinking now of the various tasks that had to be accomplished before grinding could commence.

A little flour was still left in the hoppers from yesterday's few hours of blustery weather, and I picked up a handful and crushed it to my face, feeling the rough texture of the bran against my lips. It had a warm, strong aroma that made me realise that, until now, I hadn't understood what flour really smelled like. It was a rare treat to get this close to flour so freshly milled, since, as is the case with coffee or pepper or any other ground substance, most people's contact with flour happens at a moment long after the essential flavour-bearing oils in the grain have been lost, along with a vital component of its taste.

Then I heard a shout from below, and the whole immense machinery of the mill seemed to heave a gargantuan sigh and, slowly at first then with gathering speed, the cogs and pulleys began to creak into movement. Through the window I could see the sails sweep by, hear the granite millstones scraping on each other on the floor below. It was a thrilling moment; the old mill was coming alive all around me.

'Yes, she's breathing again,' said Mrs Kite, looking around at the dust shaking silvery from the beams, hugging herself in a private little ecstasy of satisfaction.

It wouldn't surprise me if windmills appeal to one sort of personality and watermills to another. I would even be willing to bet on the possibility that if you checked up on star signs, there would be more water signs among watermillers, and air signs among windmillers.

I found Michael Thurlow and his watermill in the village of Letheringsett in north Norfolk, not far from the stretch of coast known in these parts as Chelsea-by-the-Sea, thanks to the annual influx of wealthy Londoners in search of an authentic seaside experience remembered from their childhoods, all beach huts and windbreaks and picnics in the dunes.

The watermill and its surroundings seemed a world away from the bluster of the fens. There was no wind, for a start, because this was a kind of soggy glade where the air was still but for the sound of the rushing stream that powered the village mill, and had done so, moreover, at least since 1086, when the *Domesday Book* recorded the existence of a watermill in 'Leringaseta'.

The life of the miller had a nice sort of fluidity about it that mirrored the flow of the millstream. For twenty years he was in the Royal Navy (water again). Then, during a stint as lorry driver for an animal feed distribution company, he was making his regular delivery to Letheringsett Mill when he was asked, out of the blue, whether he would like to take it on. 'You don't get many opportunities like that in a lifetime,' he told me. So the mill was rescued from its threatened future as a block of flats, restored completely and in 1984 returned to its former use, an old Ruston Hornsby oil engine having replaced water power after the Second World War.

It was a many-floored old brick building dating from 1802, with all the milling machinery in immaculate condition. You could see the great arc of the water wheel, sixteen feet in diameter, with its thirty-two wrought-iron buckets to catch the gush of the millstream and old sacks strewn about it, thick sacks sewn with a roll down the side and C.K. Squirrell & Son, 1951 block-printed in black on the cloth. Through the side windows was the constant presence of the mill pool, silent in its dark green depths, the millstream rushing uselessly beside the wheel until diverted towards it by a system of sluices.

Michael was in the mill office catching up on a few orders. Today's included 200 kilos for Hong Kong and two and a half tons for a Japanese health farm. Word had got out about the stunning quality of Letheringsett flour, which is coarse traditional wholemeal flour ground from old wheat varieties like Maris Widgeon and Alexandria that the miller finds still being grown, despite the virtual domination of modern high-yielding varieties in the surrounding Norfolk countryside.

'I've just found some fantastic spelt, and that's the oldest wheat in existence. The Romans used it,' he said excitedly. 'I've got a hundred tons waiting for me down the road.' Spelt wheat, I knew, was the ultra-fashionable grain that has taken the German healthfood market by storm (as *Dinkel*) since it was revealed that the tenth-century composer and nun Abbess Hildegard of Bingen apparently made her bread with it.

He does test millings for seedsmen who want to know how their new varieties behave in a stone ground process, and mills animal feed – bags of Pot-Bellied Pig Food, Hacking Mix and Quiet Pencils were piled up beside the millstones – and sells his own flours in a little shop on the ground floor. All in all, the mill was probably busier now than at any time in its 1,000-year history, and Mr Thurlow thought he knew why.

'It's the crap they put in bread, isn't it?' he said.

He ran a handful of flour through his fingers to show me how in a batch of freshly ground flour the darker flakes of bran were still present along with the stone-coloured endosperm. Even in commercial so-called wholemeal flours the bran is first removed and then put back in for the cranks. And for any run-of-the-mill white flour, of course, the grain is pulverised by high-speed roller mills until it could be plaster of Paris powder or cocaine just as easily as flour. 'The difference is, y'see, the stuff I'm milling here, it's got no crap in it.'

This was not a man given to mincing his words, especially on the subject of the modern food industry and all its works. His sworn enemies were all those powers of modern life who wilfully contaminate our food, rendering it at best tasteless, at worst hazardous to our health and to that of the environment.

'And I'm including supermarkets in that,' he said. 'I've had visits from three of them so far. But they want to change my packaging, and they want three months' credit. And they haven't got a bloody clue about real food. I just go away, get on with something, work off my frustrations milling. Or I say, "You found the way in – now please find your way out."'

Michael fetched me a loaf of bread he had baked that morning from his own-ground flour, handing it to me as if to demonstrate the possibilities. It was still comfortingly warm to the touch; it felt substantial, weightier than you'd expect for its size, and gave off a whiff of pungent, nutty breadiness – the primordial aroma, together with that of roasting meat the first food-smell of all.

I cut off a piece of the loaf. It had a hard, pitted, rust-brown surface and a stone-coloured interior, speckled with flecks of bran, from which the fragrance seemed to billow in waves as I broke into the crust. I sprinkled the slice with a little sea salt and savoured the bread like a fine wine, rolling around the resonances in my mouth, picking up suggestions of toast, fresh yeast, Virginia tobacco, riding saddles and Lindt milk chocolate. It was the best bread I had tasted in months. It made me ask myself why, with a new food consciousness supposedly sweeping the country, there wasn't more British bread as good as this.

The truth is that as a nation we have taken too little care of our bread. Craving white, wheaten bread, the whiter the better, we have connived, historically, in what Elizabeth David calls the 'cynical debauching of our bread'. It is hard to see how our millers and bakers can be wholly to blame for what went wrong – and few professions have been so vilified so unfairly, historically speaking – since all they have ever done is give the people what they wanted.

The story of British bread, like so much about British food, is determined by class aspirations. In medieval times there was white, brown and black bread, the white in fact bearing a greater resemblance to our own brown bread than to the bleached-white sweet steamed pudding that passes for industrial white bread. The finest white bread in Tudor times, called variously pandemaigne and manchet, was the top people's loaf, while the *Sun* readers lived on coarse 'black bread', heavy with barley and rye. As time went on, however, the working classes decided they had had enough of that. They wanted white bread, like the toffs ate. The eighteenth-century 'Standard' loaf, which had a higher proportion of rye, oats and barley and was a penny cheaper than the white loaf, was a conspicuous failure. Even when it was revealed that alum, lime and chalk were being added to it, sales of white bread rose and rose. 'The good people are not ignorant of this adulteration,' wrote Smollett in *Humphry Clinker*, 'but they prefer it to wholesome bread because it is whiter than the meal of corn. Thus they sacrifice their taste and their health . . . and the miller or the baker is obliged to poison them and their families, in order to live by his profession.'

And so it went on. By the time Elizabeth David's brave and

brilliant *English Bread and Yeast Cookery* came out in 1977, most British bread was made with flour from which the wheat-germ and bran had been expunged by means of giant roller mills, necessitating the addition of vitamins to make up for the damage wreaked on the nutritional composition of the flour. Two-thirds of all bread was made according to the Chorleywood process, defined as 'the replacement of the conventional period of dough maturing by a few minutes of intense mechanical agitation in high speed mixers'. Rather than baked, it was pressure-cooked in industrial steamers, giving it that familiar springy texture. It seemed that white bread, and white-bread gastronomical values, had finally conquered.

But then the tables began to turn. The healthfood/whole-food scene was finally getting the message across that handmade, pure and 'natural' foods were best. Those who could afford it now began to crave the much more expensive whole-meal and granary breads. (The poor, of course, were stuck with Mother's Pride.) There were campaigns for Real Bread in the Sunday newspapers. Briefly, excitingly, good bread once more became an issue.

As it seems to me, we have become of late a little nonchalant and self-satisfied about the staff of life. Where are the TV cookery programmes about home baking, featuring trendy young long-haired bakers and puns on the word 'knead'? Perhaps there is no audience for such a thing, when the British now eat less bread of any sort, white or brown, than any other country in Europe. Since the Second World War our consumption of bread has plummeted as our consumption of sugar, meat and saturated fat has rocketed. Why? Perhaps because, as one writer plainly puts it, 'bread is the staple food of poverty and . . . people eat much less of it when they can afford to buy meat'.

All I can say is that my travels in edible Britain turned up a few jewel-like loaves, made by men and women who care about good flour, good ovens and generous timings, but a very great deal of inferior bread. Just occasionally I found myself agreeing with Eliza Acton, Suffolk-born author of possibly the greatest of all English cookbooks, *Modern Cookery for Private Families* (1845), when she remarks on the 'singular fact that the one article of our daily food on which health depends more than on any other, is precisely that which is obtained in England with the greatest difficulty'.

As ever, there was no lack of variety. The big Sainsbury's outside Norwich, for example, positively groaned with ciabatta, focaccia, rye bread, pumpernickel, challah, sourdough, French baguettes, granary, organic multi-grain and a dozen other types. But there was a poverty at the heart of all this plenty. The Italian breads were dry, dull-tasting, and stingy with the olive oil. There was a lack of rich, toasty, aromatic bread flavours all round; poor flour, from intensively grown Canadian wheat, was probably the culprit. Too often, even the denser 'traditional' and wholemeal loaves seemed to have been infected with the pappiness of pre-sliced factory white bread. When I cut into the granary, it squashed down stickily into the bread-board, as if cowering from the knife, so that the loaf had to be pulled back into its original, attractively rustic, ball-like shape. Not like Michael's loaf, which yielded a little but sprang feistily back into place.

We climbed the stairs to the grinding room where the two great stones, the turning 'runner' and the stationary 'bedstone', had been winched apart to be reground, a service that takes place after every fifty tons of flour. I watched as Mr T. placed an old penny piece upon the top of the axle and winched the runner back down upon it. 'That's to stop any wear,' he said. These old stones, now freshly grooved in the particular way to carry the flour to the edge, were found cemented into the brickwork in a side wall of the mill.

He took off the brake and opened the sluice gates. The millstream came rushing through beneath us and the millwheel began to turn, creakily at first then slickly as the water surged faster and faster, transferring the power up the trunk of the axle tree to the stones themselves. Wholesome flour, good bread, is simply the end result of this physics of torque and mass. For a few seconds the stones stayed still: something was wrong. Now they crunched into motion with a loud, dry scraping like two enormous teeth chewing on nothing, and the whole structure began its primitive, relentless, beguiling dance.

'Now then, babies, let's *grind*,' said Michael.

Cromer = Crabs. In my mind, at least, the two elements are practically one and the same. C*romer*, squire? Famous for its crabs, squire. Go together like a horse and carriage, they do. I mean, if you was to go to Cromer, it would be for the crabs, right? I mean, why else would you want to go to Cromer?

I took a room at the Clifftop Hotel, an establishment that had more than a little in common with Fawlty Towers, mainly in the sense of everything being a little out of kilter with modernity and efficiency; something you could also say of Cromer itself. So that in the swirly carpeted hotel dining room (brown vinyl settees, Artex walls, brown-and-beige furry 3D pictures of boating scenes) the 'table de hôte' menu featured such items as brown Windsor soup, tomato juice and steak Diane. It said something to me about the state of our Food Nation that, while in London this kind of food had become a kind of postmodern joke, in another part of the realm it was still being served up with a straight face as if nothing at all had changed.

'Does this key open the front door if I come back at three in the morning?' I asked the greasy, wheezing proprietor of the Clifftop.

'Yes – and if you find something to do until three in the morning, do let me know!' he replied with a cackle.

My room had a view of the benighted promenade, blurred by rain. A series of feeble lights placed at intervals along the sea front – I supposed, a sort of massively cut-price illuminations – twisted and flickered in the wind. Oh dear. Cromer appeared to have fallen on very hard times.

Then I walked out to look at the town, along the seafront, high above the beach where the waves made arcs of lace in the darkness. From here I could see the lights close to. They were shapes formed out of lightbulbs coloured yellow, red and green: there was a starfish, a seahorse, a lobster, a prawn and a fleur-de-lys. (Why? Perhaps because Cromer is proudly twinned with the French town of Crest, an hour outside Lyon.) Finally, at the important end of the prom, nearest the little pier where *The Best Little Whorehouse in Texas* was showing at the Pavilion Theatre courtesy of the Cromer and Sheringham Amateur Operatic and Dramatic Society ('BAWDY NOT SMUTTY, RISQUÉ NOT BLUE,' the poster assured), there was a crab. A cute crab drawn in yellow lights with two red eyes that twinkled on and off.

My heart went out to Cromer with that crab in lights. It went out even further with the foyer of the Hotel de Paris, the magnificent old Victorian seaside pile built in 1820 in a commanding position high above the pier, and an authentic piece of *folie de grandeur*.

It went back in again when I began looking for somewhere to eat. The menu du jour in the Hotel de Paris sounded unpromising, unless you fancied orange and grapefruit cocktail or Scotch broth, tuna fish salad and jam roly poly and custard, which I didn't. The food revolution had not happened here. Neither had it made much impression on the Cromer Grill, recommended at my hotel as one of Cromer's finest eating places. I stood in the street, transfixed as much by the menu – Hawaiian chicken, vegetable pasta bake, devilled whitebait, spaghetti bolognaise – as by the unspeakable interior, all pinkly-purply frilly bits over wheelback chairs and scrolled ironwork partitions between the tables.

The truth seemed to be that there was little to choose from on this rainy weekday night. A little way back along the cliff, there was Bolton's Bistro. 'Bistro', of course, implying that what we had here was something a little more upmarket, a little more, shall we say, 'Continental', than the rest of the dining possibilities in this corner of north Norfolk. You could tell that from the menu, too, with its Continental specialities such as chicken breast, tortellini, Norwegian prawns, lobster thermidor and Ronaldo's ice cream. 'Plus much much more!! Come inside and see for yourself!!' the blackboard pleaded, its chalk marks dripping rapidly streetwards.

I would have been more than happy with a simple crab salad, with or without the radicchio, and a glass or two of wine, but there was nothing like that to be had. So I repaired to the Wellington pub and drank two pints of bitter. And then I did what the locals all seemed to be doing: I nipped across the street to Mary Jane's – one of the multitude of fish bars in the town (motto: 'Quality and Quantity'. Which means Mary Jane's gives you a right good slap-up feed, not one of the measly little portions you get in other places). Above the vats of bubbling oil I could see they served mushy peas, curry sauce and battered burgers. If anything proved that I was now truly in the North of England, it was that poor battered burger.

It being after eight o'clock, the frilly pink dining room was closed. So I ate my cod and chips standing up at a bar at the side of the shop, out of a polystyrene tray with a wooden chip fork, deciding while I ate that the chip fork was probably the most useless eating implement ever devised by man.

If the fish is pearly fresh, the batter crisply golden and not too doughy, the chunky chips fried in clean oil and the sprinkled vinegar a good malt – not that aberration, 'Non-Brewed Condiment' – there is nothing much wrong with a fish supper as a cheap, satisfying meal. There are various candidates for the birthplace of the dish, ranging from Portugal to West Yorkshire, but there can be no doubt at all about its wholesale conquest of the British soul. The odd thing, bearing in mind that surveys have shown time and time again that fish and chips are by far the most popular fast food in Britain, eclipsing even the might of McDonald's, is how little they figure in our national culinary discourse. Blandly tasty, of neutral colour, seductive in their very unsexiness, they seem to sum up everything we value in our own ethnic food. Fish and chips may indeed be our national dish: they have a permanence, a modesty, a loveable uninterestingness that qualify them highly.

Next day I got up early and poked around the town. In the window of the Cromer Indoor Market a row of pumpkins sat sadly on a glass shelf, like something out of an old Soviet department store. To judge by the selection in the greengrocers, people here subsisted largely on a diet of parsnip, swede and beetroot. By day, under a cold drizzle, Cromer seemed an almost more unremittingly miserable place than by night.

The one point of true excellence and splendour I could see in Crabville was, rightly and logically enough, its crabs. Never in my life had I seen such beauties: in serried ranks in fish shop displays, variegated shells of pink and cream and orange, or – the ready-dressed ones – belly up, displaying the creamy fibres of their meat.

I bought one at C. Cox and Son, a little fishmonger's in the street behind the sea front where you could buy, as well as fresh crabs, a dried specimen turned into a clock – or as the price tag put it, 'fashioned into a delightful timepiece'. The crabs are caught on a chalk bed about fifteen miles from the shore. Fresh water draining into the sea, rich in food particles, provides them with all the nourishment they need to grow fat and juicy.

'I get 'em brought in,' said Mr Cox. 'What's good about these, they've got a good quality brown meat as well as white, so you get a good mixture.'

Further along the street, the Lee family sold crabs from a cabinet outside their front room. Seeing me there, Mrs Lee came bustling out to pull back the plastic cover from the cabinet. She still had flakes of white crabmeat stuck to her hands, which were red from the cold water.

She looked tired. 'I've been up since before dawn, the crabs came in at six,' she said.

'Why are they the best?' She found it a surprising question. 'Well I've never tried crabs from anywhere else, but people do say they're the best in the world. They're ever so sweet and tasty.'

I bought another. They were only three pounds, perfectly dressed and fresh that morning; they were ridiculously cheap.

'There you go,' said Mrs Lee. 'Now you try that with a nice bread roll. Better than caviar, that is.'

Back along the coast to King's Lynn, where Norfolk turns into Lincolnshire. Outside the town, an industrial eyesore of steaming towers and a reek of old vegetables was a powerful reminder that Norfolk is not only home to Cromer crabs, Crone's cider and Leatheringsett flour but also to Dolmio bottled pasta sauces, and Campbell's – a name that is equally dreaded by generations of children brought up on its glutinous, over-salted soups as it is revered by connoisseurs of Pop Art.

We were sitting in the ante-room of the seventeenth-century house in the Saturday market place – so called to distinguish it from the Tuesday market place – that is Rococo, possibly the best restaurant in East Anglia. Since it was now 3.30 on a Sunday morning and there wasn't much else to do in King's Lynn, chef Nick Anderson and his wife Anne and I were working our way through a bottle of calvados and putting the world of British food to rights.

After the crisis of Cromer, the relief of being able to sit in a warmly coloured sitting room with deep sofas, art books on the tables and beautiful modern paintings (Anne's) on the walls, talking about good food, having just eaten a large amount of it, was strong and sweet.

Nick, a passionate individual in his late thirties, typified the generation of youngish chefs who had lived through the internationalist culinary fads of the eighties and nineties and then began to move back to basics, finding their own voice in the process. The term Modern British Cooking defines the phenomenon as well as any, despite having fallen out of use as the new openness-to-things became less of a trend and more of a canon, a series of conventions in itself, like any other cuisine worth considering.

Part of the point of the new British haute cuisine – or perhaps we ought to call it Top Nosh – is the realisation that all around us on these islands is a lot of splendid raw material, if we can only remember where to look for it. The proof of the pudding is that in terms of restaurant cooking it is beyond all doubt that there is more, better, and more interesting food in Britain than ever before.

Nick bubbled enthusiastically about the general level of culinary creativity to be found across the country. The picture he painted was of a population that could buy whatever ingredients they wanted in their local supermarket and increasingly was both aware of what to do with them and bothered to do so. 'It's fantastic now; people are thinking, "Ah, chicken Kiev. I won't buy it ready made, I'll buy a chicken breast, some garlic and butter and a packet of herbs, and I'll make it myself." It's great. People have seen all those TV food programmes, and they really are making the effort.'

When the Andersons first set up shop in King's Lynn their clientele was Norfolk worthies and their wives. 'What they wanted was, "How would modom like her steak?"' remembered Anne. 'But then it seemed to relax. People started coming in in jeans and T-shirt; they were people you felt you could have a conversation with, and I started to feel comfortable.'

I wondered whether she felt a little like a pioneer, spreading the foodie gospel up here in the sticks.

'Mmm, I do, but I also feel we're educating people, in the friendliest possible way. How about that couple on the sofa?'

It was a young local man and his girl, out for a special Saturday night. They'd been sitting next to me reading the menu while we waited for our respective tables, looking a little overwhelmed as they muttered to each other the strange litany of fancy restaurant words: 'rillette', 'millefeuille', 'halloumi', 'brioche'. What he had really wanted was a plain steak. But Anne had gently pushed them towards the venison, and after the meal, flushed a little with house red, they sat with the three of us for a while and drank a glass of calvados.

'How was the venison, then? Bet it was better than a boring old steak?' asked Anne smilingly.

And the couple glanced at each other, smiling too, and the guy actually said, in a wide Norfolk accent just like the old Bernard Matthews turkey ads on the TV, 'Bootiful, it was. Bootiful.'

I drove north into Lincolnshire, feeling absurdly like a pioneer myself. There were places here whose names I'd never heard before, yet would never forget. Mavis Enderby, which sounds like an unpublished novel by Samuel Beckett. Frisby on the Wreake. Pub quiz question: in which English county are a town called Boston and a village called New York?

Despite the Stateside connection, there is an old-fashioned

flavour about the way life goes on up here. Rural Lincolnshire still feels peaceful, under-inhabited, slow-paced, and cheap. People stand out in the street with their shopping baskets and gossip, as they used to before being busy became a status symbol. Compared to the rest of England, the traffic is not too bad. There is a notable lack of new building, but house prices are still low enough to make South-Easterners gnash their teeth.

This is an arable county par excellence. More than that, it's a land of brassicas, of beets, sprouts, cabbages and all the other members of that noble, generous, smelly family. In the blinding sunshine of an autumn day in south Lincolnshire, the fields of sugar beet looked like vast blue-green oceans, as though the sea had flooded in from the Wash along the dikes and canals and stuck there, rippling. It was a nice car game, identifying all that veg. There was a neat square of beautiful broccoli. Turnips. Red cabbage, with a purple trim around bluish leaves. A pile of sugar beet in the corner of a field, looking like a heap of rocks. And that thing with the feathery yellow bit on top? Something that had gone to seed? Brussels sprouts, perhaps. It would be apt, because at times this flat clogged landscape does feel a little like Belgium.

So much veg is being moved about here that what you see in Lincolnshire is not road kill but 'road spill'. The occasional onion rolling into the central reservation; a strewing of old sprouts, taking their revenge for having been abandoned by briefly filling passing cars with their stale farty aroma. Just outside Lincoln a half-lorryload of carrots was in the process of being crushed into a purée.

Gastronomically speaking, I had the sinking feeling that I was once again entering the badlands. An American friend of mine who had once eaten at what was supposed to be the numero uno restaurant in Lincolnshire told me it was not an experience she would willingly repeat.

Picnic-wise, though, you can do rather well in Lincolnshire, if you seek out the small range of idiosyncratic local products that have somehow weathered the storms of food history. With three times less rainfall than the west coast, this is not really dairy country, but the dairy product that proves the rule is Poacher, a good, strong Cheddar-type unpasteurised cheese with plenty of bite. Not least, there is Lincolnshire plum bread. This was once made with lard, thus finding a use for another piggy by-product, but now, sadly, margarine or vegetable shortening is used. My landlady at Greenfields Farm had told me the bakery in her local market town of Horncastle made the best plum bread of all, so I stopped off in the morning to buy some; it was moist and sticky with sultanas, currants and peel – oddly, not a plum in sight.

One of the great unknown items of British charcuterie is stuffed chine: a shoulder of pork on the bone that is salt-cured like ham, scored deeply and the gaps stuffed with parsley, and the whole thing cooked in the oven. I have seldom been more amazed by any piece of information than I was by the fact that Paul Verlaine, the French poet, counted Lincolnshire chine among his favourite delicacies. Verlaine had been working as a schoolmaster in Stickney, near Boston, during the 1870s when he came upon it among the 'roast beef, steaks, chops, Irish stews, and other dishes, one of which I have only seen there . . . It consisted of chopped herbs laid between very close pressed slices of a thick, very thick piece of salted pork. It was called a "stuffed chine" – very good indeed.'

The county has a long-standing and fruitful relationship with the pig. There are some great pork pies to be had here, and the Lincolnshire sausage, traditionally spiked with sage, is one of the few sausages to have a county name attached to it. The best stuffed chine I tasted was made by Phipps in Mareham Le Fen, one of only four butchers still making the stuff. It was salty, juicy and fresh-tasting, the immense quantities of parsley, compressed into thick dark-green stripes, giving the meat a bitter tang that must have been even more pronounced when blackcurrant leaves, nettles, even ordinary meadow grass were used as well. I fancy chine is one of those things you either love or hate. Locals seem to love it, anyway.

'Oh aye, on Lincolnshire Show days we get through, I should think, 80 chines in two days,' said the man behind the counter at Phipps – the 'Oh aye' proving beyond a doubt that I had unwittingly crossed an invisible boundary and was now once again in the North of England.

All the way up the North-East Coast, a string of little market towns; a solidly agricultural society more or less intact, more or less stable, more or less contented. I had stopped in Spilsby on a Monday morning to have a butcher's at the famous pork pies at Simon's in Market Street, and Monday happened to be market day, thus directly contravening the First Law of Travel, which states that, upon your arrival in a strange town, the market, fiesta, festival or other interesting event will always have happened the day before.

Spilsby was groaning, creaking under the weight of so many vegetables. At the centre of the market they were auctioning bags of them for prices that West Londoners could only dream of. A bag of leeks, thick as a toddler's bicep, for thirty pence.

'Sprouts, the bag, nice local sprouts, thirty, thirty-five, forty . . . any advance on forty pence? Sold to that young lady over there in the headscarf,' the young lady in question being a matronly farmer's wife with greying hair who beamed with satisfaction at this gentlemanly epithet.

Over by the podium were several crates of bright green parsley, the frizzy old-fashioned kind, not the trendy flat kind, destined perhaps to be chopped into a pulp and stuffed into a chine.

'Bag of parsnips. What am I bid? Thirty pence? Twenty-five?' called the auctioneer.

'Twenty-five,' said a man in a tweed cap.

'Thank you, sir, twenty-five. Any advance on twenty-five pence? Lovely bag of parsnips, put them in with your Sunday roast, any advance . . . Any more, any more . . . Come on, the quicker we get this over with the quicker I'm buggering off 'ome.'

A gust of gentle laughter passed across the assembled crowd of large, soft, short people with wide country faces.

'All right – thirty,' cried someone.

'Thank you very much, gent over there, Mr Moresby, I believe it is. Thirty pence.'

'I only said it to get rid o' yer!'

More laughter.

'Eeh, yer bugger!' said the auctioneer.

I met Mr Moresby in the Nelson Hotel after the auction. By the end of the morning the Nelson, an unreconstructed market-town pub with worn red plush seats and battered cream walls, was filling up with Spilsbyans in their market-day best, gratefully supping pints of Batemans.

I was sitting in Mr Moresby's usual seat, and he told me so.

'Eh, sonny, yer sitting in my seat,' he said, and I held his half while he lowered himself creakily into place, sucking all the while on a big briar pipe.

Without any preamble, Mr Moresby launched into a passionate account of the demise of a favourite shop – Moden's, the town baker's – just the week before.

'They've been in Spilsby for a hundred years, have Moden's,' he said, raising one hand for emphasis. 'The supermarkets pushed them out, you know. *Terrible* shame, it is, terrible. People don't realise, if they don't shop at their own shops they'll lose 'em. And they've just lost Moden's, ha'n't they.'

At the bar behind me, the vicar was buying a round for a group of his parishioners. 'Just a half of light for me, love. On duty.'

Mr Moresby noticed my pork pie, wrapped up in white paper and exuding a slight aroma of warm pastry.

'Aye, you'll enjoy that,' he croaked approvingly. 'Simon's, now they're a lovely butcher. They do a nice chine, 'n all. With a bit o' mustard, that'll go down a treat.'

The morning sun shone through the windows, bringing up the dust on the tables, picking out the red gleam in the old man's bitter and the furrows on his gnarly hands.

LINCOLNSHIRE PORK PIE

First make your jelly: place a pig's trotter with a bay leaf and a teaspoon of black peppercorns in a small pan. Cover with water and simmer for 3 hours, topping

up with water once and then allowing the liquid to reduce until it reaches halfway up the side of the trotter. Remove the trotter and any gunge from the surface, strain into a bowl and leave overnight in the fridge. By morning it should have set into a clear jelly: if not, boil briefly to reduce.

For the hot water crust pastry, boil 225ml of water with 225g of lard and pour the mixture into a bowl containing 500g of plain flour and a level teaspoon of salt. Fold in with a metal palette knife, form the dough into a ball and knead quickly until smooth. Don't allow the dough to go cold on you.

Now roll out three-quarters of the dough into a circle and lay it into a pie tin around 7 inches across and 3 inches deep. (The squat kind of cake tin used for Christmas cakes is perfect. If it has a removable base, so much the better.) Squish the pastry into the corners and up the side of the tin, sealing the joins well. Prick the base and sides well with a fork and leave in the fridge.

For the filling, take a 500g joint of pork shoulder with a good layer of fat (or substitute 100g of lean meat for bacon fat). Dice the meat into 5mm chunks – do not mince, as the texture should be chunky. In a china bowl, mix with 6 chopped fresh sage leaves, a level teaspoon of finely chopped mace and plenty of salt and pepper.

Fill the pie case with the pork mixture. Roll out the remaining pastry and place it on top, cutting away any excess. Seal and crimp the edges. Brush the top of the pie with egg wash (beaten egg and water). Surplus pastry can be used to make a decoration: leaves are easiest. Arrange this on top and brush with egg wash. With a sharp knife, make a hole in the centre of the lid. Bake in a hot oven for an hour and a half, reducing the heat after an hour if the pastry seems to be browning too fast.

Turn the pie out of its tin and allow to cool completely. Meanwhile bring the jelly to the boil and allow to cool. Pour the still liquid jelly through the hole in the lid. (A small funnel is useful for this.) When the cavity appears to be full, wait a little until the jelly subsides before topping up.

For best results, if you have enough self-control, leave the pie for a day or two before cutting open.

'Lincolnshire people take their food seriously,' read the brochure from the county council. Grimsby, one of the great ports of the east coast of Britain, seems to me like a comprehensive refutation of this theory.

Everything about Grimsby suggested a town pushed and pulled by the twentieth century into distorted and uncomfortable shapes. Grimsby is home to one of the most important fish markets in Europe, but this is now hidden away in an industrial complex with security guards on the gate. Meanwhile, what was presumably the old port has been tarted up into a red-brick 'quayside' with its own Sainsbury's and Texas Homecare. Bang next to the supermarket, opposite Carol's Handicrafts and Gifts, was the National Fishing Heritage Centre, one of those interactive museums that promise so much in the way of understanding and empathy with their subjects that they invariably disappoint.

In an effort to create some atmosphere, taped sounds of squalling seagulls and phut-phut engines of fishing boats blared out across the 'quay' from the forecourt of the Heritage Centre. On the harbourside itself, however, there were no seagulls to be seen, nor in fact any boats of any kind. The British have a particular skill at destroying ways of life in order to capitalise on the nostalgia resulting from their disappearance.

In the foyer of the heritage centre, among the racks of leaflets, I found a document entitled *Where To Eat*. This would be my key to Grimsby gastronomy. Grimsby, the leaflet declared, is 'known as Europe's "Food Town"'. How was it, I marvelled, that I had travelled across the Continent in total ignorance of its fabled riches? How could I have been so foolish? My salivary glands did somersaults in anticipation. Think of it! If Grimsby was everything it said it was, there would be succulent meats, cheeses galore, oysters and mussels to rival the best of Brittany, ethnic foods from all corners of the globe . . . And of course, Grimsby being the great lynchpin of the fishing industry, there would be twitchingly fresh fish unpretentiously served in brasseries thronged with pan-European gourmets.

The cover of the leaflet showed a full-colour still-life of huge grey tiger prawns piled on a chopping board, a shallot and a head of garlic and some red onions, eggs in a wire basket, fettucine in a tall jar, and a bottle of Recioto Amarone Valpolicella from Santa Lucia, that most tremendous and heady of red wines, the sort of thing described reverentially by Italian oenophiles as *un vino da meditazione*.

I perused the list of restaurants in Grimsby and neighbouring Cleethorpes, so usefully classified under nationality and style. The Amarone bottle had skewed my appetite towards Italian; however I did not think the Pizza Hut, alone in the Italian category in Grimsby, was quite what I had in mind. Among the Continental class, I passed over Swigs, Traders and the Pink Butterfly, and decided that Othello's smacked rather too much of *souvlakia* and Cypriot plonk.

Hoping against hope that 'Food Town' would not disappoint, I swept out into the night, driving for an hour around the one-way system before finding my way into what Grimsby might describe as its 'Old Town'.

On a Monday night at half past eight, the centre of Grimsby was deserted. If Shopping and Eating are the two activities in pole position in British urban culture at the start of the twenty-first century (the two go together, like hunting and gathering, reading and writing), there was every sign that Grimsby life was skewed decidedly towards the former. The streets, which had largely been pedestrianised (i.e., made pedestrian), were a compendium of Brit Shop's greatest names, from BHS to W.H. Smith.

Two teenage girls came clip-clopping by in white plastic platforms, looking as if they were on their way to a party. Perhaps there was an unsuspected side to Grimsby, all speakeasies and wild raves in deserted fish warehouses, and samizdat delicatessens where gourmets nibbled on smoked eel and Sevruga caviar behind double-locked doors.

'Soomwhere to eat. What, restronts and that? Don't rightly know. You think of anything, Shaz?'

'There's that fish place up Brighowgate. What about that Indian your mum took you to?'

'Yeah, just keep going up this street, then turn left, it's along there. We've joost come from McDonald's. Why don't you go for a Big Mac?'

Abdul's Tandoori was closed on Mondays. As was Grimsby's only approximation to the cuisine of the Far East, the Peking Garden – described in my brochure as 'Cantonese', which is only a thousand miles south and a whole different kettle of steamed whole fish with ginger and garlic from Peking, but no matter.

Tired of walking, I stopped for a pint at the Tivoli Tavern – leatherette banquettes and Laura Ashley Victorian wallpaper – reading with interest that the pub dated back at least to 1869, when Grimsby was nothing less than the world's most important fishing centre, as well as presiding over a range of highly successful industries, from ship-building to breweries. In those days, I noticed, the menu at the Tivoli offered French onion soup, hare and grouse soup, lobster, salmon, Brunswick sausages, and reindeer tongues.

It was rapidly becoming clear to me that reindeer tongues would not be on my menu tonight. At this rate, I'd be lucky to find anything at all. A trendy new bar promisingly christened Woods: Shippers of Fine Food and Wine, clearly modelled on money-spinning Southern chains like the Pitcher and Piano and All Bar One, complete with back-destroying bentwood chairs and acoustics apparently designed to amplify the braying of its customers, was to open the following week. Behind the glass box by the door where the menu would normally reside was a blank piece of paper. In my disillusioned, hungry state, it seemed symbolic of Grimsby gastronomy in general.

As it turned out, there was only one place in Grimsby still serving food at ten o'clock, so that was where I ended up. It was a big Victorian gin-palace recently given a makeover by its brewery masters, who clearly thought no one would set foot in the place unless it had bright blue walls and bright green carpets and served some sort of food. And some sort of food was all it was.

As I contemplated the menu a great weariness came over me, followed by a brief moment of rage as I realised that, in this once great fishing port, there was not a single item of fish to be had here, bar the tuna mayo sandwich. But this was not a restaurant, after all, just another of the new breed of food pubs, conjured up by the marketing departments of brewery chains in order to capitalise on the lucrative new fashion for eating as an activity parallel and simultaneous with drinking. So perhaps the lack of dishes reflecting the life and landscape of Lincolnshire was not altogether surprising. Something tasty, however, something carefully prepared with a modicum of love and understanding, surely fell within the bounds of possibility and expectation.

Poor food is always inadmissible, in any circumstances – especially in Europe's Food Town. Alone in my corner of a theme pub, with the ping! of the microwave distinctly audible above the disco classics on the CD jukebox, I toyed with a 'Combo' of mushrooms, onion rings, jalapeno poppers (sic) stuffed with coriander cream cheese and spicy spiral fries (whatever *they* were) – an absurd concatenation, everything encased in batter, badly fried, and given the final insult of a sad mini-salad made of a few frills of iceberg lettuce and a chunk or two of a cold red thing that had as much flavour as you'd expect from something forced into life and then sprayed into submission in some Dutch greenhouse.

I needn't, and I shouldn't go on. We have all been there before. The important thing is to make sure we never return.

12

yorkshire

feasting with fat rascals

I left Lincolnshire over the Humber Bridge, and felt my spirits rise along with my appetite. In Yorkshire, surely, there would be good things. How could it be otherwise, in this stronghold of traditional values in a changing world, this last real bastion of Englishness, where cricket and brass bands still occupy the cultural centre, and the practice of tea-drinking has something of the same timeless and sacrosanct quality accorded it by the Japanese?

Yorkshire food: the phrase conjured up images of plenty and plainness, of large plates of good substantial food; solid but not repulsively so; redolent of home and family. If there were ever a repository for the traditional virtues of British cookery, the modest, comfortable, nourishing food of our island, it would surely be here. Nothing fancy, mind, just roast beef and Yorkshire pudding, Yorkshire rarebits – best made with mustard and stout and a slice of grilled bacon – toad-in-the-hole, haslet, black puddings, spiced beef, oatcakes . . . The beauty of Yorkshire baking, set forth in parkins, pikelets, curd tart, treacle tart, teacakes and Fat Rascals. Strong bitter; stronger tea.

Here was another pork county – less so than Lancashire, but more than Northumberland. Yorkshire loves its pork pies and sausages and bacons and black puddings and hams – York hams, of course. It was only after living in Spain, where slippery pink slices of so-called jamón York are the ubiquitous and horrible alternative to the local air-dried mountain hams, that I bothered to think much about York ham. What exactly was it, and why did you find a bastard version all over the continent of Europe but the real thing almost never, even in its country of origin? Another example, perhaps, of a British foodstuff that has failed to profit in its own land.

It is possible that more people are familiar with the myth of York ham – that it was first smoked using bits of oak left over from the building of the Minster – than have actually tasted the real thing. I wasn't sure quite what to expect myself as I turned the corner from the Minster in search of Scott's the butcher, one of a row of wobbly medieval houses with the words 'YORK HAMS, BACON, LARD' in large old-fashioned letters above the shop window. All I knew was what Hannah Glasse had written in her *Art of Cookery Made Plain and Simple* (1747), to the effect that 'Yorkshire is famous for its hams, and the reason is this: their salt is much finer than ours in London, it is a large clear salt and gives the meat a fine flavour'.

In reality they are 'green', unsmoked hams, salt-cured and hung for anything up to a year. Scott's had banks of them, hanging proudly on hooks behind the counter. I tried a slice, and it was firm and genuinely meaty, not wet and slippy like that industrial stuff, with a nice saltiness pointing up a sweet, clean taste of pork. And I lingered at the counter, Yorkshire ladies audibly tutting and clucking behind me, to ask questions about the fine-looking tackle on display; the massive gammon steaks, each big enough to feed a hungry family of four, the pies, the Cumberland sausages and Barnsley chops – the gastronomic claim to fame of this Yorkshire town being a huge lamb chop, two or three bones thick and sometimes weighing as much as a pound.

I ran into one of those tutting clucking ladies again on the way into Betty's. She gave me a pointed look as we waited in the hallway of the legendary tea room (Betty's is permanently full), finally smiling and asking me affably, 'Did you find out what you wanted to know, then, loov?'

It must be a function of age, I thought, as I settled myself down at one of the mottled brown marbled tables, that sooner or later one ends up appreciating places like this, where up until that point they had induced in one a feeling of airless panic, like being suffocated by an old lady with a feather bolster. A function of age, and of weariness with sullen and slovenly service, that I was unoffended even by the frilly gentility of the mise en place, everything with its napkin around it and its doily underneath, and could listen with pleasure to the smarmy-charmy chap in the black jacket and waistcoat who slid up to the table and pronounced chirpily, in a fruity Yorkshire accent, the following sentence: 'Our coffee recommendation today is Hawaiian Kona, which is quite rich, and could be accompanied by a slice of toasted teacake.'

A function of age, too, and of increasing distaste for trendiness, that I should find delightful Betty's admixture of ages other than my own; the elderly gents in ties reading the *Yorkshire Post,* the young mums taking a break from shopping and husbands, the American tourists comparing the tea shops of Bath with those of Stratford-on-Avon, and the schoolboy on his own at the table in the corner, working his way diligently through a large jam doughnut.

The waitress who took my order, wearing a lacy white shirt with a frilly collar and a little black tie pinned up with a silver brooch, looked much as her forebears must have done when Frederick Belmont, a Swiss confectioner, opened the first Betty's branch in Harrogate in 1919, with the promise that everything served would be 'fresh and dainty'.

The waves of food began to arrive: the pikelet, a kind of thinking man's crumpet, thin and delicate and buttery with a crenellated edge; the rarebit, made with Gruyère cheese and Black Sheep ale, a nice symbol of the Helvetico-Yorkshire entente cordiale; and a marvellous tart filled with a silken combination of curd cheese, currants and eggs and crowned with three dollops of cool whipped cream. From the list of coffees I passed over Galapagos Islands Organic in favour of the exceptionally rare beans from the island of St Helena, of which no more than a few tons are harvested every year. Who knows – perhaps Napoleon would have been familiar with this thin-looking but pungent, almost fruity-tasting brew, sipping it silently as he gazed out over the steel-grey South Atlantic?

At a neighbouring table a silver triple-decked cake stand had just arrived, laden with fruitcake slices, scones and drop scones, chunks of dark, moist, treacly Yorkshire parkin and cucumber sandwiches. All around me people seemed in a mild state of ecstasy towards which I, too, was gradually ascending. I finished my food and sat there for what seemed like hours, immersed in a warm bath of bliss, watching the handsome young boys with their neat haircuts and black bow-ties as they carefully cleared the table vacated by a group of Yorkshire grannies so that another group of grannies, on a day trip from Thornton-le-Beans, could take their place.

The ladies on the next table were talking about tea, competing with each over the number of cups each drank per day.

'I'm a one, two, three, four, five, six cups a day person.'

'Ooh, I should think I drink six pots a day, not six cups.'

'Oh, well, you're an addict, then.'

'We never used to have coffee when I was young . . .'

'That's right, if you wanted coffee it was only that Camp stuff.'

'That liquid . . .'

'Absolutely disgusting – like a weak cup of tea.'

It was the most pejorative comparison she could think of.

The afternoon ticked slumbersomely by. A policeman in a tall police hat strolled past the window on the flagstones, checking his watch. When I dragged myself into the street with a heavy heart, the sky was almost darkening. The world outside seemed grey and cruel, and the ultimate proof of its greyness and cruelty was the note I found slapped on my windscreen. It was a parking fine, or rather a Parkin fine: thanks to Betty's, I had overstayed my welcome in the city of York by two hours and twenty-seven minutes.

High-tech luggage wasn't made for cobbled streets. The couple were having trouble, bickering as they bundled their wheely plastic pink-and-purple suitcase up the inclined lanes while simultaneously attempting to decipher the signs and symbols scrawled on a scrap of paper. There are few places to stay in Howarth on a grey weekday at the wrong end of October, when a cold wind tears across the moors and all colours but grey and brown seem to have been prohibited by law. But this is the heart of Brontë Country, and the Japanese, being romantics at heart, will do whatever it takes to feel themselves close to all that torment and mystery and passion.

I watched their awkward progress for a while, wondering how much of a shock it would be to a pair of Japanese romantics when, later, having dumped their suitcase on the bed and examined bemusedly the flowery furnishings of their room, they ventured forth in search of something to eat.

On a night like this the options would be few. If they didn't leave it too late, they might catch the pub down the road, which did fried stuff with chips. Being Brontë fans, they might prefer the Villette Coffee House, where the menu offered chicken nuggets, pizza slices, Cornish pasty and, for pudding, Arctic roll, knickerbocker glory, or something rather more *typiquement* Yorkshire: a speckled round of curranty cake decorated in this case with a glacé cherry and two strips of angelica arranged in the manner of a clock face and described as a Fat Rascal. That ought to confuse them entirely.

'*Wuthering Heights* is on every school syllabus in Japan. For them it's the novel to end all novels, the key text in literature,' said my landlady at the guest house, with the dispassionate air of one who has grown used to playing a modest part in the tourist economy. Her home, a big stone mansion with flagstone floors a mile or two out of Howarth, had a Brontë connection, which explained why, if you struggled up from the house on to windswept Howarth Moor, you could see that the footpath was signposted in Oriental characters.

What would she be serving for dinner tonight? I imagined a ribsticking meal of meat and several veg, followed perhaps by a steamed suet pudding, a jam tart, or some tinned fruit in cling syrup. I had hardly reckoned, however, on the culinary prowess of this remarkable Yorkshirewoman, who wouldn't have served up a meal like that in a month of Sundays, or indeed a lifetime of Sunday lunches.

Round the table that night was a small selection of her many friends, for whom a visit to the Hall meant a chance to eat something they knew in advance would be both delicious and wholesome and would not contain any meat. For Mrs Watkins was a vegetarian cook of great sophistication, schooled in the Cal-Ital meat-free cuisine of the famous Greens restaurant in San Francisco. Her mother had been a vegetarian in the 1940s, when to be such a thing was to be daringly avant-garde, and the custom had run in the family ever since.

'Most of my daughter's friends' families eat what I suppose you'd call "convenience food",' she said matter-of-factly as she brought to the dining-room table a tray loaded with mushroom tian and wholewheat dumplings, roasted vegetable salad and beetroot with blackcurrants. 'One long-suffering mother I know produces a dinner every night made up of each of the children's favourite dish, all on the table, or in front of the telly, at once: pizza, chicken nuggets, fish fingers, et cetera.'

'What about Sharon's mum, that time we went round and she said there were nowt to eat?' prompted her daughter, a sturdy blonde Yorkshire lass with skin as clear as the water in the stream that babbled in the valley below.

'Oh yes. The dole cheque hadn't arrived, it was a day late. But I couldn't help asking myself: did she have any onions? Did she have a packet of lentils? They might have had a tin of tomatoes somewhere, surely.' The point being that the notion of a store cupboard, supplying food for emergencies or unexpected guests, seems not to be common any more in British households.

The daughter's friend sat next to me, tucking into her dumplings with gusto.

'What kind of thing would you be eating, then, if you were at home tonight?' I asked her.

'Mum makes Yorkshire puddings,' she answered, perhaps thinking that was the answer I was after. 'But I'm a veggie, so no roast beef for me. We have a proper tea at 5.30. One of the rest of the family's favourite things is a pie and peas. Peas and pies – it's very Yorkshire, is that. Eh, Matt?'

'I wouldn't know, I were born in Lancashire,' said the big blond guy at the end of the table. 'My mum used to make a lovely hot-pot. These days she can't be bothered to go to all the trouble, since it's only her and me dad. It's funny, because my little brother was brought up by me grandmother, so he spent his first five years eating tripe and onions. And he still loves it, like. Whereas me, because I never had to eat it as a child, I can't stand all that old stuff.'

'I do know what you mean, loov,' offered a middle-aged lady who had come up from Keighley to help around the house and had stayed for dinner. 'You know what, somebody cooked up a pot of tripe and onions last VE Day in Howarth, and no one would touch it. 'Cause it smells, you know. Of course there are still some people who'll eat it raw. Specially in Lancashire – they'll eat anything over there,' she said with a mischievous wink at the big blond guy. 'Ooh, it just looks to me like a horrible big white blob of rubbery jelly.'

'But your husband's from the North Riding, isn't he? Doesn't he insist on "all that old stuff", as Matt calls it?' enquired my landlady.

'Aye, sometimes. Don't get me wrong, it's not all of it I mind. I do like a nice bit o' Yorkshire pudding. My Derek's mum used to cook it with currants and honey, as a sweet. Ever so nice, that is. Another thing we like is the dock puddings down at Hebden Bridge. Dock leaves and barley, boiled up with an egg. They make it at Whitsun, when the docks are fresh and green.'

Ah yes, I had read about these strange-sounding puddings in certain eighteenth-century cookbooks, but had never been able to believe that anyone in this day and age in Yorkshire would still be picking the leaves of the bistort or Easter ledger (*Polygonum bistorta*), with the optional addition of dandelion, nettle, lady's mantle, or blackcurrant and gooseberry leaves from the garden, and boiling them up in a muslin bag for an hour and a half with barley and eggs. Clearly however the practice still went on, if only in a public and celebratory, rather than domestic, form.

Easter Ledger Pudding

For this savoury pudding you will need to have access to the passion dock plant, also known as bistort, which is rife in much of Yorkshire and is at its best in spring.

Take equal amounts of passion dock leaves – the tender young leaves are best – and young nettle leaves. (Traditionally, leaves of Lady's Mantle, blackcurrant and gooseberry were also added.) Wash in cold water and trim off the stalks. Simmer in a little water with a chopped onion. Strain, reserving the liquid, allow to cool, and chop the leaves with kitchen scissors. In a bowl, combine with a handful of cooked oatmeal or pearl barley, a beaten egg or two, salt and pepper. Add a little of the cooking liquid and return the mixture to the pan, simmering until it thickens. Leave to cool in a square tin. When cold, cut into squares.

The pudding can either be eaten cold or fried with bacon. John Tovey at Miller Howe liked to serve it with roast lamb.

'What you should do, you know, if you want to look at some interesting food,' suggested Mrs Watkins, turning to me, 'is you should take a trip to Leeds. You'd be amazed what they've got down there these days. Why don't you nip down on the train tomorrow?'

So I did. I caught the little Metro train that chugs noisily along the valley of the River Aire, past the Saltaire cotton mill where David Hockney has a gallery and the trendy Salts Diner wouldn't serve tripe and onions unless they came with sun-dried tomatoes and grilled polenta.

The sun peeked out for ten minutes before being erased by banks of mist that were ripped away in turn by a howling gale. Sheep on the hillsides above the railway line were rosetted by the wind, and the Canada geese strained their necks on the river below.

'Loovly day today!' said a bright-countenanced elderly Yorkshirewoman, politely opening the door for me as we stepped off the train at Leeds station.

Twisting my scarf tighter against the cold, I hurried along Boar Lane to Kirkgate Market, long regarded as the exception, along with its equivalents in Oxford and Swansea and a few other places, to the general rule that the covered food markets in Britain's cities are not up to much.

I pushed through the doors at the corner of the market and found myself under a soaring roof of ironwork and stained glass, with slender columns with Ionic capitals holding it all up and a balustrade running around the side. It was like entering a cathedral, except that this ceaseless hum of activity, this glorious buzzing roar of money being exchanged for goods, would be thought sacrilegious in a place of worship.

'I used to go shopping at Kirkgate Market, wi' me mam. And now here I am again, workin' 'ere,' said a market manager from upstairs, wearing a white shirt and black tie. 'The wife still shops at Kirkgate, even though we live out in t' sticks. Course, they've got this new big megastore now at Meadowhall. She finds it dearer than here, though – and if you're talking about quality, there's no comparison. Did you know, fascinating fact here, we're actually standing in the biggest indoor market in Europe?'

On size alone I couldn't make a judgement, but as markets go this was certainly a good one, and blessed with some nice Yorkshire idiosyncrasies. Down Butchers' Alley, still flagstone-floored, I found 'cooked shanks', raised 'stand pies' made with pork meat, and a tasty-looking haslet.

'Could I give you t' recipe? Well, it's liver, sweetbreads, heart and various other bibs and bobs, ain't it, with some oatmeal and herbs and a little chopped onion, stuffed into a skin, and cooked. Got that?' said the man at Mr Smith's the butcher's, which had been with the market since it opened in 1904. On the bakers' stalls were Oulton slices and oven bottom cakes and strange floppy oatcakes made from batter cooked on a griddle. If I'd wanted fish, I could have had Scarborough Woof, Finny ('fresh, not frozen') and a pound of whelks for fifty pence.

'Go on, loov, take one,' said a large grinning fish-wife, seeing me eyeing the whelks. 'You'll be chewing on that till Christmas.'

I spent the rest of the morning peering into restaurant windows, musing on the way trendy Britfood at its worst has become a mere parade of gastronomically correct ingredients, the difference between one meal and another being a question of permutation. 'Risotto of arborio rice with sun-dried tomatoes and grilled Mediterranean vegetables with balsamic vinegar', at the ragingly chic Brasserie 44, just about had the lot. Puy lentils, porcini mushrooms, shaved Parmesan (nowadays it never comes unshaven), lemon grass and lime leaves . . . To judge by the menus at the city's most fashionable restaurants, these were exciting novelties in West Yorkshire, at a moment when as far as London foodies were concerned they could have been served up by Fanny Cradock, such was their antiquity in fashion terms.

At the Olde England Fisheries, life went on as if vitamin C had never been invented. You could have pies and peas, fish and chip butties, or the original chip butties. I had heard about these, but never quite dared to try one. There was a picture of the dish in question above the counter, the chips spilling out grotesquely from within a long white bun. The bread looked like two great blubbery lips. This you could have with curry sauce – one of the smellier fag-ends of our colonial past.

I decided against this and went instead to the opposite extreme of perfectly packaged gorgeousness. When Harvey Nichols opened a branch in Leeds there was general guffawing in the South of England, the subtext of which was 'as if women in the North ever had a clue about real elegance – all those Nora Batty types in aprons and curlers'.

If Northern women ever lagged behind, however, Harvey Nichols Leeds showed them doing their level best to catch up. The store was full of immaculately tailored women, many of whom had brought their wide-eyed mothers. As I was going up to the fourth-floor food section on the escalator I heard one of them say, 'It's not exactly a beige, more a biscuit. The trouble is, Mum, I haven't got a brown top to go wi' it,' and the mother reply, 'Well let's look for a brown top then, shall we, loov?'

The food hall, like the one in the Harvey Nicks in London, was a collection of expensive gifts that happened to be edible. No concessions to regionalism here – this was Yorkshire's first taste of germ-free pan-European eating.

A gaggle of girls were taking the mickey out of the prices.

'Three quid for a tin of biscuits!?'

'Oh go on, you can keep it as a souvenir.'

The restaurant next door to the food hall, with its wall of plate-glass windows offering an impressive urban view, was like Yorkshire's idea of arriving in heaven. 'I think I'm not in Leeds,' said an elderly lady by my side, almost faint with all this shiny modernity.

To eat anything High Up imparts a special frisson of glamour to the act. I sat at the window and stared out over the rooftops at this city suddenly so prosperous, so sure of itself, so lacking in the chip on its shoulder that others would rather like to bestow on it. It was a Friday lunchtime, and female executives were lightly lunching, judging it a good moment to nibble on Harvey Nicks's assembly food or perhaps sip a Jumbo Cappuccino. (The national drink of Yorkshire is surely tea; endless tea, with food and without. And the question 'Would you like a drink?' in Yorkshire has nothing to do with alcohol, but means 'Would you like a cuppa?' Cappuccino and espresso, however, seem set to change all that.)

There were Thai pork satay and Greek salad and a risotto of wild mushrooms with truffle oil and shaved Parmesan. There were confit and pancetta and salade tiède and the ubiquitous tarte Tatin, this time made of red onions. I wondered what the Yorkshire mothers, used to high teas and roast beef dinners, must make of it all. I ordered a roasted duck breast on bubble and squeak with a thyme and haricot jus, followed that with a comfortingly nostalgic dish of creamed rice pudding with a slice of parkin, that sweet treacly gingery Yorkshire cake, and then felt I had overdone it, when the chic order would have been a few mixed leaves and a mineral water.

The sun came flooding through the plate glass, making me shut my eyes and drift off for a minute or two, imagining I was sitting on some terrace on the Amalfi coast, with the turquoise sea spread out below me and the whole afternoon to sleep and swim and dream of dinner.

'You all right there, loov?' said a Yorkshire granny who was just getting up from the next table. When the waitress came by the granny touched her arm and pointed me out.

'He looks a little bit under the weather, doesn't he?' she said sweetly. 'Why don't you bring him a nice pot of tea, loov? That'll set him right.'

Next day I took the other rumbling Metro line from Keighley eastwards along the Aire, to Bradford – a city that is as close to Leeds as it's possible to be without the two places fusing into one.

Food-wise Bradford is not the dedicated follower of fashion that Leeds is. It is pointless to look for shiny modern brasseries and food boutiques here, because Bradford is not interested in any of that. The flavour of the city comes from its plethora of Asian restaurants, which reflect a history of massive immigration mainly from Pakistan and western India. It is a faithful microcosm of the reality of Britain as a whole, where Indian restaurants dominate the culinary landscape (at last count there were more than 7,500 across the country – in 1950 there were just six) and many people know much more about Indian cuisine than they do about their own.

'We've got 142 Indian restaurants in Bradford, aye, that's one for every 2,412 inhabitants,' said the woman in the tourist information office proudly, handing me the booklet they have edited that tells you *Where to Eat in Bradford City Centre*. The booklet did mention a few non-Asian eating places, one suspects more out of obligation than anything else. But who in their right mind would bother with the Oastler Coffee Room and Salad Garden (Homemade Fayre), when the city's offer of Eastern food is so generous, varied and reasonably priced?

I'd arrived during Diwali, the Hindu festival of light, and though the Asian community in this town is overwhelmingly Muslim the streets of the city centre were hung with signs wishing Happy Diwali to anyone who felt like celebrating it. In the Bombay Stores, the Asian answer to BHS that is now marked on maps as a tourist site worth seeing, there were Diwali greeting cards showing the elephant god Ganesh in his pink and orange livery, trunk aloft, and girls and their mums were buying pink and orange saris for the big Diwali parties in Manningham and Laisterdyke that the girls would be heading for tonight.

The Bombay is a shopper's paradise of spice mixes in jars and packets, Indian disco tapes, housewares bravely guaranteed for one year, slippers decorated with sparkles and spangles, day-glo prayer rugs; in fact, everything the modern-day Orientalist could possibly desire and more, except for food.

'For food, loov, you'd best try the Panorama,' said the girl behind the till, she of the red dot on her forehead. I walked a little further up the hill, past rows of dingy houses and a rubbish-strewn patch of grass in which a few kids were letting off bangers, to a barn-like building crammed with tins of ghee and sacks of rice, spices, breads and condiments, testifying to the enormous complexity and sophistication of the cooking of the Indian subcontinent. The flour section alone provided an elementary lesson in Asian cooking, in that flour is not just associated with wheat and rye, as in the western tradition, but also with buckwheat, chickpeas, maize, rice, coconut, lentils, peanuts, dried beans, potatoes and anything else solid enough to be pulverised.

In the food Dark Ages of the 1960s and 1970s, it was the Indian restaurants of Britain that reminded us as a nation what good food could be about. In many British towns and cities they are still the lonely outposts of good affordable eating, hemmed in by grim deserts of fish and chips and burgers. The popularity of Indian food cuts across all conceivable boundaries of class, age, region of the country, and ethnic group. It is marvellously democratic. As I waited with a friend and her daughter for a table at the Mumtaz, beside a takeaway counter terraced with bright orange and acid green squares of sweetmeats studded with nuts and fruit, there was a sudden tableau: a tall handsome black boy, a blonde clear-skinned girl and a bearded Asian guy, all sitting down to have lunch together.

'Well I don't know about you, but I'm having the mutter paneer and the pakora this time,' said the black boy, and to hear the Hindi words spoken in a Yorkshire accent inexplicably brought a lump to my throat.

The Mumtaz, one of Bradford's longest-lived and best-loved restaurants, is run by an extended family, the Akbars, who put their hearts and souls into the business in a way that only a family can. 'In Loving Memory of Our Dear Mother, Who Made All This Possible' reads a plaque above the kitchen door. The modest paan house opened by Mumtaz Khan Akbar in 1980 now seats 140 people in, to quote its entirely accurate publicity, 'sumptuous surroundings resplendent in the rich, glorious colours of the East'. It actually looks a little like a Sanderson's catalogue come to life, with swags of purple and flowery fabrics everywhere. There is a no-alcohol rule, which must be a useful way of keeping out the post-pub curry-floaters and all their works, though you can't help thinking a beer would be nice with hot Kashmiri dishes like the ones the Akbar family serve up, following recipes handed down from their own dear mother. But the food is so very good, the flavours so fresh and vibrant, the spicing so perfectly judged, that you forgive them everything. I had spinach and potatoes, karahi ghosht (lamb in meltingly tender small chunks, cooked in the two-handled metal pan known correctly as karahi, and widely but incorrectly as balti), and a bowlful of spiced salad chaat with a big splooch of fresh thick yogurt on top. In the absence of beer, I drank a jug of ice-cold sweet mango lassi. All so very good, that I decided to do what I'd never done before, and order a proper paan. The Mumtaz was a paan house, after all, before it was a restaurant.

I could see one of the brothers preparing it for me over by the sweet counter, where he was surrounded, like a wizard at his potions, with bowls of coloured powders, crumbled leaves, seeds and sugary silver balls like the ones used to decorate cakes. The paan mixture, which included fennel and coriander seeds, cinnamon, grated coconut, red betel-nut slices, and a kind of sickly pink jam, plus various unidentified seeds and powders, came on a small plate, heaped on top of two emerald green betel leaves that Mr Akbar folded into a neat parcel and handed to me, saying with an air of talking to someone who could not be trusted to do things properly, 'Put it in your mouth. But don't bite, just keep it in there.'

He tapped his right cheek. 'You see, after plenty of food the paan is giving a very nice feeling. Thank you.'

And I did as he said, and kept the tight shiny parcel stuck between my teeth and cheek for a while, hamster-style. But then, since nothing seemed to be happening, I gave the betel leaf a single chew. My mouth was flooded with a syrupy sweetness that gave way to a powerful rush of spices; then there was an intense bitterness – that would be the betel leaf – and a sweet, cloying fragrance that was strongly reminiscent of some sort of bathroom spray. I chewed again, riding a faint wave of nausea, discovered a thick sweet mush had made its way beyond the barrier of my teeth, and swallowed inadvertently, hoping to remove that bathroom pong from the proximity of my tastebuds. My mouth was full of pinky spicy redness. I remembered the way the streets in India are covered in red stains. That would be the betel nut. But what an idiot I was – of course, you're not supposed to swallow the thing, you're supposed to spit it out.

Whether it was the narcotic effect of the paan, or the relief involved in having tried something once that I would never in my life have to try again, I left the Mumtaz with a spring in my step, intending to spend the afternoon investigating the ethnic neighbourhoods of suburban Bradford. I headed up Westgate and Lumb Lane towards Manningham, passing the skeletal dome of a mosque under construction and a converted Methodist chapel built in golden Yorkshire stone that was now the Bombay Brasserie and architecturally possibly the most impressive Indian restaurant in Europe.

The further I walked the scruffier the neighbourhood became, and the more new mosques there were, and the more shops with cages to protect the merchandise and Indian disco music blaring out of them, and the more sweet centres, their windows full of stacked orange whirls of deep-fried jalebis and garish squares of sweet stuff. The housing stock was Edwardian or Victorian, now rather dilapidated. There was a bath-house in what had once been a school, with 'GIRLS' and 'BOYS' on two brick doorways. And in a classic English square, in the patch of ground where the central gardens would once have been, there were now little allotments full of coriander, mustard greens and methi. This was Manningham, once a white-collar suburb, now, in the words of the *Guardian* newspaper, 'an inner-city area of Bradford scarred by poverty and neglect'.

You could imagine that Manningham's cultural character must have changed dramatically, and at Mason's Pie, Peas and Tripe shop on the High Street the proprietor was happy to explain to me exactly how. 'I tell you what, not so long ago it was an English area around here, if you understand my meaning. We're in the minority in Manningham now. Funny, isn't it?'

I had pushed through the door into a dark and musty 1960s interior – Formica tables each with their bottle of malt vinegar – wondering whether the place was closed or simply closed down. Mr Mason, in a neck-tie and a white apron, was to be seen bending over a stove in an enormous kitchen out the back, digging about in two great aluminium pots. Though it was still lunchtime, there was no one in the shop but him.

'Business a little bit slow these days, then?' I asked.

'No, we get people in here from all over t' world,' he replied, not exactly answering the question.

On the wall behind the counter was the menu. This was ethnic food all right, though not quite of the variety I expected to find in inner city Bradford. Corn beef hash, meat and potato pie and peas, black pudding, and shepherd's pie were the most popular orders, said Mr Mason, followed by belly pork cut in slices from a joint, ham shanks, lamb's tongues, tripe and onions and udder.

'I just leave that up there for the sake of it. Udder's actually outlawed in Bradford, y' see. It can be very rich, especially off a Jersey cow, and I like it cold, with vinegar and salt. Simple is best, that's the English way. I'm sure the French would do all sorts of things to it, mess it about. But they would, wouldn't they?'

Mr M. was very much a stickler for the traditional, in cuisine as much as in society.

'No, there isn't anything in the world like old-fashioned English food,' he said. 'Trouble is, there isn't enough of it these days. I was born in 1942, in an air raid. I grew up eating cow-heel stew, boiled up with lots of carrots and onions – lovely. I used to live off that. My grandfather was the original "Pie" Mason. Here he is.' And he brought out an ancient photo from a curio cabinet of a proper old gent in a cap and smoking a pipe, and shook his head twice and tut-tutted. 'He'd be turning in his grave if he could see what's happened to Manningham.

'Now that's enough of my blather. What can I get you: a nice pie, maybe, or a slice of pork, a bit o' black pudding? I can do you a nice stick pudding, that's long and thin, or a berry, that's round and fat?'

The pies on display didn't look too bad. The pastry was crumbly and the meat inside a reasonably appetising colour. Nevertheless I was grateful I had already eaten and could honestly say I was sorry, but I could eat no more. For there was something about this place, this little ghetto of archaic English food and values, that made me glad to step outside again, among the saris and the sweetmeats.

The problem with traditional English food is not so much that it is bad for you, or that it is stodgy and boring, or any of the other calumnies levelled against it. In fact these beliefs are part of the problem. English food simply has what is known as a 'bad image', and that image is inevitably worsened when, as so often, the dishes in question are badly cooked and badly presented.

Finding a decent Yorkshire pudding in Yorkshire, for example, requires a major piece of detective work, though there is no shortage of opinions as to how exactly it should be made. In the tourist office in Bradford there was a kitchen cloth on the wall that tourists could buy as a souvenir, explaining how to make Yorkshire pudding with a batter made with milk and eggs. I told this to a friend of Mrs Watkins back at the guest house, and she tutted with disapproval at the suggestion of the milk.

'You don't need to use milk, loov, and that's the honest truth. Water's the thing. Not many people understand this, but I'll tell you fer nothing, what's going to make that pudding rise isn't baking powder, self-raising flour or anything else, but *steam*. That's why you need a really good roasting oven – to get that steam going, so the surface bubbles up.'

'Oh, I don't know, loov. I don't think water gives as good a flavour, you know,' said another Yorkshirewoman, a petrol-pump attendant I got talking to in Skipton, on the way up to the Dales. 'My mother used to make it with milk and water mixed. She used to pour it in with the roast, so you'd get the meat sitting in a proper lake o' pudding. Mmmmm! What pump are you on, loov? Cash or card?'

'You should always whisk it up nicely, get some air into it, that's what my granny used to tell us,' said the girl who brought my tea at the café in Horton-in-Ribblesdale. 'I wouldn't make it myself, I have to watch me weight. I'd rather have a pizza, to be honest; one of them nice crispy ones.'

'Women these days can't be bothered to make Yorkshire puddings, and I can't say as I blame 'em,' said the man at the

Yoredale Cheese Shop, where I'd stopped to locate one of the two or three Wensleydale cheeses still made on-farm in the dale. 'There's so many other things to do, weekends. I mean, who wants to be faffin' around in the kitchen when you could be bobbin' out to the shopping centre, tekkin' kids to the theme park? The proper Yorkshire Sunday lunch, that'd be once a month these days, not once a week. And the Yorkshire puddings you'll find in pubs and restaurants, they'd be frozen.'

'Whisk it, not too much, with a fork, that way you keep the lightness,' said the waitress at the King's Arms in Askrigg. They didn't actually serve Yorkshire pud in the pub, she was sorry; that wasn't really their thing. 'Mexican fajitas with roasted Mediterranean vegetables' or 'timbale of sun-dried tomatoes and halloumi cheese' were more their thing, she said.

The thought of anything at all being 'sun-dried' in the Yorkshire Dales made me giggle. 'Rain-sodden' would be nearer the mark.

'Is your Yorkshire pudding fresh or frozen?' I asked the barman at the Dog and Duck in Scagglethorpe.

'Frozen,' he said flatly.

'I'm afraid it's frozen,' said the landlord at the Bear in Buttercrambe.

'Frozen. We make it up in batches, slice it up, then defrost it when a customer orders it,' admitted the lady at the Bell in Wombleton.

I was beginning to despair of Yorkshire cuisine entirely. Imagine finding only a frozen cassoulet in Toulouse, or frozen paella in Valencia. There would be a national outcry; angry editorials in *Le Monde* and *El Mundo*. Quite apart from that, it was getting close to two in the afternoon, and two in the afternoon, as many a lazy weekender-in-the-country has found out to their cost, is the terrible curfew hour when pub kitchens across the land clang shut with all the grim finality of a castle portcullis.

Out on the A684, just past the Wensleydale Cheese Visitor Centre, there was a tableau of Dales life, so perfectly timed that it might have been arranged to coincide with my visit by the Authentic Touches department of the Yorkshire Tourist Board. A Wensleydale milk lorry pulled out from Catriggs Farm, loaded with that morning's milk. But the road was blocked with a flock of cantering, baaing sheep, funnelling themselves through a gate towards the pastures of the valley floor, the farmer's wife running in front of them, the farmer with a crooked stick and an eager young sheepdog bringing up the rear.

I asked about the pudding as I made my way around the county, and it was in Helmsley, a small but well-fed town on the edge of the North York Moors, that I finally received the most completely truthful answer to my question.

'We can't do it fresh – that's a home thing,' said the cook at the Royal Oak. 'When we make it for us, it's straight in the oven, straight out, Sunday lunchtimes. When it's not for ourselves . . .'

'It's frozen?'

'Unfortunately, yes.'

So I gave in and ate some of the frozen 'tourist' pudding at the Royal Oak, with onion gravy and a Barnsley chop, and if the truth be known it wasn't bad, though I hankered for the extra-special article the natives reserved only for their tribe; I imagined it a deep golden colour, fading to brown and crispy round the edges, blessed with an added dimension of savouriness by the meat juices dripping from the joint of mutton roasting on the rack above it.

If pudding was a Yorkshire dish in suspended animation, at least Yorkshire curd tart was thoroughly alive and well. I stepped across the market square at Helmsley after lunch, having heard that the Castlegate Bakery was one of the county's better pastry shops and thinking I might snap up something here for food-loving friends and family in the South. And I was pleased to find an Eccles cake better than any I had tasted, melting flaky pastry crunchy with sugar and juicy with currants, and a fine real Yorkshire parkin, dark and treacly, and a crumbly, creamy, delicately cheesy curd tart, made from scratch with fresh milk curdled on the premises, the whey drained off and the curd mixed with eggs and sugar and butter and currants and a delicious little spark of nutmeg.

Yorkshire Curd Tart

For the pastry, rub 125g of butter and a pinch of salt into 250g of plain flour. Add a little cold water to bind. Leave in the refrigerator for half an hour before rolling out the pastry and lining a greased flan tin with it.

For the filling, cream 50g of caster sugar with 75g of unsalted butter. Stir in two beaten eggs, 75g of currants and 25g of ground almonds. Mix gently with 250g of fresh curds and spoon the mixture into the pastry case.

Bake for 25 minutes in a hot oven until the filling has set and turned golden brown.

I picked up a trio of tarts: two for friends and family, and one for me to eat tonight, back in the West Riding and my Brontë B&B. It almost made up for the frozen pudding.

Tradition is a touchstone in Yorkshire life, and that goes for eating as much as anything.

The Box Tree restaurant in Ilkley, where I ate my best Yorkshire dinner, is one of the last bastions of a certain kind of traditional luxury and decorousness that used to be much more widespread in Britain, until the combination of contemporary design and modern manners came along and almost wiped it out altogether. It has become an institution, like Betty's. So that were anyone to try and do away with the old-fashioned decor and style of the place, the legions of customers who have measured out their lives in grand and glorious old-fashioned Box Tree meals would probably take to the streets of Ilkley in protest.

It was a faultless meal, one of the very few such meals I had eaten so far. But this wasn't the perfection of asceticism, but of generosity. It was eager to please, but not desperate to do so. It wasn't flashy, you didn't feel your powers of culinary appreciation were under scrutiny, and you weren't aware, thank heaven, of any media cult around the person in the kitchen. All you knew was that you were in safe hands.

The menu was in English, though the chef was French. It listed Starters, Main Courses and Desserts, but the language of plain English cookery – breast of partridge, lamb cutlet, steamed fillet of brill – was made piquant with *pipérade, galette, ballotine* and *farce*.

There was a subtle and mutually respectful kind of rapprochement going on here. Cream of pumpkin soup with parmesan and herb gnocchi was velvet smooth and delicate, with the gnocchi hinting at English dumplings. Sautéed Cornish scallops came with a fruit chutney and a lemongrass sauce, which seemed almost an affectionate parody of Modern British Cooking, with its constant movement between nostalgic harking-back and anxious reaching out for some kind of exoticism. Terrine of duck foie gras with prunes took things right back to South-West France, and stunned me with its cool luxurious excellence. The dining room, though full, was almost silent, but you could sense the concentration and the pleasure.

There came a group of seven main dishes, each substantial, attractive, irresistibly well conceived. There was heartiness in the roasted rump of veal with spinach and girolles, glorious extravagance in the fillet of Aberdeen Angus with wild mushrooms, madeira and truffle sauce, a brilliant restraint – if that isn't a contradiction in terms – in the fillet of brill with a raviole of langoustines, braised leeks and celery.

I left the Box Tree after consuming all that, plus a classic soufflé omelette with raspberry sauce, a whole bottle of Burgundy, several strong black coffees and a plate of petits fours. It was hard to imagine eating better, at this level of artistry and expense, anywhere in Yorkshire, or perhaps even anywhere in Britain, I thought as I stepped out a little dazedly, into cobbled streets glazed with recent rain.

I was in Whitby on the North Yorkshire coast, sampling the

superb kippers from Fortunes smokehouse, when a fascinating article appeared in the newspaper.

'North-East top of junk food table,' ran the headline.

A survey had shown that the Newcastle area, an hour or two north of here by car, had the worst diet in Britain. According to this survey only a third of the population of the North-East ate anything approaching the recommended intake of vegetables, fruit and fibre. The other two-thirds lived on the overdose of saturated fat, starch and sugar provided by fried fish, fried sausages, fried burgers, pizzas, pies, chips, kebabs, chocolate and sweets.

In a nice piece of synchronicity, the same newspaper also bore a short article about the antics of Paul Gascoigne, the famous footballer. It transpired that Gazza, who is known to hail from Newcastle-upon-Tyne, had been seen out and about the night before a big match. He'd had a few drinks, and then, rather than go out for a civilised dinner somewhere, he had headed for the nearest late-night fast-food stall and gorged on a doner kebab, leaving a trail of shredded iceberg lettuce as he stumbled down the street to his hotel.

Despite the unfortunate equation Geordie = junk food, the city of Newcastle, which fancies itself these days as a thrustful design-led loft-living metropolis along the lines of Manchester or Glasgow, was evidently not quite the culinary desert it had once been. There was now, apparently, at least one really good restaurant. It served beef fillet made with a Newcastle Brown Ale sauce and Newcastle Brown Ale ice cream.

I should like to have tasted that beef fillet and that ice cream, though perhaps not both at the same meal. But I never made it to the city centre; I got helplessly lost in the jungle of the Tyneside satellite cities, took a wrong turning off the A194 somewhere outside Gateshead and ended up on the fringes of a post-war estate, tombstone housing blocks managing to look stained and dingy even in the dim autumn sunshine. A few kids played ball on a patch of rough ground above which plastic bags floated and tumbled like desert grasses.

A child skidded up to me as I parked the car and locked it and said amiably, 'Wha' you fookin' want, mate?' His teeth, I couldn't help noticing, were an interesting shade of greenish-grey.

What I wanted was to know exactly what he ate, and what his friends ate, and what his parents ate. From the look of those teeth I feared the worst.

Blackbirds Estate possessed a basic pub, the Lion and the Unicorn, a chemist, a small supermarket and a chippy. I made straight for the supermarket, where the British wines, the Brown Ale cans and Thunderbird were kept in a cage behind the cash desk, and the cash desk itself had a special cage all of its own.

Even the worst London corner shop was better than this. There were no green vegetables, only a few shrivelled carrots, potatoes and onions. What there was in abundance was a familiar panorama of packaged processed convenience food; packet soups and tinned soups, corned beef, instant coffee and Fray Bentos pies, gravy granules, own brand baked beans, industrial (Danish) bacon, plastic-wrapped (Canadian) Cheddar, crisps and snacks from here to eternity and a giant freezer packed to the brim with fish fingers, pizza, burgers, crabsticks, Birdseye Mini Chicken Kievs, Bernard Matthews Turkey Roll, McCain Oven Chips in giant plastic sacks, more fish fingers, pizza, burgers . . .

I wondered what kind of creative solutions I might come up with, in the unlikely event of my becoming a resident of the gastronomically challenged Blackbirds Estate. I supposed I would end up shopping for those shrivelled roots and making a lot of nourishing soups with pulses and bacon that would bubble on the stove for hours and keep the kitchen warm. I would ransack the spice rack and make dhals and kormas. I would melt the Cheddar with a little Brown Ale and eat it with boiled potatoes – a kind of Newcastle raclette. There would be ways and means of eating well, though I couldn't deny it would be tough.

The chippy next door offered cod, huss, haddock, rock, saveloy, spring roll, 'budgie', all cooked in the same time-honoured chip-shop way. Sometimes I think frying and battering ought to be made a crime, like assault and battery. And there at the end of the menu, between pickled egg and curry sauce, I finally saw it: 'Mars + chips'.

The horror! The horror! Finally I was face to face with one of the notorious demons of British life. For a long time I had suspected from the 'friend of a friend' character of the anecdotes told about it, that the deep-fried Mars Bar was nothing more than an urban myth, like the dog in the microwave. There was no mistaking the black and red box behind the counter, however, nor the sweet sickly chocolatey aroma that mingled with the shop's other smells of frying oil and Non-Brewed Condiment.

The guy in front of me had just ordered something I had never seen before: a deep-fried slice of pizza. But I knew the job I had to do, and in a minute the Mars Bar was in my hand – an object of rock-like appearance, entirely covered in a solid carapace of yellow batter and gently steaming on its polystyrene tray.

'Er, what do I do with it?' I muttered, sounding posh.

'Ye fookin' eat it, don't ye!' said the cook, thinking this was hilarious. 'Wan' any vinegar, like?'

I shook my head and took a small gingerly nibble, and then, since this had got me no further than the batter, I took a bigger bite. The gooey fattiness of the toffee and melted chocolate, combined with the pappy yellow batter and the faintly rancid oil that seeped from it, created a uniquely disgusting taste sensation.

I must have grimaced.

'Dinna like it then, di-ye?' laughed the guy with the pizza, licking fingers that glistened with grease. 'Wheer ye from anyway like? South of England? You fookers don't know what's good for ye. All them fookin' TV chefs wi' their fancy Southern shite. Fried Mars, man, that's reet good Northern scran that is. 'Cause you're in the North of England now, and ye better not forget it.'

I left the offending item in a seeping, oily mess outside the door, barely able to believe I'd tasted so much as a mouthful of it. It was time to take my custom elsewhere. It was time to go south.

13

london

plenty and polenta

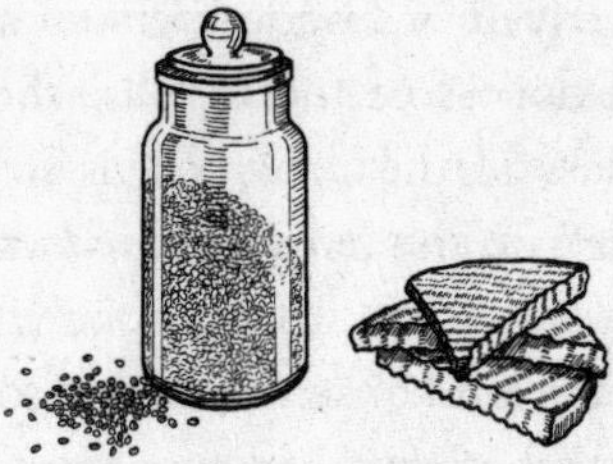

When a man is tired of provincial food, with its fussy, fusty notions of good taste, its shy mimicking of urban fashions that were already passé anyway, and its hellish ways with batter and corn oil, he may as well aim for the one place in the United Kingdom that could never be accused of provincialism – except perhaps in the context of European food, where it still seems a little over-earnest, a little over-excited by the new horizons that have opened up before it.

London is the great laboratory of British eating; where food fashions first come to the boil, only to curdle and go sour not long afterwards; where most of the food writers live, that gobbling scribbling army; and where the newspapers that cultivate and nourish them have their headquarters. London is the point of origin of most of the 700 new cookery books published in

Britain each year, and of most of the dozens of TV cookery programmes. Yet despite the prodigious creativity of its chefs and cooks, this is a capital of consumption, not production. It grows nothing, makes nothing, but, like a gaping maw, sucks down into its gullet the produce of the provinces, and sends them its fads and fashions in return.

On the day I arrived in London, elated and nervous to be back in this harsh doily-free metropolis where much of what passes for high class in the provinces is here nothing better than kitsch, I picked up the *Evening Standard* and saw it in the headlines, in black and white. To someone who had been away for a while, it was the kind of sentence that sounded so unlikely that you wondered whether it had ever been formulated before in the history of language. LONDON – FOOD CAPITAL OF THE WORLD? it shouted, a curious phrase, at once swaggeringly assertive and yet questioning, as if left in doubt by the very grandiloquence of its claim.

It is certainly a claim that, if you'd tried to make it at almost any other time in history, would have been immediately laughed out of court. London food has more often failed to impress than otherwise. The Reverend Dr Trusler, in his *London Adviser and Guide* of 1786, warns readers that they 'will not relish the vegetables and fruit generally sold in London'. The eighteenth-century French traveller M. Grosley was ready to back him up: 'All that grow in the country about London, cabbages, radishes, and spinnage, being impregnated with the smoke of sea-coal, which fills the atmosphere of that town, have a very disagreeable taste . . . I ate nothing good of this sort in London, but some asparagus.' Grosley, evidently something of a gourmet, was surprised to find the meat in London very inferior to that of Paris. London bread has traditionally come in for some tough criticism, too. Smollett's Matthew Bramble called it a 'deleterious paste'. Bread-making expert Frederick Vine wrote in 1897, with a nice dose of sarcasm: 'To describe some of the tackle sold as bread in London as anything else than batter would be to stretch a point in its favour.'

In these days of plenty and polenta, it is shocking to remember just how poorly so many Londoners have eaten for so much of the city's history. Friedrich Engels's still riveting account of the *Condition of the Working Class in England in 1844* contains descriptions of the London poor scrabbling in the streets for rotten vegetables and potato peelings. Half a century later, a survey of poverty in the East End found the children of Bethnal Green being fed almost exclusively on bread, 83 per cent having no other solid food for seventeen out of twenty-one meals in the week. Rickets, dental caries, scurvy and other diseases caused by malnourishment were rampant. Milk, meat, bread and water were routinely contaminated. Even those Londoners who could afford to eat in restaurants didn't always have a better time of it. As the author of *The Memoirs of a Stomach, Written by Himself, That All Who Eat May Read, edited by a Minister of the Interior* (surely one of the best-titled food books of all time) recalled in 1853: 'I have dined at eating-houses, the effluvia of which, steaming up through the iron gratings made me qualmish before eating, and ill all the day after . . . I have groped my way down hypocausts in Fleet Street, and dined in cavern-like taverns, wishing myself a thousand miles away the moment the eternal joint was uncovered.'

It would surely be safe to say that London was never really a great place for food until the end of the twentieth century, when it suddenly transmogrified into (possibly) the Food Capital of the World.

The last time I took a good long look at food here had been in the 1980s, an era that felt terribly shiny and sophisticated at the time but in retrospect seems innocent and breathlessly enthusiastic. All things were possible, as long as you had the cash, and this was as true of food as anything else.

Suddenly there seemed to be good places to eat on every street corner. Notting Hill, newly gentrified, and Soho, newly purged of sleaze, blossomed amazingly. My favourite restaurants of the time were Alastair Little in Frith Street, pioneer of Mediterranean simplicity; Clarke's in Kensington, pioneer of Californian chic; the Greenhouse in Mayfair, pioneer of Modern British Cooking; and Chez Nico in Victoria, pioneer of bolshy superchef shenanigans, where rumour had it that a customer was once ejected from the restaurant for ordering a gin and tonic before their meal. I also loved Kensington Place and the River Café.

For six months in the late 1980s I worked as a waiter at L'Escargot in Greek Street, where in those days the legendary Elena Salvoni was still hostess. Everywhere then was a prototype of something, and under Elena L'Escargot was the prototype of the media restaurant. The menu, carefully chosen to appeal to up-to-the-minute media people, offered such delicacies as avocado and mango salad, deep-fried Camembert with blackcurrant sauce, salmon fishcakes and porcini mushroom risotto with shaved Parmesan. The wine list, put together by up-to-the-minute wine person Jancis Robinson, was one of the first in London to give bin space to the new generation of exotic wines from such places as Oregon, Israel, Canada and England.

Not everything was hunky-dory, though. It was still hard to get a decent cup of coffee anywhere else but Bar Italia in Frith Street. (This at least has undeniably changed for the better. The new generation of coffee houses, Starbucks and Coffee Republic and Aroma, have finally democratised good coffee.) The licensing laws irritated foreign visitors and embarrassed their hosts. Much of the food served was pretentious and modish. There was a feeling of tentativeness, of an awkward but nonetheless passionate urge for self-improvement.

Would any of those gastro-ghosts, I wondered, still be haunting London?

I left the car at a friend's house in Bow and stepped out on to the streets of the West End, Trafalgar Square a white marble camposanto of turrets and towers and dazzling stucco against a powder-blue sky. Though it was midweek, this morning had a Sunday serenity about it. I couldn't remember ever having seen London look so clean, so sparkling, so *designed*. Even the last leaves in the square looked as perfect as if they'd been stuck on individually, by gangs of window dressers, perhaps, at the dead of night.

At the National Portrait Gallery there was a small exhibition of photographs of Famous Food People. That fact alone amazed me, for in Britain until not long ago Fame and Food were not words you saw together very often. I was surprised, too, at how important and full of gravitas these people had been made to look, as if the photographer had wanted to underscore their status as proper Personalities, not just anonymous denizens of the kitchen. Here was Rick Stein, holding a large fish in the half-light of Padstow harbour; Franco Taruschio of the Walnut Tree Inn, in a Welsh landscape, emerging from behind a tree; Marco Pierre White, smart and serious, looking like the businessman he had become since those far-off days at Harvey's in Wandsworth; Fay Maschler, the Frank Rich of the London restaurant scene, whose yea or nay can make or break a youthful eaterie, sitting placidly at a table for one, as if Isigny butter wouldn't melt in her mouth.

I walked up to Piccadilly, stopping to take a look at the most beautiful restaurant interior in Britain, the pseudo-Byzantine Criterion Brasserie, whose soaring ceilings glitter with gold mosaic. (Since I was last in London Mr White, now regarded as the country's most influential and brilliant restaurateur, had brought the place into his expanding empire along with Mirabelle, the Titanic, MPW in Canary Wharf, the Grill Room at the Café Royal, and the Oak Room at the Meridien Hotel, over which three Michelin stars now shone.) Into Soho: L'Escargot and Alastair Little were still there, little changed apart from their prices. Shoppers poured out of Camisa, the Italian delicatessen, some bearing the little white pots of homemade pesto that I remembered buying ten years before. But there was a slew of new places, each more designy and fabulous than the last. In Wardour Street, formerly almost a no-go area strewn with a variegated foliage of tarts' cards, club flyers and fast-food wrappers, there were three chic new restaurants in all of 100 yards: Satsuma, an orange and textured-concrete split-level Japanese noodle refectory, of a type made trendy by the wonderful Wagamama, a mile to the north; Spiga, a cool shiny Italian; and Mezzo, a huge and glittering place that from the outside, if you didn't know any better, you might almost have confused with the offices of an advertising agency whose work on the Tizer account was the dernier cri.

I'd arranged to have dinner that night with a friend who ate out three times a week and knew all the gossip. I needed a crash course in the post-Food Capital restaurant scene, and Sue seemed like the person to provide it.

'Where d'you want to go, then?' she asked me on the phone.

'Somewhere nice. Somewhere fashionable, not too expensive. Somewhere that hasn't been open long?'

'Trouble with something that hasn't been open long, you'll never get a table at this short notice. We could try Mash. But that's been around for six months, not quite so "now" any more. How do you feel about the Hoxton Square scene?'

I had to tell her I was not familiar with it, though I understood the East End in general was on the way to becoming to the 2000s what Soho and Notting Hill had been to the 1990s.

'Yes, it's kind of the latest thing. There's the Lux Bar and Grill, the Great Eastern Dining Rooms, the Electricity Board Showrooms . . . All very cool. There's somewhere there I'd like to try, though, a new sort of bar/restaurant/hangout type place. Shall we go for it? Okay, let's meet at Home at, say, eight-thirty, nine?'

I almost asked her what her address was, and wouldn't it be better just to meet in the restaurant, before realising of course it wasn't home she was talking about, but Home.

So we met in a dark basement in a desolate East London backstreet, and found our way through a dark bar room furnished mainly with scuffed old leather sofas and cheapjack 1970s shelving. There were twentysomethings lolling about everywhere, looking oddly 1970s in their dowdy browns and blues. Further down the same street, said Sue, there was a bar with filthy windows and jumble sale furniture and a single light bulb hanging from the ceiling. If this was the New Drabness, thank goodness it didn't extend to the food served at Home. You could see the cooks darting to and fro in their cramped underground kitchen; they were young spiked-haired girls and boys, drawn from the same sort of constituency and age-group as the customers. Through the hatch came a succession of highly accomplished dishes that wore their influences admirably lightly: a chunky terrine of rabbit and pigeon with red onion jam, a kind of salade tiède of chargrilled fennel and leeks, juicy and sweet, with capers and red pesto; a fragrant bowl of noodles in broth with tiger prawns, oyster mushrooms and green beans; then a pan-roasted cod fillet with saffron beurre blanc and spring onion mash – mashed potato flavoured with a member of the allium family was all the rage this year – and a plainly roasted, but utterly delicious, breast and leg of free range chicken. With a bowl of good fat chips, it was altogether a most un-1970s dinner.

'So you want to know what's happening in the London Food Scene?' Sue began, with a comical groan, as the starters arrived.

'Well. You've got the guys at the top getting more and more starry – in all senses – and more and more respectable – in all senses – and richer and richer – in all senses, probably, too. Gordon Ramsay, well, you can't get a table for the next century. Marco White's sold out to Granada and become a millionaire. Okay, the best posh restaurants in town are the Mirabelle, the Ivy, Pierre Koffmann's La Tante Claire, Gordon Ramsay, who's just moved to where Tante Claire used to be, Aubergine, which is where Gordon Ramsay got his first two Michelin stars, Chez

Nico, the Square – this is just my opinion, right? Mmm, this fennel thing's great.'

My mind already swam a little, and it wasn't only the massive dry Martini I'd just finished. The world of London restauration was always a merry-go-round of openings and closings, buy-outs, and chefs changing horses halfway through the ride. But since my last visit to the funfair the carousel had been cranked up into a rollercoaster.

'You wanna know about fashions? Well, Pacific Rim sort of came and went. The Sugar Club has lost its cred. Wacky ingredients are just not what people want. Fusion food's still around. Vong's good. The Birdcage is bonkers fusion stuff, a mad mixture of Thai and Italian. And Nobu – fabulous, expensive food, thrilling really, Latin American meets Japanese, I love it, there's nothing else like it in London.

'Italian's still massive. I've been to half a dozen fab Italian places in London recently. Grano, Maremma, Assaggi. The Spanish boom never really happened, though the tapas thing had a boost when Antony Worrall-Thompson opened Wiz. Japanese has exploded. Indian has gone regional, Goanese, Keralan, blah blah blah. The latest thing is Indian chefs putting their names to restaurants and charging accordingly.'

'Tell me about the gastro-pubs. Didn't somebody say they might turn out to be the bistros of British catering?' I asked, referring to a decade-old phenomenon whereby gloomy old boozers were stripped of their swirly carpets and nicotine-impregnated curtains and turned into restaurant-bars where you could eat informally and cheaply, drink wine or beer, and hang out on Sunday lunchtimes with your friends and their children.

'Oh, the gastro-pubs, don't worry about them, they're doing fine. A new one opens up every week. When they work, like the Cow or the Eagle or the Ram, they can be a great way of eating out for not too much cash. But now we're on the subject; do you want me to tell you the biggest problem about London food?'

'Okay. Why don't you tell me the biggest problem about London food.'

'The biggest problem about London food is it's still too élitist. We still really need more good places to eat that are also affordable, for God's sake. There's a lot of fab food at the top end, but my God you pay for it. And that's where ethnic eating comes in, you see. The good thing about London was always that, partly because we didn't have our own cuisine I suppose, you could get fantastic Indian, Italian, Chinese, Thai, Japanese, Turkish, you name it – the only thing we haven't got is Mexican – at an accessible price.

'There's some wonderful cheap food out there in the sticks. I'd say that's where the real action still is, not in some overpriced TV chef's restaurant in Mayfair where the guy spends his whole time at business meetings. I'd get out to Zone Four if I were you. Get yourself a travelcard, I would, and go for it. Oh, and don't whatever you do miss Dalston. Hot tip.' And she put her finger to her lips, in a gesture that I took to mean both 'tasty food' and 'Ssssshhhhh . . . Keep this one a secret, would you?'

As if in London, a city with both eyes firmly on the main chance, anything as good as a great cheap meal could be kept a secret for longer than it takes to say, 'A table for two at eight-thirty.'

*

London the inscrutable, incomprehensible, inexhaustible, insufferable . . . Where other cities are like fried eggs, with a discernible neat logic of 'centre' and 'outside', London is an enormous dish of scrambled eggs, made with eggs that were not very efficiently mixed so that the yolks and the white and the seasoning ended up unevenly distributed across the plate. Even in Defoe's time it was 'the disaster of London . . . that it is thus stretched out in buildings; and this has spread the face of it in a most straggling, confused manner, out of all shape, uncompact, and unequal.'

In food terms London is a little like Britain in miniature: certain areas might be opulently varied and sophisticated, while others are sunk in a sad sort of sensuous poverty. So that while Kensington, Islington, Soho and now Clerkenwell and Old Street appear to have seen the light, huge swathes of London are still plunged in the deepest gastronomic gloom. Where are the agreeable restaurants, the go-ahead grocers bursting with good breads and British cheeses and charcuterie, where are the fine pastry shops and coffee houses in (to pluck out a few names quite at random) Roehampton, Lewisham, Tottenham, Bromley, Neasden, Earlsfield, Kilburn?

The salvation of the suburbs, and possibly London's true richness as a food city, is what you might call immigrant cuisine. I taxied it to Southall, way off the end of the Underground beyond the last stop on the District line. People who live in Chelsea or Mayfair or Marylebone have a medieval sense of the Tube map as their picture of the known world, and places like Southall as a terrifying unexplored land where, for all they know, the inhabitants probably have two heads and walk backwards.

I stopped the cab opposite the Gurdwara Sri Gwo Singh Sabha, a Sikh temple with the air of a warehouse, all arched windows and bright flags fluttering in the forecourt. Just over the road, the old Victorian pub on the corner (licensee: Mr M. Dhaliwal) had been painted with pictures of brave Sikh warriors in fancy turbans, and now served tandoori dishes from Lahore, Pakistan having been the point of departure for most of Southall, though Indians, West Indians, Kenyans and Somalians also shop, eat, live and worship, cheek by jowl, in the same square mile.

To be so near to Western culture, and yet so far from its food, was an exhilarating aperitif for the mind. There was a kind of liberating un-Englishness here, sensual, noisy, fragrant, that felt like a million miles from Tesco Metro. The great Indian superstore in the Broadway, like all its equivalents across the UK, aspired to the condition of the bazaar. No Western anomie and antisepsia here: shoppers bustled and shouted, tweaking the vegetables and fingering the bags of pulses, and the aisles were pungent with henna, joss sticks, sweat and fenugreek leaves.

Shops in this borough clearly catered to a refreshingly different set of needs from those of SW3 or NW3: you could buy sitars, T-shirts that said 'Proud to be Sikh', CDs of *Your Twenty Favourite Marriage Songs* and alarm clocks made to look like mosques that woke you with an electronic muezzin's call to prayer. I was in a state of shopping ecstasy. Simone de Beauvoir was right when she wrote, in *The Second Sex*, that 'buying is a profound pleasure, a discovery, almost an invention'. Tempted beyond resistance by a bottle of Black Seed Oil that came with a recommendation from none other than the Prophet himself –

'use the black seed indeed, for it is a remedy for all diseases except death' – I splashed out a pound or two and bought some, thinking that it might make an original addition to a salad dressing, especially since Austrian Roasted Pumpkin Seed Oil was now so terminally uncool.

The food in Southall was so fascinating, so good and so deliriously cheap, that, in true Asian style, I found it hard to stop snacking on it: first a masala dosa and a lassi in the A Sweet, then a dish of lambs' trotters in a glutinous spicy gravy at Gifto's (the names round here are hilarious), then an iddiapam, something like an Asian crumpet, and a sour fish Maldives curry at a Sri Lankan place further up the road. Then, nicely set up for the morning, it was back to the A Sweet for a chaat and a chat with Bobby, whose dad came over from Lahore thirty years ago.

'We were the first 'ere, innit. That's my dad, on the wall there,' he said proudly, pointing to a photo of a serious gentleman in a smart black suit and a turban with a garland of marigolds around his neck.

Unlike telephone boxes in other parts of London, those of Southall are not decorated with prostitutes' visiting cards, but carry publicity of a different sort. 'Are you going to the Punjab?' asked one advertisement, offering a big car to take you from Delhi airport to your home village, with a FREE visit to the Golden Temple at Amritsar if you booked the return trip.

The Punjabi Sikhs and their cooking, based on use of the tandoor and karahi, are the gastronomical cornerstone of Southall. Yet there are many other flavours in this melting pot. Like the Somali breads and stews, aromatic with wot, the East African essence of onion, garlic, butter and spices, consumed by sad-eyed Somalis in a dingy drop-in café called the Salaam; and the Indian food made with African ingredients like mogo (cassava root) and tilapia (a freshwater fish now farmed in the East African lakes) brought over by Kenyan and Ugandan Asians when they came to England in the 1960s, and now served up at Brilliant, regarded by curry-heads as one of London's finest Indian restaurants. Being an enterprising sort, some of these subcontinentals have branched out in new directions: South Indian snacks at the Pakistani chai stalls, tandoori chicken at the Kenyan Asian curry house opposite the drive-thru McDonald's. (How anyone could prefer a Big Mac to a masala dosa I do not understand.) The Tandoori Kebab Centre, I noticed, even had a halal Chinese restaurant in the basement. I loved the idea of halal Peking Duck, and a picture flashed across my mind of the squawking, outraged bird being pointed in the direction of Mecca.

It is not just that London now has a range of national cuisines almost as wide as New York's; without looking too hard, I have found Eritrean, Peruvian, Tunisian, Bulgarian, Georgian. It is also that, confusing though it may be to our snooty sense of propriety (foreigners ought to attend to their own cuisines, thank you very much, and not spend time dabbling in other people's), there is these days a certain amount of blurring at the edges.

In the gastronomic Gobi Desert of Colindale, at the same sort of distance north as Southall is West, someone had once told me about a curious establishment, part superstore, part pan-Oriental food warehouse, where the concept of Asian eating seemed on the point of coalescing into some glorious, myriad-flavoured whole.

An hour and another cripplingly expensive taxi ride later, and I was there, cruising through the windswept uplands of Far North London, past ranks of drab grey 1930s semis under a drab grey sky, a landscape neither suburban nor truly urban, culturally as well as tonally indeterminate, and apparently devoid of all human life, of whatever ethnic origin.

Architecturally speaking the 'largest Oriental food store in Europe', as it advertised itself, was basically just another B&Q industrial warehouse, except with Forbidden City roof tiles stuck on at the edges. The building sat directly on the roaring Edgware Road, one of outer London's major highways to hell. The old Sikh sitting motionless on a bench outside looked as though his yellow-grey beard had become polluted by passing traffic.

Inside was an explosion of colour. I made first for the Japanese bookshop, where Britain's one and only glossy food magazine, now run by a supermarket chain, sat alongside a dozen well-fed and fleshy equivalents from Japan, one of which was entirely devoted to the subject of soup. An avenue of shops selling bamboo furniture and silk cheongsam jackets suddenly opened out into a great covered patio where the noise and the sudden mass of humanity made me stop in my tracks. Say what you like about London, and I do, it certainly knows how to spring the occasional pleasurable surprise by way of recompense for the massive demands it makes on its inhabitants.

Around the walls of the Food Court, arranged in the manner of a market, were the food stalls, a dizzying array of tradition and language and culture that could take you from Beijing to Bali, if you so desired, in a couple of steps. All of a sudden I knew how I would be spending the afternoon. I and my palate would be going on a leisurely tour of the cuisines of the East, being sure to expend the absolute minimum of physical effort in so doing. And I wouldn't be the only traveller on the road. In the vicinity of my table were Chinese and Japanese and Indian families, children shrieking and scrapping on the ethnic boundaries, and a Jewish couple from nearby Golders Green, and a trio of giggly black girls – why stop and gossip in the grey streets of Colindale, when you could do it here? – and a scattering of lone white males like me, greedy for a little afternoon delight.

The dim sum house, the noodle kitchen and sushi bar were only the start. Thereafter, one could stop off at the Malaysian/Singaporean café, the Vietnamese diner, the Indonesian, the Korean, and the North Chinese takeaway, the Chinese bread shop and sweet shop, the Japanese cake stall selling neatly wrapped buns and sweetmeats made of red beans and rice, the tropical juice bar and the place that sold bento boxes with bits of everything. I sat sipping a cold glass of coconut and kiwi, wondering at which end of the continent to start. Perhaps I should begin, like the black guy over there with Rasta plaits and tartan trousers, with a nourishing bowl of ramen noodles. Or maybe that Indian family had the right idea, and a nice plate of sushi might stimulate the appetite for the pan-Oriental snack-fest to come. At the Food Court there were no borders anymore, nothing to stop anyone from anywhere enjoying the food from anywhere else. The bourgeois notion of culinary authenticity, of the decorous separation between one culture and the next, was as meaningless here as in the fusion-food temples of Mayfair. This, in a warehouse in Colindale, was the melting pot at a good, rolling boil.

*

The catalogue cover showed photographs of TV chefs larking about with items of food as oversized as their egos, one leaning over a giant tomato, another holding up a broccoli spear the size of a chef's hat, and a third perched on the edge of a bowl of pasta. A trade fair was running for a few days at Olympia, showing off all the glamour and grooviness of the new gastronomy – 'the action-packed world of food', no less – and making you wonder at times how much more there was to the revolution in British eating than wave upon wave of breathless, relentless, multicoloured hype. Washington Apples, French Cheeses, Wines of Germany, A Taste of Sweden ('Have you tried our great new Swedish stir-fry?') . . . There was so much PR in the air you could practically smell it.

Outside the Super Theatre I met a friend who, since she moved to the far reaches of East London, sometimes had cause to wonder whether the revolution had actually happened at all.

'There are only a few actual food shops in my area, and those shops have very little of what I would describe as actual food,' she used to say.

On the occasions I went to visit her, in the dark days of the last recession, we would tramp reluctantly up to Chrisp Street Market, or Limp Street as we had mockingly re-christened it, fantasising aloud about persimmons, mizuna and Moroccan mint. The market had a rickety, bombed-out look; the fruit and vegetables were sad, old and extremely cheap. Sad old ladies haggled over a few shrivelled turnips; downtrodden families lugged boxes of frozen chicken legs. Rarely, you might find a head of garlic, a beetroot or some fresh spinach, and these were occasions for rejoicing.

Now we stood by the Super Theatre and watched the

crowds roll in to see the shiny happy TV chefs, and reflected on the irony involved in the fact that the cookery shows, supposed to encourage us all to get in that kitchen, were interspersed with tastings of cook-chill meals from supermarkets.

'I'm not against convenience foods – in their place. And their place is very, very small,' said Diana.

At a restaurant space beside the theatre a group of slightly less famous trendy chefs, of the sort that might have their own TV show in a year's time if they kept on networking, cooked up their frenziedly cosmopolitan assemblies: risotto fritters with balsamic mayonnaise, seared beef with Thai spices and cucumber relish, grilled cinnamon quail on roast carrot and ginger salad with pomegranate. It was time for lunch. Some of this stuff sounded tempting enough, but as a place to eat there are few more uncongenial places than the Great Hall at Olympia. So we hailed a black cab in the street and made for Dalston. It was already past three o'clock, but Turkish time is not quite as unforgiving as London time, and there would even be a chance to do some shopping and snacking at the Turkish Food Centre before tucking into a big, late lunch across the road from the Best-Tat Cash and Carry on Arcola Street at the barbecue place that Diana swore was probably the best restaurant for its price in the whole of London.

There was an aromatic flavour of the East, these days, in the East End. Like tourists who had strayed off the beaten track somewhere in downtown Istanbul, we peered at the strange words and went a little mad, snapping up bags of dried mulberries, sumac and black onion seeds, tins of salted sardines, bottles of lemon vinegar and sour grape juice, and pots of *ajuar*, the Bulgarian/Turkish/Macedonian mixture of roasted peppers, aubergine and onion, and boxes of Turkish delight with walnut, hazelnut and pistachio, and a ewes' milk cheese from Cyprus. Meanwhile we nibbled on lahmajoun, the perfect fuel for a shopping session as animated as this, because you could roll up the thin flatbread into a tube and the surface of chopped onion, parsley, sumac and minced lamb stayed where it was until safely inside your mouth.

The Mangal was built around a great rectangular charcoal grill from which clouds of fragrant smoke billowed up into the industrial-sized fan-duct above it. The grill was so big that there was only space in the tiny blue-tiled dining room for four small tables. We grabbed one and sent out the smart boy waiter to buy us a couple of beers.

There was no menu, but we let them bring us whatever they wanted, which turned out to be kuru fasulye, beans in tomato sauce, and a salad of beetroot and long bars of white radish, and another salad of chargrilled aubergine and peppers, thickly dressed with olive oil and sour cream, and a series of juicy chargrilled kebabs, shish with onions and sweet peppers, spicy suçuk sausage, and a whole boned chop impaled on a stick, like a meat lolly. On a corner of a dingy side street in Hackney, this was glorious food, and so eye-poppingly cheap that you could pay for a taxi ride from Chelsea and back with the difference between a good meal in the East and a bad meal in the West.

'I've lived in London most of my life and been interested in food for half of it,' said Tom Conran as he poured the morning caffe latte at his Kensington flat.

'I guess you could say for the last twelve or fourteen years I've been keeping a pretty close eye on what goes on. And one of the things I've noticed is how Fay Maschler focused on how well you can eat in the kind of cheap ethnic restaurants you've obviously been hanging out in these past few days. What she did was create a market which grew and grew. For what it's worth, I still think that's where the best food in London is. The Turkish scene in Dalston, for instance. Hottest ticket in town.'

This was a man who knew whereof he spoke. Tom and I and four other friends once spent a week holed up in a farmhouse in Snowdonia. We were several hundred miles from the nearest deli, and there was no out-of-town hypermarket anywhere near. But Tom had been thinking ahead, and brought with him several dozen oysters, a rabbit or two, a whole smoked salmon, a box of Manx kippers, a big leg of mutton from Pipers Farm, half a Llangloffan cheese, two crates of champagne, a pig and a custom-built metal spit upon which to roast it. So that at least we managed to keep body and soul together in that farmhouse, until the main bulk of the supplies arrived.

Even in combat trousers, sloppy black long-sleeved T-shirt, and a fortnight's growth of dirty blond beard – regulation Ladbroke Grove uniform that year – Tom exuded the charm and chutzpah proper to the scion of a successful family, the cool self-assurance that says, 'No worries. I can get things done'.

Which he can, and had. To be precise: a shop, eponymously named, in Westbourne Grove, where *le tout* Notting Hill buys its bread and cheese. A café above the shop. And a magnificent pub, the Cow, famous for its oysters and Guinness, which a few weeks earlier had held a festival of regional English cooking; pies, meats, hot-pots, puddings.

'I've made a great discovery,' he said, eyes lighting up. 'You can get Staffordshire oatcakes in the Cromwell Road

Sainsbury's. You can wrap them around whatever you want, baked beans, Cheddar cheese . . . Brilliant fast food. By the way, I saw the other day that fish and chips are still the number one takeaway in the UK – much more than McDonald's – which at least shows there is a little bit of life left in our traditional British grub.'

I sat down gingerly on a white acrylic seventies-style capsule chair. There on the smoked-glass coffee table was a glossy food magazine. I flicked through it idly, noticing a feature about Alice Waters, doyenne of California cuisine and founder of the great Chez Panisse restaurant in Berkeley. 'I'm really excited about what's happening in England,' she gushed. I imagined she really meant 'what's happening in London', since it was difficult to imagine Alice tripping excitedly around, say, Liverpool, or Lowestoft or Leeds.

Fashion and fashionableness are an inevitable part of the urban flux and reflux. In no other branch of the creative arts, however, does fashion reveal its essential absurdity as in cooking. In a way it actually mitigates against creativity, because as long as you are flambéeing your crêpes Suzette (1970s) or tarte Tatining the fruit or vegetable du moment (1990s), you are failing to think for yourself. On the other hand, perhaps a repertoire of national dishes is nothing more than fashion that's congealed, 'set', as it were, like a terrine into a mould.

'Oh, it's nonsense, the fashion thing, I know. People want to live in the right area, buy the right car, be seen at the right restaurants, and eat the right food. It's a bit shallow, but there you are. A lot of it's got to do with insecurity. What fashion does is take away some of the responsibility for making your own decisions.'

Tom had his opinions as to the great unsolved mystery of whether people in Britain actually cook at home, or whether they merely glue themselves to some celebrity chef TV show while, as Fay Maschler once put it, 'a pre-prepared, manufactured dish bought at a supermarket circles gloomily in the microwave'. Most people cook, in the fullest sense of the word (which is the only sense that really counts), no more than once a week, he believed, often simply replicating a favourite recipe from the cookbook of their favourite restaurant.

'You see them out on Saturday afternoon, buying the gear for their big meal,' he said. 'Which is fine, of course. But to cook properly you need to know a bit about what you're using. It's like being a painter, you need to have techniques. I can't see anything changing until people really start to learn about food, not just regard it as a lifestyle thing and an occasional hobby, like buying some designer clothes and wearing them out to a club on Saturday night.'

From Tom's place I walked down Gloucester Road to the Cromwell Road, where a glittering new Tesco stood on the corner, a plate-glass palace apparently deliberately placed within trolley-throwing distance of the older mega-Sainsbury's further along the road. Several of my London friends had been shopping at this Sainsbury's for many years and regarded the siting of the parvenu Tesco's as an act almost amounting to treachery. The new store had made for a certain amount of complication in their lives, since though they were prepared to concede that Tesco's possessed a fabulous sushi counter and a gorgeous range of ready meals, Sainsbury's had the edge for overall variety. And variety, as far as supermarket food is concerned, is not merely the spice, but the meaning of life.

What kind of picture of British eating habits would you take away from the Cromwell Road Sainsbury's if you were able to spend a couple of hours merely looking, instead of frantically doing what comes naturally in a consumer society?

First and foremost, perhaps, of a society that wants for nothing except even greater choice, even greater quantity, even more immediate gratification. I gazed along the miles of white aisles, to see people peering at the shelves with a mixture of dazzlement and puzzlement, for such immensity of choice is simultaneously pleasing – such riches, all for me! – and problematic, because it brings with it the tiresome burden of justifying the choices you make. Did I prefer the fine beans from Guatemala, or the fine beans from Zimbabwe, or would the *extra* fine beans from the Gambia add an extra West African finesse to my cooking? Among the exotic fruits – dodhi, gisoda, eddoe, chow chow, prickly pear, physalis and tamarillo – which would add greater glamour and fragrance to my fruit bowl?

If I wanted a good olive oil, the choice from Provence, Catalonia, Andalucia, the Peloponnese, Crete, and Italian oils from Apulia, Lazio, Tuscany, Basilicata, Puglia and Sicily would be overwhelming to anyone who had not taken a university degree in the subject. 'Oh my gosh. Aren't they all Italian? I should think they're all much of a muchness,' said a jacketed supermarket official when I asked her for help.

There was little doubt in my mind that quantity, here, was of considerably greater importance than quality. On the one hand, never in my life have I seen so many crisps – sacks of the things in a multitude of palate-crinkling flavours, stretching away into the distance – nor so many bottled sauces and pre-packaged meals-in-a-moment, many of them endorsed by celebrity cooks who ought to know better. It seems odd, in a country bombarded with cookery books and TV cookery shows, that there should still be a demand for a pale pink gunk containing every gum, glucose and glyceride known to science that if you add to potatoes creates an 'instant' dauphinoise.

On the other hand the fruit, though fabulously varied, was often shiny, hard and aroma-free. The cheese was all chilled into a corpse-like lifelessness. Why will supermarkets – or why can they – not sell ripe cheeses? The less said about the pathetic fish counter, in a wealthy neighbourhood of the capital of a land where one is never further than fifty miles from the sea, the better. Even in the famous Sainsbury's organic vegetable section, signalled by an image of a rustic scarecrow in a moth-eaten tweed jacket, everything was embalmed in most unrustic plastic. The entire shop shone and sparkled with plastic under its merciless white neon lighting. Plastic made almost the shop's only sound, a soft but omnipresent rustle and crackle and creak in the trolleys and under the hands.

'We've got to get out of here,' I heard an Australian woman mutter to her husband as they steered their laden trolley with increasing desperation around the maze-like aisles of this enormous windowless space. I too was feeling the onset of panic, and took deep breaths of air-conditioned air as I made my way towards the ranks of tills, pausing only to cast my eye over the contents of a nearby trolley and wonder for how long the human frame could survive on a diet of extruded potato snacks, sausages, Viennetta ice cream and Diet Coke.

London was once a city of great markets. There were once meat markets at St James's, Leadenhall and Newgate, butter and cheese at Clare Market, fish at Billingsgate and of course the great vegetable markets at Spitalfields and Covent Garden, built by Inigo Jones in 1630. Almost all have either gone or are on the way.

The markets that London still possesses are street markets, the best ones being Brixton, Berwick Street, Chapel Market, Ridley Road and Shepherd's Bush, and these remain alive largely thanks to the city's Caribbean and Middle Eastern and Asian populations, for whom market shopping forms another crucial link in the chain of good food and life. They are seldom permanent, covered markets, more often a row of stalls that appears once a week in the street. As supermarkets extend their tentacles into every corner of our lives, the street food markets of London will surely disappear just as the neighbourhood grocers and butchers and fishmongers have vanished before them.

When I was in London, however, something seemed, at last, to be stirring. The organic movement, fuelled by widespread disenchantment with the machinations of the food industry, was fusing with the new interest in traditional and regional British food, and the result was a number of farmers' markets at which producers of organic and/or artisan food could sell directly to the public. This had been happening for years in the United States, but had never really occurred to anyone here until now.

There are some things in London that if you live there you can somehow never afford the luxury of doing. It was when I was on my way to look at the famous tomb of John Gower, the fourteenth-century poet, in Southwark Cathedral, that I came upon the Food Lovers' Fair. There has been a food market in Borough High Street since 1276, and the handsome pillared market buildings date from 1851, though the market itself is wholesale and normally closed to the general public. But the Food Lovers' Fair, held at Borough Market once a month, was something new – a chance for small-scale real food producers from all over Britain to sell their wares directly to a populace that cannot get enough of them. In a few years, maybe even months, one could imagine this area becoming one of London's gastronomic centres of excellence. At the time of writing, it was planned to run the real food market only once a month, which seems almost too infrequently to create the sense of gentle, pulsing routine that a real market ought to have.

I wandered among the green-painted, airy halls amid an excited, chattering throng of food lovers. There were so many things here that I coveted, so much that was fragrant and earthy and real and ripe, that before long I was laden with British breads and cheeses and charcuterie and fine vegetables and fruit, as it is only right that a food-loving Briton should be. A nutty, fruity, aromatic apricot, hazelnut and raisin loaf from Sally Clarke's shop in Kensington, believed by some to bake the city's finest bread, would provide the basis for my London picnic, and small amounts of some of my favourite British foods would adorn it. Slices of Denhay Farm's air-dried ham; smoked salmon from Summer Isles; baby round carrots, radishes, and mangetout peas as sweet as candy; a mixed bag of apples from Brogdale Orchards.

In the streets adjoining the market itself the real good food continued, spilling out like some benign amoeba into Bermondsey. At Neal's Yard Dairy, run by Randolph Hodgson, one of the flag-wavers for proper on-farm British cheeses, I was able to put together a compilation of the greatest hits from my gastro-travels: Kirkham's Lancashire, Lord of the Hundreds, Isle of Mull, Capricorn. It felt good to have seen some of these cheeses at an earlier phase in their existence, to have trod the pasture that made them. At Konditor and Cooke, an impeccably modernist deli that looked like a hip sunglass store but where the pastry was as beautiful as the architecture and the whole shop was full of the sweet aroma of good fresh butter, I bought a brioche and some chocolate truffles, which with the rest of my booty were as much as I could carry.

As I staggered over London Bridge at dusk the river seemed to glow beneath me, reflecting a big-city sky that was gently turning orange, like a ripening truckle of Double Gloucester.

There was one question that, when I lived in London, vexed me more than any other. It was the question that friends from America or Continental Europe would put to me as part of the visitor's anxious interrogation of the native. Having amassed a satisfying list of sights, confident now in their new knowledge that, for example, Highgate Cemetery can only be visited as part of a guided tour and that the best street market is Brick Lane on Sunday mornings, I could feel the question coming, as inevitable as coffee and mints.

'And where in London do you go for real English food? Not the tourist version; you know, the real thing?'

It was a question that begged so many others. What exactly was English food anyway? Was it distinct from Scottish and Welsh food, or did English really mean British? Presumably 'Modern British Cooking', catholic and many-faceted, wasn't what the visitors wanted at all. On the other hand, perhaps it reflected the reality of modern Britain more faithfully than pies and puddings. Thank God they hadn't asked about 'typical

London dishes', as you might enquire after the rich culinary repertoire of a European city like Venice, Marseilles or Madrid. For, if it ever had a food tradition of its own, London had long ago traded it in for a dizzying, fashion-crazed heterogeneity.

Yet there is at least one 'typical London dish'. A group of dishes, forming a neat little culinary cul-de-sac, might be nearer the mark. This little niche of London cooking has nothing at all to do with fashion; on the contrary, it could hardly be more repellent to the bruschetta set. Rather surprisingly, despite everything, however, it shows few signs of wanting to lie down and die just yet.

Perhaps I could send my foreign visitors here. Not the elderly or nervous, nor those of a delicate constitution, but certainly the curious, the adventurous and those on a tight budget. Across Tower Bridge, past the coach park and the turning into Tooley Street, home of the London Dungeon, and you just keep going, into the grimy hinterland of Bermondsey.

Like several places of its ilk in other parts of South, East and South-East London, the restaurant bears the name of Manze's. The Manze family arrived from Naples in 1878, and originally traded at No. 85 Tower Bridge Road as Ice Merchants and Confectioners before buying up the shop next door. More than a hundred years later, Manze's is still serving up the old cockney food: jellied eels, stewed eels, meat pies and mashed potato. Of the couple of dozen eel and pie houses in London, this is the oldest trading, the most historic, the grandest, a kind of cathedral.

One can only wonder what those Italian immigrants must have thought of this indigenous London cuisine, with the red and gold glories of Neapolitan cooking still fresh in their minds.

Ironically, of course, this sort of thing – the gelatinous textures and bland colours and neutral, Northern flavours – looks a good deal more foreign nowadays to British eyes than pizza napoletana.

Manze's was a white-and-green-tiled shop with high ceilings and a long marble counter with wooden booths opposite to which you took your white bowls of food to sit beside the other scoffers. On a cold day an old-fashioned ceiling radiator, a complicated thing of flaps and panels, gave out a powerful blast of warmth. Along a shelf behind the counter were photographs of 'famous' Manze's customers, most of which produced only the dimmest glimmer of recognition in my mind.

The menu was written in white plastic letters on a blackboard; a topos of the greasy spoon café. Some of the letters had fallen off and had not been replaced – perhaps the boards aren't made any more – so that the dishes available, a kind of mathematical permutation of the same four items, were pie and liquor, 1 pie and mash, double ie and ash, eels and mash, jellied eels and liquo . . .

The pies looked and tasted horrid, the meat gristly and of indeterminate provenance. What intrigued me were the eels – distant culinary cousins of the elvers of Somerset and Gloucester, and survivors of a sizeable swathe of history. The *Domesday Book* records the existence of an eel fishing industry on the Thames around Twickenham, which is also where one of the first eel pie houses was founded, on a small eyot or island in the river, ever afterwards known as Eel Pie Island. Until the twentieth century, when pollution killed off the population of sharp-nosed Thames eels, *Anguilla acuhirostia*, they were the fish used for the pies. Now, I was informed, they come mostly from Holland and Lough Neagh in Northern Ireland, and are sold to the pie shops already killed, gutted and beheaded.

A plate of stewed eels. These would have been the filling for the pie, I surmise, before the original dish died out in the 1940s. And the girl reached down into a great metal pot in the window and ladled the chunks of meat in their thin sauce into a white soup plate. With that came mash, two creamy smears over the side of the plate, and a ladleful of the famous 'liquor'. This had an unearthly green colour that, as it seemed to me, was unlikely to have been the result merely of a large quantity of chopped parsley.

'What's in the liquor, anyway?' I asked the girl in the neat green cap and coat.

'Parsley,' she said brightly.

'And . . .?'

'Food colouring, flour and water.'

Yuk.

A serving of jellied eels – but mainly for the purposes of research. The girl served them up gingerly, a wobbling bowlful, with a look as if to say 'rather you than me'.

'I hate eels, I can't even bear to look at them,' she said with a grimace. Another instance of a curious phenomenon: the intense dislike of a traditional British foodstuff by the very person who, as its salesperson and therefore in some sense its promoter, you'd expect to have the opposite view.

Nevertheless, I saw her point. With the best will in the world, one could hardly have described the dish as a thing of great beauty. The jelly was cold and rubbery, and the eel chunks, when you finally got to them through the jelly, were bony and tasted of mud. What could be better, Jane Grigson once asked, than a bowl of jellied eels served out of an old white basin and a glass of white wine to go with them? It was a rhetorical question, prettily phrased, but I answered it mentally as I sat at that marble-topped table: a number of things, Jane, a number of things. Even the stewed eels, meaty and savoury, were much nicer than the jellied, especially when messed up with a bit of potato and a generous sprinkling of pepper.

I finished my cup of orange tea and took a bus back up through the City to Smithfield Market, another fine relic of Victorian London, filigree ironwork now gaudily painted in pink, purple and blue, surrounding a severely clean white inner cell: the meat market itself, echoingly empty at midday.

The restaurant St John, in St John Street, in a street adjacent to the market where glossy new eating places were two a dozen, had been sold to me by a food lover I knew who respected the chef, Fergus Henderson, for his determinedly anti-food-fashion stance. As it happened, St John had recently become one of the most fashionable restaurants in town, besieged by wealthy young bohemians, young City men and their fathers and media people who recognised a neat idea when they saw it.

The neat idea was this: within a minimalist space of white walls and sanded floors, possessing an atmosphere akin to a Victorian hospital dining room, diners would be offered a series of dishes that trawled the very depths of our national culinary subconscious. The menu would be based around charcuterie and offal, as indicated by its logo, which showed a pig flying through the air with its various cuts marked out A to E. On a given day there might be liver, ox heart, sweetbreads, Bath chaps, bone marrow, pig's spleen, pig's tongue and whichever part of the pig the chitterling is. The back-to-basics theme would be continued with variations on game, native shellfish, and good old British vegetables such as beetroot, celeriac, Jersey royals, kale, watercress, none of your rocket and radicchio, thank you very much, and rounded off with Eccles cakes and rhubarb fool. It is the kind of cooking that appears to have been designed to appeal to our grandfathers. Odd, then, that it's the sons and daughters who have turned to it in their droves.

English food in restaurants used to mean Simpson's in the Strand: plush, clubby, gold-trimmed, waiters bowing and scraping and juggling with silver domes. The deliberately austere, institutional drabness of St John was a way of letting you know that this had nothing whatever to do with that. As was the staccato briskness of the menu, which gave you the lowdown in unembroidered style: haddock and lentils, grilled squid and dandelion, pigeon and turnips, ham in hay.

Whatever Modern British Cooking was taken to mean, I began to see that St John did not fall under its brightly coloured umbrella. This was a restaurant that fell into a category of its own in which it was, so far, the only occupant: Ancient British Cooking. I ordered Bath chaps, pigs cheeks braised with crunchy pickled shallots and a watercress salad, and roast bone marrow, which arrived wrapped in a white linen cloth and accompanied a long-handled metal implement that resembled a particularly gruesome piece of surgical equipment, for the purpose of scooping the beige-coloured goo from the interior of the bone. Since the outbreak of bovine spongiform encephalopathy it was illegal, strictly speaking, to serve a dish like this, beef marrow being a major breeding ground and cradle of the disease, but this merely gave the experience a frisson of danger that made up in part for its distinct lack of gastronomic value.

I could perhaps have stopped there, but this was the kind of ethnic British food, authentic, gutsy and inventive, that I had dreamed of for months. I needed to try it all: the Gloucester Old Spot chop, sweet and musky, unlike any other pork I'd ever tasted, and the lambs' tongues and broad beans, and the magnificent rabbit and fennel and whole heads of garlic and slabs of cured ham, served in a great basin that would comfortably have fed a family of four in any other culture at any other moment than our own Western Utopia.

The afternoon had turned sad and grey, the winter rain coming in against the skylights. British food in its traditional guise, I realised, having just dispatched a large amount of it and pondering the wisdom of a final spoonful of Bakewell Tart and a large malt whisky on the side, is essentially comfort food, an emotional and physical insurance policy against the climate.

There would be no dinner for me today. As night stole across the City and the commuter trains rumbled out of Fenchurch Street, I would creep back to my lodgings and devote all my energies to digestion.

What I had to digest, however, was more than a single enormous lunch, more than a hundred enormous lunches and dinners and breakfasts and picnics on clifftops and nibbles of cheese and charcuterie and all the other items in a store cupboard of such surprising excellence. Had they any idea of its quality, the French and Spanish and Italian friends who believed

'British gastronomy' to be a hilarious joke would have had the smirk wiped off their faces.

What I had to address was a series of questions I had been postponing for too long. There was nothing oxymoronic about British cuisine, that much was now dazzlingly clear. Neither are we, as a gastronomic culture, at the nadir any more, nor at the triumphal summit of the curve, but, perhaps, at a point somewhere on its gentle upward slope. But are we nearer the bottom or the top? And at what speed do we move: racing madly towards a kind of Byzantine exquisiteness, or limping sluggishly towards a point at which the population at large finally learns to take a little more care of what it eats?

I lay in my bed in Bow, trying to make sense of these dyspeptic animadversions. What I had seen on my travels had sometimes been hard to stomach, it was true. Food in Britain, a little like the British character, you might say, runs to extremes of crassness and refinement, of penury and opulence, that make it sometimes hard to believe that both elements can co-exist under the same flag. There is something a little tragic about a nation that once had a fine food culture, mislaid it out of carelessness, and then realised to its horror that the rest of the world regarded its eating habits with contempt.

There is something heroic, by the same token, about a nation that makes up its mind that a fine food culture is what it will have once more, whatever it takes to acquire and maintain. Taking stock of the situation, it saw that the foundations were decidedly flimsy: its rural, regional tradition, the basis of all the great cuisines, had almost disappeared. But it shook itself down and set about rebuilding the structure using whatever materials were to hand: a few bits of its colonial inheritance, things that it had picked up on holidays abroad, plus a few odds and ends that were still lying around from before. The Frenchwoman on the Newhaven ferry was right: having no altar to kneel at probably did allow for a certain freedom of movement. But the British, or the section of them that cared about such things, had a series of other advantages too. They had a few glorious ingredients. They were possessed of an apparently unquenchable energy, curiosity and appetite. Keeping their minds and their mouths firmly open, they got on with forging a brave new world of food.

As far as London food went, however, there was a piece of the puzzle I still hadn't yet put in its place. I still hadn't eaten in a great London restaurant, the sort of place that justifies both hype and prices and the right of this town to call itself the food capital of the planet. The sort of place where art takes over from artifice and gives you a little champagne buzz of excitement as part of the cover charge.

For my last big meal in London and Britain, I would have to aim high.

I pondered the myriad choices and came up with a shortlist. I then set to ringing around, quickly finding that most of the top places were as fully stuffed with Amex-wielding clients as a canard farci aux truffes. The demand for stratospherically expensive meals in places fêted by the London-based restaurant critics of the moment was seemingly inexhaustible.

Only in one restaurant, a grand and fashionable establishment in the heart of West One, was there a table for one at the time I wanted it on an ordinary weekday lunchtime in November. This restaurant did not appear to trade on a glamorous celebrity chef, since the man in question had not thus far appeared on TV and conspicuously, gratifyingly, failed to emerge from the kitchen on my visit.

The word around town was that this was a grown-up restaurant, though the jury was out on what exactly that might mean. Did it mean that grown-ups went there, people with neat straight suits and neat straight careers? Or did it mean that the style of the restaurant in some sense represented a maturing, a coming-of-age? Possibly the latter, in as much as this didn't seem a restaurant in which either the food on your big white plate or the quietly elegant surroundings called attention to themselves particularly.

There was something nicely serendipitous about my last three meals, it struck me as I settled myself in my chair and received into my hands the last menu I hoped to peruse for a very long time. There was the pie and mash house, the nostalgic Britfood brasserie, and now this, a discreet and expensive Mayfair restaurant whose own claim to Britishness was made, it had to be said, with a greater subtlety than either.

The roots of the dishes showed, but they were covered over with comforting English moss. Fillets of plaice with parsley mash and buttered spring vegetables was an exalted version of the kind of thing a good British home cook might serve her children, the kind of thing, in fact, that my mother served me. Ragoût of turbot and oysters with an open raviolo of crab might have come straight from Mrs Beeton, were it not for the open raviolo. And Chateaubriand with Sauce Béarnaise was pure old-fashioned Café Royal.

There was a sensibleness here, a taking stock, an intelligent retreat from the food-fashion frontline. There was even a hint of the kind of déjà-vu that might suggest the gradual formation of a tradition. Nothing was modish here. How could it be, when salade Niçoise and wild mushroom risotto and tarte Tatin had been reproduced all over town in a myriad guises ever since the Food Revolution began way back in the 1980s?

But what was really revolutionary was the *uninterestingness* of the food, its lack of startle. Could it be, I wondered as I sipped on a macchiato, that the difference between the food culture of Britain and that of France, Italy, Spain or Greece is that food in those countries is less obsessively *interesting* to their inhabitants, who have no need of the palate-tickling novelties that so occupy us here? Could it be that the moment when good food ceases to be news, when it stops needing to impress with its wild cosmopolitan flair, is also the moment of maximum achievement, when the page can be turned at last on the peculiar history of our national cuisine?

For it is a hard thing to say, but fine food is far from the most important thing in the world. It is not really a question of reaching perfection – that would be too much to ask – nor of lotus-eating, but of finding and maintaining a level of confidence in the food we eat day by day that enables us to get on with the rest of our lives. I forget who said it, but the phrase could apply perfectly well to the food of Britain: 'We have more than enough masterpieces. What we need is a better standard of ordinariness.'

Beyond the plate glass windows of the restaurant, a café offered two eggs, beans and fried bread and a cup of tea for £2.50. A few inches from where I sat, a motorcycle messenger chewed his way through a Big Mac, the yellow polystyrene container flapping in the cold wind.

The Christmas lights were going up on Bond Street.

Somewhere in the depths of Norfolk, one hundred thousand turkeys shivered on death row. This year, for once, I might spend the festive season in the land of my fathers, if my metabolism had recharged itself sufficiently by then to deal with the onslaught of bread sauce, Christmas cake and brandy butter.

I paid the bill and left in a hurry, happy to empty my mind of eating. From here to Epiphany, there would be nothing but cabbage soup and memories.